D1038592

E.L. GODKIN
A BIOGRAPHY

OTHER BOOKS BY
WILLIAM M. ARMSTRONG

E. L. Godkin and American Foreign Policy, 1865-1900
The Gilded Age Letters of E. L. Godkin

Copyright by
C. Kruell 90.

Godkin in 1890

E. L. GODKIN
A BIOGRAPHY

William M. Armstrong

2 Oct. 1831 - 13 May 1902

State University of New York Press
Albany 1978

First published in 1978 by
State University of New York Press
Albany, New York 12246

© 1978 State University of New York
All rights reserved

Composed by
Typography Services
Loudonville, New York 12211

Printed in the United States of America

Library of Congress Cataloging in Publication Data

Armstrong, William M
E. L. Godkin.

Bibliography: p.
1. Godkin, Edwin Lawrence, 1831-1902.
2. Journalists—United States—Biography.
I. Title.
PN4874.G5A87   070.4'092'4 [B]   77-12918
ISBN 0-87395-371-1

PN
4874
.G5A87

To NORMA
and great-hearted souls everywhere

p 010.1 c.2c

CONTENTS

List of Illustrations

ACKNOWLEDGMENTS

This book could not have been written without the help of many persons. Foremost, I wish to thank the Houghton Library of Harvard University and the Bodleian Library of Oxford University for courteously providing me with microfilm of their Godkin holdings, indispensable because of Godkin's almost undecipherable handwriting. Of the many fellow scholars who aided me, four stand out: James M. McPherson and Martin Duberman took time to extend me favors beyond the demands of academic courtesy, mainly through supplying me with mentions of Godkin in their notes from the correspondence of others, and I deeply thank them. The late Allan Nevins, a long-time admirer of Godkin, on short notice generously put aside an evening to discuss him with me, besides faithfully answering my questions by mail. Lastly, D. S. Porter of the Division of Western Manuscripts of the Bodleian Library, Oxford University, went out of his way to answer my many inquiries and to facilitate my acquisition of Godkin materials from that institution. To a larger assembly of scholars I owe more than perfunctory thanks for patiently answering my queries or sharing with me their knowledge in person. They are Hans Trefousse, Louis Filler, Nathan Smith, Richard B. Hovey, Alan P. Grimes, Robert Muccigrosso, Richard E. Welch, Leon Edel, Arthur P. Hogue, Gordon Milne, Michael Burlingame, George Arms, Morton Keller, Elizabeth Wallace, John K. Reeves, Frederic C. Marston, and J. Albert Robbins.

The bringing to completion of this biography has been a long task, and many of the persons who first helped me are dead. Among the descendants of persons dealt with in this book, I particularly wish to acknowledge the kindness of the late Cornelia Godkin, who supplied me with photographs, books, and other mementos of her father-in-law and who gave me permission to publish Godkin's letters, besides promptly answering my inquiries. The late Frederick Law Olmsted, Jr., offered me his oral remembrances of the Godkins and helped me to cut through the scholarly red tape that initially prevented me from getting access to the Olmsted Papers in the Library of Congress. Edith Perkins Cunningham and Marian Hague helpfully supplied me with their written recollections of the Godkin family, and Margaret V. Bryce tendered me permission to publish letters of her uncle, James Bryce, to Godkin. Susan S. Hammond provided me with oral and written information about her father, Arthur P. Sedgwick, and Rosamund Gilder generously loaned me copies of letters, then in her possession, from Godkin to her father.

From archivists and librarians in the United States and the British Isles I received so many courtesies that I cannot suitably acknowledge them here. I especially wish to thank E. Taylor of the John Rylands Library and D. Flanagan of the British Library of Political and Economic Science, W. D. Coates of the [British] National Register of Archives, Anna Hackel of the British Association for American Studies, John Alden of the Boston Public Library, Frieda C. Thies of the Johns Hopkins University Library, Ruth E. Ballenger of the Rutherford B. Hayes Library, Carolyn Jakeman and William A. Jackson of the Houghton Library of Harvard University and Mr. Jackson's successor W. H. Bond, T. D. Seymour Bassett of the Wilbur Library of the University of Vermont, Alice H. Bonnell of the Butler Library of Columbia University, Kimball Evans of the Harvard University Archives and his successor, Harley P. Holden, W. E. Bigglestone of the Oberlin College Archives, Dorothy W. Bridgewater of the Yale University Library, Margaret Hackett of the Library of the Boston Athenaeum, Charles Penrose of the Clarkson College Library, Mrs. Graham D. Wilcox of the Stockbridge, Massachusetts, Library, Mrs. Matthew Josephson of the American Academy of Arts and Letters, Stephen T. Riley of the Massachusetts Historical Society, George A. Schwegmann, Jr., and Katherine Bland of the Library of Congress, Angela Rubin of the University of Chicago Library, Robert W. Hill of the New York Public Library, James J. Heslin of the New York Historical Society, Josephine L. Harper of the State

Historical Society of Wisconsin, John E. Buchanan and John Wertis of the Mann Library of Cornell University, Herbert Cahoon of the Pierpont Morgan Library, and Marian Clarke of the Watkinson Library of Trinity College.

Some material herein appeared previously in my *E. L. Godkin and American Foreign Policy, 1865-1900* and in my *The Gilded Age Letters of E. L. Godkin.* For identification of Godkin's editorials I have relied on Daniel C. Haskell's invaluable *Nation Index,* plus my "Additions to the *Nation Index,*" [*Bulletin of the New York Public Library* 73, 4 (April 1969)] and my "The Writings of E. L. Godkin" [*Bulletin of the New York Public Library* 72, 5 (May 1968)].

Finally, I wish to thank the American Philosophical Society and Clarkson College of Technology for providing me with research grants that helped make this book possible. For the painstaking accuracy of June Broughton, who typed the final draft of the manuscript, I have nothing but admiration. Thanks of a kind that cannot adequately be put into words are due my former wife Norma C. Armstrong for her unselfish labors during the primary stages of the research for this volume.

WILLIAM M. ARMSTRONG

Potsdam, New York, 1976

INTRODUCTION

There is good and bad in every one, although biographers sometimes overlook this. Oversimplification is one of the vices of authorized biography. The family-retained biographer, by selecting from amongst his subject's words and deeds, can reconstruct his subject in any dimensions his employers wish. That, to a degree, is what happened to E. L. Godkin in 1907 at the hands of Rollo Ogden. Because Ogden's *Life and Letters of Edwin Lawrence Godkin* occasionally reveals Godkin's warts does not raise it in the scale of literary importance. Ogden, in his preoccupation with showing his subject as a crusader for righteousness, failed to show him as a human being with human failings. As William Dean Howells noted, of the many legitimate criticisms of Godkin, being a "prig" is not one of them.

In presenting an intensively researched biography of a man who has been nearly forgotten for over half a century, I am conscious that I open myself to the suggestion of taking my subject too seriously. But as scholars of the Gilded Age know, a biography of Godkin is overdue. Most of them are aware that the *Nation*—the weekly New York journal of opinion that Godkin helped father in 1865 and which he exclusively directed after 1866—significantly shaped the historical judgments of his contemporaries. Yet Godkin himself remains partly a mystery.

When I began this book, I was aware that more than half a dozen persons had begun biographies of Godkin only to abandon them. For some, it was disillusionment with the captious editor; others threw in the towel for lack of material. The most difficult part of my task was to find accurate, unbiased information about Godkin, much of that in print about him stemming from invincible admirers or confirmed detractors. One tantalizing finding early emerged; announced admirers of Godkin are sometimes critical of him in their private correspondence. For example, in 1907 William Dean Howells gave in to the urging of Charles Eliot Norton and eliminated some derogatory remarks about Godkin from his review of Ogden's *Life and Letters of Edwin Lawrence Godkin*. In doing so, Howells made it plain that, although he had always appreciated the *Nation's* kind treatment of himself, he was not enchanted by Godkin's editorial attacks on others "quite as deserving."

In the end, my research produced a less sympathetic Godkin than the one who emerges from the pages of Ogden's study. Godkin's courage and independence as an editor won him a coterie of followers, but few fast friends. Boston's Henry Lee Higginson spoke for part of the genteel community when he vainly opposed the establishment of an annual Godkin lecture series at Harvard University—a scheme conceived by Godkin's son in concert with William James—and denounced the editor as a carping slanderer of "great conceit, arrogance [and] evil temper."

Outwardly Godkin's heavy-handed resort to personalities impressed fans more than it did the unrepentant objects of his editorial scolding, some of whom did not deign to reply to his attacks. Once he circulated in the *Evening Post* the rumor that Tammany Hall was planning a physical assault on him; yet the closest any of the victims of his verbal onslaughts ever got to seeking physical satisfaction was when a New York street car conductor whom Godkin was upbraiding shoved him from his car. Innumerable persons have testified to his icy personality. This is not to assert that Godkin lacked charm, especially in the drawing room, but to point out that his geniality was reserved for the company of his equals. Still, argue his admirers, his brusque exterior and petulance ought not to obscure his contribution to journalism.

It is to this question, the accuracy of Godkin as a journalist, that older historians have too seldom addressed themselves. Scarcely had I gotten into my study of him many years ago than I became aware that the then-orthodox view of the Gilded Age was freighted with opinions of mugwump historians who were disciples of Godkin and the *Nation*. But, aside from dutifully reporting this, together with my finding that Godkin was neither a deep nor an original thinker, I had no desire to take from him his just fame as an editorial writer. Godkin's prejudices were the prejudices of the genteel society of his age, and it is as a man of his age that his stature must be weighed. The same present-day measuring stick that can be used to condemn him would also condemn William James, James Bryce, Albert V. Dicey, James Russell Lowell, Charles Eliot Norton, and a host of other later nineteenth-century thinkers who acknowledged their debt to Godkin.

Reviewing a doctoral dissertation about Godkin and American foreign policy that I published some years ago, Howard Mumford Jones expressed puzzlement that, despite my negative findings about Godkin, I concluded that on the whole he is to be admired. This is what I wrote:

> The world in 1900 was probably the better for Godkin's having lived in it. Impulsive, hypercritical, and intolerant though he sometimes was, his volatile pen may have had a distinct sobering effect on an age that needed forcefully to be reminded of its shortcomings (albeit some of them, said Rutherford B. Hayes, "are not what the *Nation* supposes").

Further research has not caused me to alter that judgment.

E.L. GODKIN
A BIOGRAPHY

Chapter One
Irish Beginnings

*John Stuart Mill was our prophet,
and Grote and Bentham were our
daily food.*

"A stout old Englishman" was John Fiske's impression of
E. L. Godkin at thirty-six.[1] This underscored the fact that,
although the Godkin family traced its Hibernian roots back
seven centuries, Godkin seldom acknowledged his Irish past.
Characteristically he went to pains to conceal it. If George L.
Stearns had known Godkin was an Irishman representing
himself as an Englishman, Stearns told Boston friends, he
would not have financed the *Nation*.[2] But with the Irish-born
James Bryce Godkin was more candid. "I am an Irishman of
English ancestry," he told Bryce in 1882, "bred in strong
attachment to the English government, educated at an English school and Queen's College Belfast. I have lived in Ireland only four years continuously since I was thirteen."[3]

The above testifies to something about Edwin Lawrence
Godkin, but it sheds little light on his forbears. For over
thirty generations, in fact, Godkins had inhabited the Emer-
ald Isle; no modern record could show when they had not
been there. According to family history, the first Godkin
appeared in southern Ireland during the twelfth century
where, in company with one Ram, he became the nucleus of a
small colony on the coast of County Wexford in what became
known as the Barony Forth. Owing to the presence of Scottish blood, the colony throughout most of its history spoke a
dialect similar to lowland Scottish. The colony became Protestant during the Reformation, survived the Cromwellian
period and the Restoration, and persisted in Wexford into
the nineteenth century, when as late as 1870 the Domesday
Book showed a Godkin among the landed proprietors of the
Barony Forth.[4]

Yet by the nineteenth century the Irish Godkins were in process of disappearing. Edwin, the best known of his line, proved to be nearly the last; his only sons and his only brother would die without heirs, and there is no mention of male cousins. Moreover, as has been noted, Edwin infrequently admitted to anything but Anglo-Saxon antecedents, although his relatives acknowledged that through the centuries in County Wexford the family had taken on a rich admixture of Irish blood.[5] "To the Irish strain may be attributed his humor and pugnacity," supposed an acquaintance, "to the Scottish his shrewdness and invincible common sense, to the English his tenacity of purpose, and to all three his courage and independence. . . ."[6]

Nothing is known about Godkin's distant forbears, but his paternal grandparents appear to have been middle-class Wexford farmers of adequate education and means. It was near Gorey, in County Wexford, that in 1806 their son James Godkin was born.[7] James entered the world at the close of a dismal decade of Irish history that had seen the failure of two abortive insurrections, together with an Act of Union that stripped Ireland of her native parliament and moved the handling of Irish affairs to London. The insurrection of 1798 had been waged with especial ferocity in Wexford, where maddened Catholic peasants took to the field armed with pikes. Though the two principal leaders, Wolfe Tone and Robert Emmett, were dead—felled by self-inflicted wounds or by the hangman—around hearths in Wexford their memories were still green.

The Godkins did not suffer many of the hardships that the land system inflicted on the tenant farmers of southern Ireland, but as young James grew to manhood his eyes could not overlook the grinding lot of the peasantry at the hands of absentee landlords in London and elsewhere. Although his parents taught him to take pride in his Anglo-Irish heritage, he early became persuaded of the injustice of the land system and of English rule. The most degraded victims of London's policy were the disenfranchised Catholics, but the Protestants of County Wexford, neighboring County Wicklow, and the six counties of the north shared Catholic resentment toward the crown. Thus it was not strange that the

1798 rebellion of the United Irishmen was conceived by adherents of both faiths; nor was it strange that the adult James Godkin emerged as one of the concerned Protestant voices in the fresh wave of disturbances that swept Ireland in the 1840's.[8]

James received a better education than most Irish youngsters of his day, and in his early twenties, while a candidate for orders in the Church of Ireland, he married Sarah Lawrence, the daughter of Anthony Lawrence, a comfortable proprietor in neighboring County Wicklow who traced his descent from English settlers who came to southern Ireland during the Cromwellian era. It was at the country home of the Lawrences near Moyne that on 2 October 1831 the Godkin's first child was born. They named him Edwin Lawrence.[9]

Except for periodic family moves, Edwin's childhood was not much different from that of other middle-class Irish children of his day. His father, a talented and well-motivated but restless man who would occupy a succession of Irish pulpits and editorial chairs, was often away from home, and the task of rearing his son fell mainly on nursemaids and maternal relatives. Throughout the successive changes of family residence, the Lawrence country place at Moyne — near the "meeting of the waters," the Vale of Avoca celebrated by Thomas Moore in his haunting "Irish Melodies" — remained "home" to Edwin and to the sisters who began to follow. There they saw their grandmother Lawrence and, on a nearby estate, their aunt and uncle Courteney.

Tim Healy, a family retainer, had a fondness for young Edwin; in Tim's infirm old age Edwin and a sister would occasionally favor him with small gifts. Another retainer was Thomas Doyle, the Lawrences' steward, whose son "Young Tom" was Edwin's favorite playmate.[10] Listening to Edwin read aloud from his books—he had inherited from his father a fondness of history—opened to the Doyle children vistas usually denied to lower class Irish youngsters.[11] And Edwin thereby began a life-long ritual. (Late in life he told an interviewer that he found no evening at home pleasanter than when he was reading aloud to a captive audience.[12])When not showing off in this way for the Doyle children, Edwin romped with "Young Tom" through the fields of Moyne. After he was grown and in college, he never ceased to stop at one of the Doyle cottages whenever he came "home" to Moyne.[13]

On the surface Edwin's childhood was a happy one— "harrowed with laughter," he told William Dean Howells— but he had difficulty accepting his father, an upright though somewhat disputatious man, from whom Edwin acquired some of his traits.[14] The Reverend James Godkin was comparatively free of religious bigotry, but dissent was in his marrow. Soon after Edwin's birth, he broke with the Episcopal church and, on being ordained a Congregational minister, was elected to a pastorate in Armagh, northern Ireland. But although preaching was James's chosen vocation, dissenting journalism was becoming his passion. He had already published a religious tract, "A Guide from the Church of Rome to the Church of Christ," that would go into several editions. A forceful writer, James bequeathed to his oldest son a pejorative ability with words. But James's polemics lack the humor, personalities, and biting sarcasm of his son's. From his father Edwin acquired a commendable hatred of hypocrisy, but, less fortunately, he failed to inherit that clergyman's "readiness to form the most kindly estimate of individual character."[15]

From this point on, accounts of the Godkin family vary. Edwin learned to read at home, and evidently at the age of seven he entered a grammar school at Armagh. His father joined the Irish Evangelical Society, and for the next several years he led a seminomadic existence as a missionary to the Catholics. His duties took him all over northern and western Ireland, and occasionally young Edwin came with him, once even to Scotland.[16]

After Armagh the Godkins divided their time between Newry—near which they lived for a time—Moyne, and Belfast, where James obtained a pulpit and began conducting a controversial and short-lived weekly, the *Christian Patriot*.[17] Meanwhile he continued to produce nonconformist tracts, two 1842 ones bearing the titles, "The Touchstone of Orthodoxy" and "Apostolic Christianity: or the people's antidote against Romanism and Puseyism." The latter tract sought to refute the ritualistic doctrines of Edward Pusey which, along with the Oxford Movement, were winning adherents in the Church of England. Had James chosen to ignore the political travails of Ireland and concentrate on theological issues, he might have become an important religious controversialist.

Belfast, the "Athens of Ireland," boasted one of the better Irish schools, the Royal Academical Institution, and when Edwin was about nine, his father put him in it. The lad's master was Abraham Hume, barely on the threshold of his career but to the impressionable Edwin "an object of more awe . . . than any other human being has ever been."[18] For reasons not stated—it may have been the floggings, or it may have been Hume's ardent championship of the established church—within a year James and Sarah transferred their son to a school for the sons of Congregational ministers in Yorkshire County, England, near Leeds. Reportedly James made only one request of the school authorities—though an unusual request for his day—that Edwin not receive floggings.[19]

Young Godkin stayed at the Silcoates School for nearly four years. No rival to Rugby, it had scarcely forty pupils and scanty resources. Its curriculum was classical—Latin, Greek, English, French taught by a part-time instructor, Euclidean geometry, algebra, and geography. Godkin never thought highly of his education at Silcoates, but perhaps his thirst for personal comfort prevented an objective estimate.[20] Classes were held in the bare upper floor of an old farm building outside the little city of Wakefield. A small distance away sat a house that served as a dormitory. For a playground, bounds were fixed a short distance on either side of the school building, plus the front yard, which was railed in from the high road. A former pupil recalled the school:

> I remember well how we hopped on cold foggy mornings up the little lane from the back of the house to the schoolroom and shivered there breakfastless from 7 to 8 over the slates on which we worked our sums, and in the evenings went through "preparation time" by the light of a few tallow dips, which it was the monitor's duty to look after, and in regular rounds through the evenings to trim with a pair of snuffers.[21]

Despite the unpretentiousness of Silcoates, life there was

not always dull. When Edwin was in his third year, the
pupils divided the school into legal districts, each with its
own court of law empowered to summon and try offenders.
Edwin, who could recite from memory passages from the
Irish courtroom speeches of Daniel O'Connell and John Cur-
ran, was one of the barristers. Another time the boys amused
themselves by starting newspapers. One lad established his
imitation of *Punch;* two others parodied the London "Thun-
derer" with "Our Own *Times.*" Godkin's paper, its name lost
to history, was said to be the biggest of all.[22]

In the spring of 1845 Edwin was almost fourteen. Long on
proscrastination, he was not doing as well in school as his
parents wished; he complained of his health, and he was
suffering from emotional problems. Being an Irish boy in the
midst of English children may have been a factor, but more
central was his growing estrangement from his father, accompanied by a mounting streak of arrogance. James and
Sarah took their son out of school and allowed him to pursue
his own devices for a year. Part of this time he seems to have
received tutoring from a maternal uncle, and in 1846 he may,
as some suggest, have attended the Belfast Academy. But
mostly he looked forward to his holidays at Moyne. There a
foxhunting relative taught him to ride and shoot, foreshadow-
ing the drill with fire arms that he would give his own son
thirty years later. Long-remembered by Lawrence employees
was the day Edwin accidentally discharged his rifle inside
the cottage of "Young Tom" Doyle's uncle, leaving a lasting
hole in the ceiling.[23]

Meanwhile, Irish political affairs were approaching a new
crisis. Daniel O'Connell, leader of the Irish party in the
British Parliament, had recanted his Burkean conservative
position and was leading his fellow Catholics in a movement
to repeal the Union between Ireland and England. Two of
his radical young supporters were Charles Gavan Duffy and
the northern Presbyterian writer and political agitator John
Mitchell, whose sister was a neighbor of the Godkins near
Newry. To Belfast went young Duffy in 1842 to become a
Catholic journalist in that Protestant stronghold, and there
he met the Reverend James Godkin. The two met as opponents on the religious question, but, discovering that they
agreed on the land question, became allies.[24]

In the fall of 1842 Duffy, with Protestant writer Thomas Davis and John Blake Dillon, launched in Dublin the *Nation,* the literary vanguard of the Young Ireland movement. A literarily innovative, but to the English politically seditious, weekly, the *Nation* was warmly welcomed in the Godkin home; Edwin took delight in reading it to the children of the family nursemaid. (Later it would inaccurately be reported that he named the New York *Nation* after it.) When the ardently Catholic O'Connell voiced objection to the *Nation,* he alienated supporters like James Godkin who, in concert with Duffy, was now participating in the activities of the League of North and South. The league's goal was to attack the land problem by restoring the interfaith cooperation that had animated the United Irishmen in 1798.[25]

Irish Protestants had always shown more zeal than Catholics to repeal the Act of Union; O'Connell may have been influenced to take up the cause of repeal by his dislike of British Prime Minister Robert Peel. But whatever the Liberator's motivation in leading the agitation, the Peel ministry moved in 1844 to end it by arresting and trying O'Connell and some of his followers, among them Charles Gavan Duffy. Through a legal technicality their convictions were overturned, and their Loyal National Repeal Association went on the next year to sponsor a competition for essays in support of repeal. James Godkin submitted an anonymous entry, "The Rights of Ireland," and won third prize.[26] In announcing his essay in the press, he described it as "a hearty defense of my beloved country, and I am willing to bear whatever it may cost me." One idealistic passage is evocative of Mazzini and cultural nationalism. Pointing to what he termed the "signs of the times," Godkin portrayed the Irish struggle as part of a great "revolution of ideas" that was lifting "the mass of mankind to importance and power, and, in fact, to the eventual government of the world."

> It is a revolution which goes alike beyond all former examples in history and principles in philosophy. None was ever so universal, so profound, or so powerful. . . . What is now presented to the world, is not as formerly, kingdoms convulsed, or navies wrecked upon the shore, but that time in the affairs of men, that slow rising and gradual swelling of the whole ocean of society, which is to bear everything upon its bosom.[27]

By this time the restless preacher's political activities
were causing evangelical tongues to wag. When with his
consent his authorship of "The Rights of Ireland" became
known, his connection with the Irish Evangelical Society
abruptly ceased.[28] After preaching for a time in an independent pulpit, in 1848 he abandoned the ministry, the British
Anti-State Church Association publishing his final blast at
established religion, "The Church Principles of the New
Testament."

While James was thus immersing himself in the Irish protest, his oldest son was entering the newly founded Queen's
College of Belfast and charting for himself a different course.
Against Irish nationalist opposition, Parliament had recently
voted funds "to enable Her Majesty to endow new colleges
for the advancement of learning in Ireland." Although
Queen's College, Belfast was open to all faiths, its administration was pro-English and its tiny student body was mainly
Protestant young men "of narrow means and broad ambitions."[29] Admitted on a legal scholarship—no doubt because
his father was a clergyman—Edwin was not a diligent student at Queens, but there he did improve his use of Latin
and French and the writing skills he had acquired from his
father. In 1850, during his third year, he was elected president of the newly founded college literary and scientific
society (which celebrated its fiftieth anniversary in 1900),
and he was "considerably puffed up" to be allowed to read a
paper on Lord Eldon to the student body.[30]

When Godkin entered Queens, he was still reading Duffy's
Nation, but he was beginning to have doubts about the
movement it espoused. Young Ireland was a romantic movement that, like its counterparts in other countries, emphasized ethos and noble ideals. Adhered to by idealistic young
men at Trinity College in Dublin, the movement proposed to
cleanse the national mind of class, regional, and religious
divisions and to stimulate understanding and brotherhood
among nations. A minor rivulet in the European stream of cultural nationalism, Young Ireland owed little to Irish thought,
or even to the prevailing doctrines of English philosophical
radicalism, but a great deal to Guiseppe Mazzini, Thomas
Carlyle, and Charles Gavan Duffy.[31] Both Carlyle and the

editor of the *Nation* had initially been attracted to philosophical radicalism, but each now had reservations about
utilitarianism. "To make our people politically free but bond
slaves to some debasing social system like that which crowds
the mines and factories of England with squalid victims, we
would not strike a blow,"—declared the *Nation* in 1848. It
was in that year of European revolutions that Duffy escorted
Carlyle on a tour of famine-desolated Ireland.[32]

This kind of moralizing was ceasing to attract young Godkin, who by nature was neither a sentimentalist nor an
idealist. Talk of proletarian revolution made him flinch, and
even Mazzini's middle-class slogans about "humanity" were
starting to sound to him like cant. With mounting impatience
he rejected Carlyle's allusions to what the Sage of Chelsea
called the "dismal science" of political economy, growling
on one later occasion that Carlyle's disciple Ruskin had a
"screw loose."[33]

It was at Queen's College that Godkin found the philosophy
he wanted, mainly through the instrumentality of William
Neilson Hancock, holder of the chair of political economy
and jurisprudence. Hancock used Jeremy Bentham's *Principles of Morals and Legislation* as a textbook, teaching that
human institutions should be judged not by fixed moral
criteria but by "expediency," i.e., by whether or not their
utility justifies their continuation.[34] From Hancock and his
colleagues young Godkin imbibed the outlook of the typical
English Liberal, later so well articulated for the British upper
middle classes by R. H. Hutton and John St. Loe Strachey in
the *Spectator*. "John Stuart Mill was our prophet," Godkin
recalled, "and Grote and Bentham were our daily food."[35]
Political economy, Godkin learned from his professors, was
law, and laissez faire was its iron decree—since classical
economics satisfied the utilitarian definition of expediency
—unalloyed by humanitarian considerations.

Despite his ultimate rejection of Mill—because of the leftward direction of the philosopher's later writings—Godkin
throughout his life clung to the Liberal, upper-middle-class
social philosophy he acquired at Queen's College.[36] Representative government he found to be the province of the
"intelligent classes," which is to say the entrepreneurial

classes. (During the brief ascendancy in 1871 of the Paris
Commune, he complained that "veritable workingmen sit in
council in the gilded saloons of the Hotel de Ville and are
waited upon by lackeys in livery.")[37] Not inconsistently, he
endorsed—with limitations—the broadening of the suffrage
in England. Revolutions were allowable if they did not
threaten private property, since only a weakling would look
to the state for support. Indeed, held Godkin, one of the
purposes of revolution should be to liberate society from the
fallacy that the state is concerned with the collective well-
being of its citizens.

From his reading of David Ricardo and James Mill at
Queen's College, Godkin was converted to the anti-Aris-
totelian abstraction that man is an economic animal who
exists solely to accumulate wealth on the most favorable
terms. Expediency rules; morality, justice, patriotism, and
the needs of society have nothing to do with it. Forty years
later in an essay, "The Economic Man," Godkin continued to
argue for the worship of the Economic Man on the grounds
that economic laws determine human activity as absolutely
as natural laws govern the motion of matter.[38] In his economic theorizing Godkin was fairly consistent; as admirers
pointed out, he gives the impression of being an exact and
logical thinker. But this is not to say that he was an original
thinker. An acquaintance and business associate, Brander
Matthews, found him a "very clever," "clear headed" but
"never open-minded man" who

> seemed to many of his admirers to be an original thinker
> because he was able to apply to American conditions the
> principles he had absorbed in his youth. . . . [but he] was
> impervious to every new idea in sociology or statecraft; when
> he died he was limited to the beliefs he had held when he
> immigrated to America.[39]

Whatever the abiding value of the education Godkin got
at Queen's College, he left there firmly convinced that the
abolition of the Corn Laws augured the triumph of laissez
faire throughout the world. Regarding his college experience, he wrote that

> at that period, in England and Ireland at least, political econ-
> omy was taught as a real science, which consisted simply in

the knowledge of what man, as an exchanging, producing animal, would do, if left alone. On that you can base a science, for the mark of science is that it enables you to predict. Since then, what is called political economy has become something entirely different. It has assumed the role of an advisor, who teaches man to make himself more comfortable through the help of his government, and has no more claim to be a science than philanthropy or what is called "sociology."[40]

While Edwin was thus approaching maturity, the Godkin family continued to increase. There were now several sisters, Georgina, Kate, and Maria, as well as little brother Anthony, born about 1844.[41] Ever since Silcoates days, the somewhat headstrong Edwin had been away from home much of the time, and the girls—who found their brother a "mine of learning"—looked forward to his visits. They forgave him his brusque ways, this handsome, witty, proud lad with a "fiery temper, but lovable and affectionate" all the same.[42] Self indulgent—he had been spoiled by Lawrence family retainers who treated him like a "young prince"—the thirst for leisure never left him.[43] To the family he was constantly wearing the appearance of delicate health while defaulting on his obligations.[44] Once, recalled a sister in a critical letter about him most of the contents of which have been destroyed, his fondness for parties got him so far behind in his school work that "he had to study so hard to make up for lost time that he brought on a fever."[45]

Godkin as an old man often returned in his thoughts to his childhood. After his funeral in 1902 his widow set about to visit Ireland to see the fondly remembered scenes of his youth. Godkin's surviving sisters advised against the visit, pointing out that in her distraught condition his widow would not see County Wicklow through the eyes of an Irish boy. Edwin, explained his sister Georgina, had "one Celtic quality, at least—love of the soil where he was born, and probably exaggerated the beauty of the country."[46]

Two young Americans, Frederick Law Olmsted and Charles Loring Brace, learned the truth of the adage that no outsider can see Ireland from the jaundiced perspective of an Irishman when in 1850 they set out from New Haven with Olmsted's brother for Belfast on the last leg of a walking tour of the British Isles. Charmed earlier by the English

countryside with its neat cottages, well-trimmed hedges and
high level of cultivation, Ireland proved a shock to them.
Along the Irish coast, where many wealthy landowners lived,
they encountered neatly whitewashed peasant cottages and
handsome park gates, but as they moved into the interior
of Ireland the appearance of the country changed. They
found pigs intermingling with people in the halls of some
living quarters and fields "filled with weeds or entirely
neglected. . . ."[47]

But this, the primitive Erin of Godkin's youth, had its
compensations for at least one of the travellers. Olmsted
and Brace carried a letter of introduction to Robert Neill,
a merchant of Belfast who had entertained in his home the
American abolitionists William Lloyd Garrison and Frederick
Douglass; and at Neill's home Brace could not take his eyes
off his host's daughter, Letitia.[48] Edwin Godkin was a friend
of Letitia and her brother William, but he apparently did not
meet the American visitors on this occasion. (Later, after he
migrated to the United States, he found in Brace and Frederick Law Olmsted unselfish patrons.)

From Ireland Brace, a newly ordained clergyman, and the
Olmsteds made their way to the continent, Brace lingering,
after his friends departed for home, in Germany for the winter. The spring of 1851 he ventured into Hungary, where the
Austrian authorities briefly jailed him as a sympathizer with
the Hungarian revolutionary Louis Kossuth. Thereafter he
tarried a while in London and there seems to have met young
Godkin, who had taken rooms in Richmond for the summer
with young Neill. Brace, now in the process of becoming
engaged to Letitia Neill, had begun a book on his Hungarian
experiences that found Godkin an interested reader.[49]

With the opening of 1851 the nineteen-year-old Godkin
was contemplating his future after college. He had reached
young manhood with no discernable religious convictions—
he was an announced skeptic, although for social convenience he adopted the Episcopal faith—and he had no intention of following his father into the pulpit. His declared
goal was a legal career. Like his father, who was now in
Londonderry editing the Derry Standard, he had newsprint
in his blood, but journalism was a trade that did not offer him

the social status he craved. One option was to go to Dublin and study law at the King's Inn, perhaps financing himself with part-time work on Duffy's *Nation* or on the *Freeman's Journal,* the famous old Dublin biweekly to which his father contributed after 1846.[50] Instead he decided to confront the barriers of English society and seek his fortune in London.

Young Godkin was no stranger to London, for after his father gave up the pulpit, James spent nearly two years there writing for the *Standard of Freedom* and for provincial papers like the Belfast *Independent* and the *Freeman's Journal.*[51] In the middle of 1851 Edwin moved his belongings to London and in the fall, in a "sanguine eager" mood, he set about studying law at the Middle Temple.

The Middle Temple, one of the four Inns of Court where young men prepared for the English bar, boasted its own hall, a stately sixteenth-century Elizabethan building. Godkin took rooms with another student in nearby Garden Court and settled down to spend the three years usually required before being called to the bar. But not for long. His roommate was a budding journalist—J. C. McCoan, later editor of the *Levant Herald,* and the lure of the newsprint beckoned Edwin.[52] He took himself to Ludgatehill to his father's Radical acquaintance, John Cassell, publisher of the *Standard of Freedom* and several working-class magazines, and Cassell gave him a post on one of his new magazines, *The Workingmen's Friend.*[53]

An unpretentious, rudely designed penny weekly containing travel sketches, tales, verse, and home instruction, *The Workingmen's Friend* nonetheless boasted among its contributors the young Jules Verne, Fredrika Bremer, and Harriet Beecher Stowe.[54] Publisher Cassell's credo was similar to the one James Godkin had tried to instill in his children. James's concern for the downtrodden victims of the Irish land policy had its counterpart in Cassell's pacifism and interest in the English working classes. None of these concerns evoked strong interest in Edwin, whose Radicalism was middle-class.[55] But he embraced two of his father's teachings—education unhampered by sectarian control and editorial adherence to "truth, freedom and justice, irrespective of party interests."[56]

Throughout late 1851 and 1852 young Godkin served as a subeditor of The Workingmen's Friend. Between this and leisurely, fun-filled summers in Richmond with William Neill, there was no time for law studies.[57] Because he was not compelled to strive for effect in a worker's magazine, his writing is free of much of the pretentiousness that distinguishes his later productions. One contribution to The Workingmen's Friend is his only known venture into fiction, a short story entitled "A Christmas in Rathnagru."[58] A bizarre tale of a college duel, interwoven with the visit of a banshee to a country home, the story is rather skillfully executed and indicates that, had Godkin wished, he could have excelled his sister Georgina as a writer of minor fiction.[59]

Godkin was conceived during the revolutionary upheavals of 1830; he came to manhood during the second great wave of revolutions to sweep Europe in the nineteenth century. The revolutions of 1848, to the extent that they were led principally by middle-class men attached to the interests of property and trade, fired his imagination. By the spring of 1849 the contagion that had begun in France the previous year had spread to Hungary, and the Austrians only with difficulty quelled the resulting uprising. Two years later Godkin, following in the footsteps of his father, who wrote on historical subjects for Cassell, commenced a series of historical sketches of Hungary in The Workingmen's Friend.[60] The sketches, which came as Brace was completing his Hungarian book, appeared regularly in the magazine between November 1851 and February 1852. After extensively rewriting and expanding them, using material on the 1849 Hungarian uprising from the military memoirs of General György Klapka and articles by Boldenyi and de Lansdorff in the Revue des Deux Mondes, Godkin in 1853 published The History of Hungary and the Magyars.[61]

The central theme of this 380-page book is the tyranny the Austrians had imposed on the Magyars. Frankly intended to capitalize on the Kossuth excitement sweeping the English-speaking world, the book went through several printings, including an American edition, and it earned its twenty-two-year-old author the thanks of a group of Hungarian patriots. The History of Hungary and the Magyars, unlike the somewhat sophomoric sketches from which it is derived, is well written, but it is a tract for the times rather than a work of scholarship. Godkin acknowledged in his introduction that he did not expect the book to "satisfy all the requirements of criticism." One passage, which reflects the hortatory style that characterized his writing, tells of the unsuccessful uprising of 1848 in Vienna and of what followed after the rebel leaders surrendered the city to the authorities:

> The Austrian government was busily engaged in the work of butchering the unhappy rebels, a species of employment for which its army has always shown itself better adapted than for conflict with a foreign foe. The history of its campaigns is but a list of defeats and disgraces; it lays down its arms to an armed enemy, and eagerly takes up the axe and the cord against its fellow-countrymen, or the unfortunate peoples whom the arbitrary decrees of diplomatists have flung, bound and helpless, at its feet. . . . The city was abandoned to the rage of the military, who were chagrined at their former defeat and pusillanimous flight; and the inhabitants lived for weeks in a state of terrorism and suspense more horrible than the dangers of actual hostilities. Innocence was no shield, for the courts-martial seldom took the trouble to sift evidence. To be arrested was, in most cases, taken as ample proof of guilt.[62]

In another passage Godkin alludes to the vicissitudes of Brace at the hands of the Austrian authorities in Hungary in 1851. Brace, although "extremely guarded in his conversation and inquiries . . . soon drew down on him the suspicion of the authorities, was arrested, tried secretly by court-martial, browbeaten and bullied by coarse and brutal soldiers, and at last thrown into a dungeon." After being released through the intercession of the United States consul, the American

> bore testimony to the utter prostration of the people under the grinding tyranny . . . the ferocious insolence of the police, the unchecked brutality of the soldiery, the crowded state of the dungeons—crammed with wretches who had lingered in agony for months and years . . . the torturings, the beatings with sticks, the daily fusillades on the glacis, and all the other horrors and enormities by which tyranny heaps outrage on humanity, and blasphemes God. But he bore testimony, too, to the reverence with which Kossuth's name and memory are treasured in the hearts of the people; to the pride with which they look back to that surpassing struggle in which the valour

of their sons and brothers so long baffled the rage of despots.
. . .[63]

Judging by the fact that it went through several printings,
including an American edition, Godkin's first book was a
popular success. Its author had made no extravagant claim
to scholarship, and he need not have sorrowed over the conclusions he reached in it, but sorrow over them he did. His
enthusiasm for Kossuth and democracy passed, and he dis-
carded The History of Hungary from his shelf. It had been
composed "in a flush of enthusiasm," he answered a query,
and was a book he no longer wished "to own or have recalled."[64] Keeping silent thereafter about his part in the
"Kossuth craze," as he now called it, he censured those
who, as he put it, went "nearly crazy over the Hungarians
and, indeed, over one party of the Hungarians [Kossuth]
which Hungary has since rejected."[65] It would be more than
forty years before Godkin would attempt another book about
democracy, and this one would be as penetrating in its
criticisms of the democratic ideology as the first one had
been unstinting in its praise.

Chapter Two
War Correspondent with the Turks

> The Allied armies, if I am not greatly
> mistaken, were not sent out here to
> form a huge paving board, or act as
> Health or Town Commissioners, but
> to restore the Principalities to the
> Porte.

The same year that Godkin published his *History of Hungary*, the long-smoldering Eastern Question burst into flames, when Europe's perennial invalid, Turkey—egged on by England and France—sent an army to oppose Russian encroachments along the Danube. A number of English leaders, including Prince Albert and Radical politicians Richard Cobden and John Bright, deplored the clamor of the British press for intervention on the side of Turkey. Especially disappointing to them was the prowar stance of the liberal *Daily News*.[1]

Godkin, although a firm supporter of Cobden's Free Trade doctrines, had never embraced the Manchester politician's pacifism. Moreover he was caught up in the popular antipathy toward Russia, partly because the czar had intervened in 1849 to assist Austria in crushing the Hungarian independence movement. In the fall of 1853 Godkin addressed a letter on the Eastern Question to the *Daily News* which paved the way for an invitation to him to serve as that paper's special correspondent in Turkey.[2] Several days later Turkey declared war on Russia and Godkin packed his suitcases and left for Constantinople.

In Rumania, in the meantime, the bloody engagement of Oltenitza had been fought. In December Godkin tarried in Constantinople long enough to learn that more Russo-Turkish hostilities were expected on the lower Danube and then boarded a steamer for the Bulgarian seaport of Varna. From there he traveled overland, with a servant and two guards

provided by the local pasha, to the Turkish army headquarters in the Bulgarian town of Shumla, where the commander-
in-chief, Omer Pasha, was encamped with the main body of
his army.[3] Godkin succeeded in getting an interview with the
Croatian soldier-of-fortune and sent lavish praise of him to
the *Daily News.*[4] (Critics of Omer Pasha charged that as
Michael Lattas he had deserted his post as a paymaster in
the Austrian army after embezzling money and that in the
Turkish army his soldiers went hungry while he pocketed
money for their rations.)[5] Godkin was also impressed with
the Turkish soldiery, whom he found singularly free of
"brawls or irregularities of any kind" as well as "most of the
other vices of European soldiers."[6]

Scarcely had Godkin arrived in Shumla than word came
that the Russians were moving eastward from Bucharest to
attack Kalafat, a fortified Rumanian village on the Danube
garrisoned by about 15,000 men under Achmet Pasha. The
correspondent joined forces with Captain Maxwell, a British
military observer who was serving as a special correspondent of the *Morning Chronicle,* and another British officer;
riding day and night they reached the Bulgarian village of
Widdin across the Danube from Kalafat two days before
Christmas.[7] The three took a cottage on the outskirts of
Widdin, and Godkin commenced sending letters to the *Daily
News* under a Kalafat dateline—although it would be days
before he and his companions would cross the river to see
the Turkish encampment. They were soon joined by an earlier arrival, Joseph Crowe of the *Illustrated London News,*
who accepted the assignment after Thackeray reportedly
declined it. One of the highlights of their stay, Crowe subsequently remembered, was their indefatigable Greek servant,
Spiro, who cooked with what purported to be fresh butter, "a
whitish tallow, run, after melting, into a goatskin, to which
the hair internally adhered." To cook with it one picked out
the hair, yet "nothing could clear it of the taste conveyed by
the skin."[8]

The expected hostilities were not long in coming. In January 1854 Achmet Pasha led part of his garrison out of Kalafat
and surprised the Russians at Cetatea. Godkin, who did not
witness the action, nonetheless gave his readers a graphic

description of it. The Russian soldiery he found contempt-
ible; the dreaded Cossacks proved useful only as scouts
"and generally take care to keep themselves out of reach of
danger," and the artillery could hit nothing but by accident.
On the other side, the Turkish artillery showed exceptional
accuracy, and the soldiers of the sultan gave ample proof of
their discipline.[9] But Godkin would soon moderate these
sophomoric judgments.[10]

The action at Cetatea temporarily halted Russian plans for
an offensive in that region, and the special correspondents
at Widdin, hungry for copy, turned to other subjects. In one
dispatch a sexually frustrated Godkin complained of the
unattractiveness of Bulgarian women, "veiled and draped
figures that glide like phantoms through the streets."[11] In
another he found fault with the Turkish army's medical service, supposing it to be "composed almost entirely of roving
adventurers of every . . . profession but the one they practice
—Italians and Germans mainly, jugglers, outlaws, runaway
bankrupts, and, in short, men who in most cases had shut
themselves out from all hopes of an honorable existence in
their own country."[12] But at the prompting of a recently
made Italian friend, he visited a Turkish military hospital
and to his surprise found the Italian medical staff reasonably
competent. Later he returned to his original estimate of the
Italian doctors as "impudent mountebanks who had followed
all sorts of vile callings at home."[13]

The military inactivity bred growing impatience toward
the British and French governments for not declaring war on
the czar. "Every one," asserted Godkin, "feels convinced that
an Anglo-French army, acting in conjunction with the Turks,
would clear the Russians out of Moldavia and Wallachia in
one campaign, and dictate peace to the Czar on his own
territory." He underscored Russian military ineptitude, as-
suring his readers that a sizeable part of the czarist armies
were Jewish conscripts who would hardly fight, "as your
good Hebrew has always in modern times shown a thorough
distaste for the calling of a soldier."[14]

Even as Godkin was writing this, England and France were
declaring war on Russia with the announcement that they
would carry the conflict to the Danube. Godkin's pleasure

at this was diluted by the news that Austria had joined the allies. Better she ally herself with Russia—even though it prolonged the war—so that final victory "would see Austria wiped out from the map of Europe, and some fifty millions of men delivered from a slavery that surpasses in vileness all that is recorded in history."[15]

With February came improved weather on the Danube, and the Turks began sending heavily armed reconnoitering parties into the Russian-occupied Rumanian countryside around Kalafat. Occasionally the special correspondents— they had grown to four with the arrival of a Frenchman, Guys of the *Illustrated London News*—joined the sorties, usually led by the fierce-looking soldier-of-fortune, Iskender Bey. "Venez avec moi, mon cher," Iskender invited Godkin, "je vous menerait dans un endroit bien chaud."[16] Godkin, Maxwell, Crowe, and Guys, together with several English military observers, received their baptism of fire when they joined a Turkish reconnaissance-in-force of a Russian-occupied village. Riding in company with a troop of fierce *bashi-bazouks*—the ill-disciplined Turkish irregular cavalry—they came in sight of some Cossack outposts. While the *bashi-bazouks* spurred their horses in pursuit of the Cossacks fleeing amidst the hayricks into the village, the Englishmen reined up alongside a precipice and Godkin dismounted to heed a call of nature. Suddenly, to everyone's astonishment, the *bashi-bazouks* returned, "running home in wild confusion" followed by a troop of Cossacks "scrambling up" the precipice on their left. Adding to the Specials' discomfiture, the *Daily News* correspondent was not ready to mount his horse. "A certain button on his dress," recalled Crowe, "seemed to give him endless trouble." Finally Godkin was ready, just as the Cossacks were upon them, "with lances to the front." The Englishmen wheeled their mounts just in time to escape.[17]

With the declaration of war, England, France, and little Piedmont began readying expeditionary forces to send to the Danube. An impressive-appearing Piedmontese military observer, Captain Govone, later Italian minister of war, arrived at Widdin and moved in with the special correspondents. Sometimes he, with Godkin and Maxwell, would cross the

Danube and spend the night at the Turkish camp at Kalafat.[18]
On one such excursion across the river early in March, Godkin took time to note the plight of the refugees stoically encamped on the bank awaiting passage to Widdin, their entire
possessions piled on bullock carts, "pots, pans, bedding,
Indian corn, gourds, in one heterogeneous mass." "I . . . must
say it would be hard to witness a more pitiable exemplifica-
tion of the horrors of this war," noted the young correspondent, "brought upon peaceful Europe by the accursed ambition of the Muscovite despot."[19]

With the arrival of spring and the Russians still making
no offensive movement toward Kalafat, the allied military
observers departed for Rustchuk where new hostilities were
expected. Crowe, Godkin, and Maxwell were preparing to
follow them when Maxwell fell ill. After some debate Godkin
consented to remain with him, whereupon the correspondent of the *Illustrated London News* left, leaving behind two
resentful companions. Maxwell was soon able to travel, and
late in March 1854 he and Godkin made their way on horseback out of Widden.[20] Enroute to Rustchuk they passed
through Bulgarian villages heavily populated by Rumanian
emigrés—Wallachians who had fled their homeland, wrote
Godkin, "to escape the tyranny of their boyards, who are,
without exception, the most worthless aristocracy in Europe." At Plerna they lodged overnight at a private home,
where their host's two attractive daughters rebuffed their
attempt at flirtation. But their carefree mood changed to
a more business-like one when they learned that the Russians had crossed the Danube and were launching a major
offensive.[21]

Reaching the Bulgarian town of Rustchuk early in April,
Godkin and Maxwell found it grimly prepared for war.
Perched on a sloping southern bank of the Danube, it overlooked the Russian-occupied Rumanian town of Giurgevo
across the river. Some inhabitants had refused to flee and
had excavated caves under their homes for protection from
bombardment. To Godkin's irritation, the troops were reliev-
ing their boredom by firing their cannons and carbines at
each other across the river. Pointing out that a Turkish
soldier "who was strolling about had his arm broken in this

way," he moralized that "a soldier does not fight to kill, but to win. . . ."[22]

The western press was now becoming critical of the conduct of the war, and the military authorities were showing reluctance to let the Specials into the war zone. So far Godkin had been laudatory of the Turks or else circumspect in his criticisms of them, but now he joined the rising chorus of disapproval.[23] Moreover he was censorious of the European press for what he termed its "mania for the home manufacture" of war news. Much of the press coverage of the war, especially the Austrian, was "either pure fiction, or truth so disguised or distorted as scarcely to be capable of recognition."[24] Even the good, grey *Times* of London, he pointed out, had swallowed the Viennese newspaper falsehood that Omer Pasha had occupied and burned Bucharest.

With the Russians across the Danube and marching in force on the Dobrudja, the Turks evacuated Rustchuk and fell back on Shulma, where Omer Pasha was encamped with the main body. Godkin and Maxwell joined the withdrawal south.[25] As they wound their way down the steep heights through the hilltop entrenchments overlooking the northern edge of Shumla, the correspondents found their progress slowed by throngs of soldiers, "ruffians of every stamp," snorted Godkin. There were the colorfully garbed *arnouts*, irregular infantry of the Turkish army, "ten of whom are not worth one regular soldier of any nation in the world save the troops of the Pope, or those of the King of Naples"; there were the rapacious *bashi-bazouks*, whom vicious beatings ordered by Omer Pasha had not tamed.[26] In the *Daily News* Godkin urged Omer Pasha to march the *bashi-bazouks* before firing squads, suggesting that a "few fusillades on a large scale would inspire more . . . terror than all the sticks in the Balkans."[27] Yet not uncharacteristically his sympathies came to the front when Omer Pasha heeded this advice and ordered the execution of a number of *bashi-bazouks*.[28]

In Shumla the *Daily News* correspondent and the *Morning Chronicle* correspondent were reunited with Govone, and they presented a letter of introduction from Iskender Bey to Sadyk Pasha (the Polish Count Chikoffsky), intending to remain in that town until the arrival of the allied expeditionary army. But deciding after a fortnight that nothing would happen in Bulgaria until the arrival of the British and French, they left and with Govone went to Constantinople, where they remained two weeks, part of this time at the allied camp at nearby Scutari.[29] To his readers Godkin acknowledged the superiority of the French army over the British, yet he conceded that the sight of the young, unbearded Britons aroused "a thousand conflicting emotions" in his breast, "pride or pity, hope or regret, to see these fair-haired Saxons sauntering along the shores of Asia Minor, the defenders of a people whom their ancestors shed so much blood to exterminate or repel. . . . how very few may ever set foot on English soil again!" He noted the sprinkling of British wives at Scutari, observing that "the devotion which makes a woman follow her husband into Bulgaria, with even a slight knowledge of what awaits her, is certainly something nobler than the valor of the bravest soldier."[30]

Returning to Varna early in May, Godkin, Maxwell, and Govone settled down in that Bulgarian port city to await the arrival of the British expeditionary force. One evening Godkin and Maxwell joined the elderly Paton of *The Times*—*The Times's* colorful William H. Russell had not yet arrived in Bulgaria—at a dinner given by the British consul, Colonel Neale, in company with Bairam Pasha (General Cannon) and the commander of *HMS Banshee*. Godkin was keeping a diary at this time, and some of his entries colorfully depict his hatred of the British aristocracy. In one he describes the arrival aboard the *Banshee* of the quartermaster general of the British army, Lord de Ros, "the oldest baronet in England, in reality a thrust-up, whippersnapper about town . . . Oh England! Oh my country! . . . oh, this slutten aristocracy!"[31]

With the further advance of spring the Russians laid siege to Silistria, the Danubian fortress at the northeast corner of the Bulgarian quadrilateral. Although its Turkish and Egyptian garrison put up a spirited resistance, Silistria, it appeared, would fall unless the allies relieved it. But the allied expeditionary army marked time in Turkey. As the foreign correspondents in Bulgaria waited impatiently for its arrival, they stepped up their criticisms of the conduct of the war.

In the *Daily News* Godkin turned to sarcasm:

> We are told every day of the wonders that are being wrought
> by the Allied troops at Gallipoli, of the regular cleansing of the
> town, of the establishment of cafes, European baths and wash-
> houses, and, for aught I know, libraries, penny news-rooms,
> and model lodging-houses; of the astonishment of the Turks at
> French activity and vivacity, and the wonderful effect which
> this spectacle and example is likely to produce upon them;
> but, if anyone supposes that all this will do anything towards
> driving the Russians out of Bulgaria, he is egregiously mis-
> taken. The Allied armies, if I am not greatly mistaken, were
> not sent out here to form a huge paving board, or act as Health
> or Town Commissioners, but to restore the Principalities to
> the Porte.[32]

Unless the allies took the offensive before winter, Godkin
warned his readers, the sultan would have to accept peace
on Russian terms; for the Turks were weaker north of the
Balkan mountains than their pride let them admit. "Ten
thousand men in their mouths became twenty, and so on in
regular progress till one ends by having an army large
enough to overrun Europe." Yet Godkin sympathized with
the Turks in their weakness; ". . . all in all, in docility, obedience, fidelity, patience under hardships, bravery in action,
no troops in the world surpass them. Officer them well, and
establish a good commissariat, and the Crescent might again
make Europe tremble."[33]

On 19 May a British war ship arrived at Varna bearing the
allied supreme commanders, Lord Raglan and Marshal St.
Arnaud. Omer Pasha rode over from Shumla in all his osten-
tatious finery to meet them, and together the three generals
journeyed back to Omer's headquarters for a hurried inspection of the Turkish army. Cynically Godkin noted the event in
his diary: "The big-wigs landed and drove around the town
on Friday. The same evening at midnight they started for
Shumla. What for? God only knows."[34] His irritation arose
chiefly from the fact that the foreign correspondents were
not invited to the ceremonies. Afterwards Govone, who was
leaving Varna to join in the defense of Silistria, came to dine
with Godkin and Maxwell and amusingly described his pre-
sentation to the allied commanders-in-chief.

The visit of the allied commanders signified that the allied expeditionary force intended soon to be on its way to Bulgaria. In Varna harbor an allied fleet lay at anchor, while at water's edge British sappers were hastily constructing a pier.[35] At the end of May came the first allied troop transports.[36] As Godkin watched the troops disembark, he swelled with imperialistic pride at "one of the most hopeful facts of our time, that the armies of the really great and free states of the world are becoming the pioneers of civilization and the arts, instead of being the emissaries of violence and destruction." The allied expeditionary force was "a great company of missionaries who teach civilization" through example, from which the Turk was learning "what he never could have learned in any other way—the folly of the pride which made him fancy himself the *élite* of mankind, and how immeasurably inferior he is to the Christians. . . ."[37]

Thus although Godkin still enthusiastically endorsed the allied intervention, like the other special correspondents he had scant praise for its commanders. One reason was the coolness of Lord Raglan and his staff toward the press. Lacking access to news at allied headquarters, the Specials relied on enlisted men's gripes and café rumors, nearly all critical of the conduct of the war.

One of the correspondents' targets was General Sir George Brown, an old Peninsula veteran, who, although a brave soldier, was regarded as a martinet. Brown, in young Godkin's view, was in the war theater solely "to see to it that the army was ruined according to the regulations." "Nothing has excited so much indignation," he asserted in the *Daily News* in July, "as General Brown's conduct with regard to the sick." Owing to poor rations—bad beef and bad bread— dysentery was widespread in the Light Division, yet Brown was ordering his men into the field "with no medical supplies except brandy and distilled water."[38] Another festering problem, the baggage question, brought a stern admonishment from Godkin: "Let officers and men carry as little baggage as possible, as few changes of dress, &c., as the dirtiest cynic can desire; but by all means shelter them at night and feed them well."[39]

It soon became evident that Lord Raglan and Marshal St. Arnaud did not intend an early campaign in the Balkans.

Godkin and Maxwell, disinclined to mark time at the allied encampment near Varna as William H. Russell of *The Times* and other correspondents were doing, set out north to visit the Turko-Russian front. At Rustchuk they found the military situation changed since their last visit.[40] On 6 July 1854 a Turkish force, learning that the enemy, under Austrian pressure, was withdrawing from the north bank of the Danube, crossed the river and engaged the Russians on an island between Rustchuk and the Rumanian shore. After a day of savage fighting, in which several English officers and scores of Turkish soldiers were killed, the Russians evacuated the Rumanian town of Giurgevo and set up a new encampment two and one-half miles distant. Omer Pasha followed up the Turkish advantage by bringing up the main body of his army from Shumla, and English sappers set about throwing bridges across the Danube.

A few days after the battle, Godkin crossed the river with Govone and another Italian friend, Crespi, to inspect Giurgevo. The inhabitants had fled *en masse* with the Russians, but to Godkin the Rumanian town was a pleasant contrast to "wretched, tumbledown, filthy, ill-favoured Rustchuk." The three men inspected the surrounding Turkish outposts and then settled themselves for the afternoon in the town's principal hotel.[41] Relaxing over bottles of iced champagne, Godkin spotted his old fellow lodger, Crowe of the *Illustrated London News,* "looking very healthy and nasty." Inevitably the conversation turned to the troubles of the press. Govone mentioned that Colonel Symonds, the British commissioner to the Turkish army, had advised Omer Pasha to expel the foreign correspondents. That night Godkin angrily exploded in his diary: "Symonds is a thorough humbug. He has all the airs and impertinence of a Jack-in-office, and is, I believe, as incompetent a Jackanapes as lives, which is one way of accounting for his hatred of the press."[42] But in the *Daily News* he charged that it was Lord de Ros who was turning the Turkish commander-in-chief against the foreign correspondents.[43]

With the Russians withdrawing northward, the inhabitants of Giurgevo began filtering back to their homes, and life returned to normal. Godkin, Maxwell, and Govone com-

mandeered an empty house, furnishing it with effects that its
owners had stored in the cellar. The poet Moritz Hartmann,
special correspondent of the Cologne *Gazette,* joined them.[44]
Godkin had fallen victim to an intermittent fever, "from bed
to the cafe — and from cafe to bed," but he was enjoying his
friends' companionship and the scanty attire of the Rumanian females. The weather was hot, and the coolness of the
feminine *dishabille,* he happily informed his readers, was "a
complete and triumphal answer to all objections that may be
made to it on the score of propriety."[45]

But the charm of Giurgevo, like that of Varna, proved
transitory. Especially frustrating to Godkin was the inactivity
of the allies. "Not one step had been made during the whole
summer towards the great object of the war," he complained
in August, "the mutilation of Russian power." Additionally
galling was the recently signed Turkish-Austrian accord. In
it, alleged Godkin, the Turks bowed to Austrian demands
and surrendered to them two Hungarian refugees, showing
that the price of collaborating with Austria was "to wallow in
the same mire, and smear one's self with the same filth."[46]

Godkin, Maxwell, and Crowe had been the first English
special correspondents to enter the war zone, but now nearly
all the London papers were represented, and rivalries were
developing. At Varna Godkin met *The Times's* much-publi-
cized William H. Russell. A likeable Irishman with a fund of
droll stories, Russell impressed Godkin as a "welcomed guest
at every mess table" but an object of resentment among the
other correspondents because *The Times* had used its influence to have him housed and provided with horses at
government expense.[47] After cholera struck the British Light
Division encamped near Varna, the *Daily News* carried a
sneering account that Russell had "bolted" the camp in fear
of the plague "and was not likely soon to return." When
Russell learned of the story, he notified *Daily News* editor
Knight Hunt that he would "trounce" the "lying" Godkin the
next time he saw him, and he addressed a similar threat to
Godkin. Godkin replied with a denial that he had written the
offending piece, whereupon Russell handsomely apologized.
"You have overwhelmed me with shame and regret," he told
the younger man, adding that the whole experience had been

a lesson to him "not to act on hearsay evidence."[48]

Under renewed Austrian pressure, the Russians continued their withdrawal northward and began evacuating Bucharest. In the *Daily News* Godkin, ignorant of the reasons for the evacuation, credited the Russian withdrawal to the Turks, stating that they had negotiated "with more firmness, tact, and decision, than all the European diplomatists put together," and then, when negotiations ceased to be fruitful, "fought with unexampled energy and bravery."[49] Early in August Maxwell, Godkin, and Hartmann requested permission to accompany the Turkish advance guard under Iskender Bey to Bucharest. The Turkish authorities refused, but the correspondents hired a coach and went anyway.

Godkin and Maxwell were in their hotel room in Bucharest—the Jewish Hartmann found it necessary to stay with friends—when Rumanian police confronted them with a warrant for their arrest for illegal entry. Determined to resist, Godkin ordered his horse and set off at a gallop, with two lancers in pursuit. "Enroute," as he related in the *Daily News*, "my pistol jumped out of the holster and left me without arms; and having a very limited acquaintance with the town, I speedily lost my way, and . . . began to promenade up and down the streets, the lancers still at my heels."[50] Maxwell joined him and the two tried to reach the English consul, but they found their way barred by Rumanian soldiers with drawn bayonets who encircled them "with a very amusing display of martial ardour" while the two, according to Godkin, entertained the gathering crowd by yelling epithets at the soldiers.[51] Finally the prefect of police arrived and ordered the soldiers away, explaining to the correspondents that the order for their arrest came from Bucharest commandant Sadyk Pasha, on orders of Omer Pasha. Thereupon Godkin and Maxwell demanded an audience with Sadyk Pasha, who declined but agreed to free them on parole while they pleaded their case by mail with the Turkish commander-in-chief. Angrily Godkin fired a despatch to the *Daily News*: "No man can have a higher respect for Omer Pasha than I, but I must state frankly that no man in the Turkish dominions, be he who he may . . . shall outrage me with impunity."[52]

Because, hitherto, Godkin had been allowed to move freely about the war zone, he concluded that the Bucharest incident meant that British official circles were now deliberately hamstringing the press. "Lord de Ros, the Quartermaster-General, who makes no secret of his monomania on the subject of the press," he asserted in the *Daily News,* "did all in his power to prejudice Omer Pasha against us, he even implored him to send us away, and pointed out in a most feeling manner the prodigious evils that resulted from our presence." Lord de Ros and his fellow English officials "ought to have been ashamed to talk thus to a foreigner of the greatest glory of their country—the newspaper press."[53]

At length Godkin and Maxwell were granted approval to remain in Bucharest, and they settled down in a cottage on the grounds of a hotel with a good restaurant. Though they found Rumania politically debauched, its capital city had its special compensations, such as the Warmburg Gardens, the favorite summer gathering place for the *soirees* and promenades of the fashionable.[54] One of the fascinations of the city for Godkin was the sexual life of the married women. His readers learned that wifely infidelity carried with it "the most perfect impunity, as far as public opinion is concerned," so that during the Russian occupation czarist officers, "with all the polish with which a Russian knows how to cover his barbarism, were vastly more successful in the boudoir and the salon than . . . on the battlefield."[55]

Less pleasing to the young bachelor was the Bucharest rumor mill. Besides the German language papers at work manufacturing "*canards,* fables, and inventions" about the war, the foreign consulates, together with a Greek cafe, teemed with false reports.[56] "In the Greek cafe . . . I am persuaded a committee sits nightly for the invention of lying reports, and employs agents for their propagation on the morrow." He mourned: "Oh Greece! oh, Greece! how much enthusiasm was poured over you . . . without making you any less a brigand and a liar. . . ."[57]

With the withdrawal of the Russians from the Principalities the stated object of the war had been attained, but England and France now decided to destroy the Russian power in the Black Sea by seizing the Russian fortress of

Sebastopol, Crimean headquarters of the czar's Black Sea fleet. To this end in September the cholera-decimated allied army debarked from Varna for the Crimea, leaving Godkin and the bulk of Omer Pasha's army behind.

Except for a brief journey into Moldavia, Godkin spent the rest of 1854 with the Turkish army of occupation in Bucharest. With emotion he described in the *Daily News* the tug-of-war between the Turkish and Austrian occupiers for control of the city.[58] When the Austrian troops entered the city with great pomp in September 1854, his scorn was unrestrained. They were all "brilliance, insolence and assumption," whereas those Turks whose uniforms were threadbare were refused permission to parade, "hiding their rags in their tents while the best beaten, oftenest-thrashed troops in the world were taking possession of Turkish conquests...."[59]

Should the allies fail in the Crimea, believed Godkin, Austria would dishonor her commitments to the alliance.[60] While he anxiously awaited the news from the Crimea, he pondered the allied mismanagement of the war: "It is hardly necessary to go back to last April—to condemn the needless delays at Malta, the delay of two months at Scutari and Gallipoli, the delay of two months more at Varna, as if everybody in office and authority was labouring might and main to give time to the enemy."[61]

As weeks went by with Sebastopol still in Russian hands, Godkin's criticisms grew. In November he demanded an investigation of the British ministry, implying that it had "tacitly connived" in the Austrian "treachery" by which the Turks were prevented from prosecuting the war against Russia in the Principalities. In the *Daily News* he declared:

> The blood of all Englishmen that now moistens the soil of the Crimea cries to Heaven for vengeance, and it is high time for their countrymen no longer to trust to the bragging and fine words of diplomatists, but to insist once and for all upon having a clear and concise explanation of the extraordinary circumstances that in a war undertaken on behalf of Turkey, the Turkish army, 80,000 strong, in an excellent position, was allowed to remain idle for three months, while the Russian army opposed to them was allowed to retire unmolested before them, and make a march of six weeks' duration, and then fling themselves *en masse* upon the English and French in a distant corner of the Crimea.[62]

The disclosure of the role of the English and French governments in kowtowing to Austrian villainy, predicted Godkin, would fill the public with permanent contempt for diplomacy.[63]

At the end of the year Godkin and his companions left Bucharest and returned to Varna, preparing to follow the Turkish army into the Crimea. His dispatches to the *Daily News* now reflected a thorough disillusionment with allied leadership. The British army in the Crimea, he reported, was in a horrible state, men "dying like cockroaches" and the "most horrible and disgraceful confusion" everywhere.[64]

Early in February 1855 Omer Pasha's army disembarked in the Crimea and occupied the coastal town of Eupatoria, north of Sebastopol. Godkin, following in a troop transport, arrived in time to be the only European correspondent to witness the bloody Russian sortie against Eupatoria two weeks later, scoring a beat over the other London papers with the news of the Turkish victory. The Turks now dug in at Eupatoria in preparation for a long occupation, a bored Godkin reporting to his readers in April: "The soldiers are getting quite sick of this eternal digging."[65]

Ever since Bucharest Godkin had been having difficulties with the military authorities. Like all of the special correspondents he expected them to supply him with transportation; when it was not forthcoming his criticisms grew.[66] Late in March an incident occurred that further ruffled relations between the press and the military. A troop of *bashi-bazouks*, ordered out of Eupatoria for a reconnaissance of the countryside, attacked some Cossack outposts and, according to Godkin in the *Daily News*, massacred some of the wounded without mercy.[67] The next month, as Omer Pasha prepared to send a sizeable contingent of his army by sea from Eupatoria to join the allies before Sebastopol, Godkin and a correspondent of *The Times* were refused cabin accommodations on an English transport, even though, charged Godkin in the *Daily News*, a cabin was given "without hesitation to a German Jew, an adventurer from New York, who was roaming about, probably seeing whom he might devour."[68] The other *Daily News* correspondent, headquartered with the allied forces in the Crimea, rushed to Godkin's defense, expressing to the paper the opinion: "It is high time that [Colonel Symonds] should be personally and publicly made responsible for his underhand intrigues against his countrymen in Omer Pasha's camp."[69]

Ironically no sooner had Godkin reached Omer Pasha's headquarters near Sebastopol than he was disabled by a recurrence of his intermittent fever and evacuated to the British military hospital at Scutari. He did not rejoin the Turkish army until June. From this point onward his dispatches are mostly critical of the Turks, especially the Turkish leaders. Omer Pasha, he concluded, had not twenty officers under him with "a particle of courage and honor."[70]

Except for a few days in June when Godkin detached himself from the Turkish army in order to witness the illstarred allied attack that month on Sebastopol, he remained most of the time at the Turkish headquarters near Sebastopol until the fall of the Russian fortress in September. It was not all personal hardship. He saw much of his friends Crespi and Govone. With Crespi he traversed the Balaclava Plain, joyfully shouting, as their horses reached a gallop, "Siempre avanti Savoia," the motto of Crespi's regiment, the Cavalerie Legere d'Aosta. At the battle of the Chernaya he watched breathlessly with Govone while the bersaglieri (infantrymen of the Piedmontese army) "little men, with cock's tails in their hats and dark green uniforms," retook a bridge at great cost.[71] Nights he spent in his own tent, wangling dinner invitations from assorted pashas and local officials and avoiding the enlisted men's mess. Although Godkin felt that the caste system in the British army had much to do with its inefficiency, his own genteel tastes would not permit him to rub shoulders with the common soldiery.[72]

With operations before Sebastopol virtually at a stalemate, a rumor arose in July that Omer Pasha, his vanity wounded by the refusal of the allied high command to consult with him, would take his army back to Bulgaria. Godkin eagerly welcomed the prospect: "Give us back Bulgaria and Wallachia, says everyone; if we must have war let us have war en regle, with marches . . . villages to occupy, women to make love to . . . ."[73] The next month Omer Pasha stepped down in disgust, leaving his command to an "ignorant and brutal old pasha" who, reported Godkin, hadn't the slightest notion how to deploy an army.[74] The departure of the Turkish commander-in-chief gave the *Daily News* correspondent a chance for the first time to report his true feelings toward him. Omer Pasha, he alleged, was consumed by "inordinate personal vanity"; he would sacrifice any cause to his own ambition. "I must add," Godkin found it expedient to explain, "that when acting alone these defects were by no means striking — It was long before I detected their existence."[75]

The departure of Omer Pasha in August 1855 constituted a clean sweep of the original allied supreme commanders. With the exit of Lord Raglan, General St. Arnaud, and Omer Pasha and the revolution in public opinion toward the war that now was occurring in England, the fall of Sebastopol to the allies the next month was anticlimactic.

Shortly after the fall of the Russian stronghold, Godkin left the Crimea for Constantinople. From there he wrote his last dispatch to the *Daily News* before turning homeward in October.

How shall Godkin be evaluated as a war correspondent? Certainly no assessment can ignore his personality. Although he set for himself loftier standards than most journalists of his day, his temperament overrode his objectivity. Analogies are unsafe, but one might, for the sake of comparison, visualize Godkin's equally compulsive acquaintance, Theodore Roosevelt, trying to play the role of objective reporter of the Spanish-American War. Indirectly Godkin confessed his limitations as a war correspondent when he later wrote of the profession: "As soon after the declaration of war as the correspondents have reached the ground active operations are expected to begin, and delay is treated as a sign of fraudulent intent, or of some sort of humbug on the part of the belligerents. . . ."[76]

Equally important in any assessment of Godkin's stature as a reporter of the Crimean conflict is that, with the passage of time, the climate of ideas in international relations changed, and so did Godkin. For instance, in 1899 he editorially described the Crimean War as an unprovoked aggression by England and France on the czar for sensibly trying to remove "the terrible stain on our civilization that was Turkey."[77]

Godkin's youth and inexperience, plus the fact that he represented a newspaper with less power and circulation than The Times, put him at a disadvantage before a more talented and mature correspondent like William H. Russell, whose paper enjoyed a near-monopoly of influence with the public.[78] Otherwise there is not much to distinguish them as war correspondents. Both Godkin and Russell were ignorant of military tactics; each was prone to misstate facts and to misuse evidence. Both held inflated notions (for their day) of the rights of civilians in a war zone, especially the right of civilians to supply newspapers with sensitive military information. On the more positive side, each performed a service by alerting British readers to the inexcusable mismanagement of the allied effort in the Crimean War. Of the British army and the role of war correspondents during that conflict, Godkin at the end of his career perceptively wrote:

> The British army then suffered, probably more than any Continental army except the Austrian, from the evil . . . of good family connections. It has needed time and much experience to impress upon the modern world . . . that on the field of battle all distinctions vanish. I therefore cannot help thinking that the appearance of the special correspondent in the Crimea, to whatever evils and abuses it may afterwards have led, was a troubling of the waters which was a good thing for the British army and people. It led to a real awakening of the official mind. It brought home to the War Office the fact that the public has something to say about the conduct of wars, and that they are not the concern exclusively, as that delightful old charlatan, Lord Beaconsfield said, of "sovereigns and statesmen."[79]

In 1855 reform was overdue in the British army, and Godkin could take a certain satisfaction in his role, however small, in pointing to the need for a change.

Chapter Three
Belfast to America

> [Americans] have been so long ac-
> customed to look upon a democracy
> as affording the largest measure of
> liberty, that they cannot as yet bring
> themselves to see that a man's neigh-
> bors and friends may prove much
> more troublesome and vexatious ty-
> rants than any king or emperor.

Skirting Greece on his leisurely way homeward, Godkin
halted in Italy to call on friends of Govone in Turin. Months
of fraternization with Govone and Crespi had instilled in him
a liking for upper-class Italians that he would retain into
middle life. His subsequent "monkey and hand-organ man"
characterization of the Italian and his call for a halt to Italian
immigration to the United States testifies as much to Godkin's class bias as to his racism. Years after the Crimean
War, when Govone, now Italian minister of war, committed
suicide after allegations were made against his probity,
Godkin declined to believe that there were flaws in his
character.

From northern Italy Godkin proceeded to France where,
among other stops, he visited a younger sister in school.
Then he crossed the channel to the British Isles, from which
he had been absent two years. A brief, discouraging, London
period followed, reflecting the love-hate courtship he had
carried on with England since he was fourteen. As his friend
Henry Holt remarked, Godkin would happily have remained
in England if he had been born to the peerage or close to it,
but finally convinced that he could not surmount the walls
of English society, he returned to his native soil.[1] He went
first to Dublin, doubtless pondering a reconciliation with his
father, who was now editing the *Daily Express* there. But
while James Godkin took a measure of pride in his Irishness,

35

his oldest son did not. Whatever the real reasons, father and son did not get along, and before long the twenty-four-year-old Edwin was on his way north to Belfast.

March 1856 found him in that northern city giving public lectures on the war.[2] That Northern Ireland should be the magnet, when Godkin's hopes for preferment in England faded, was not strange. Although he took perverse pleasure in ridiculing the Irish, viscerally he was a son of Erin.[3] In Belfast lived many of his acquaintances and exclassmates, such as Tom Ingram—whose brother John was acquiring laurels as a professor at Dublin University—David Cross, R. J. Arnold, and S. Girdwood.[4] Belfast, of course, was the home town of his London chum and benefactor Neill, who in 1853 had encouraged him to seek the job of special correspondent in the east for the *Daily News*. And just returned to Belfast for a visit was Letitia Neill, now Mrs. Charles Loring Brace.[5] Letitia, at her parents' home in Belfast while Brace was in London for an international convention for children's charities, reported that she found Godkin charming.[6]

Other attractions for Godkin in Belfast were the Finlays, Francis D. Jr. and his popular sister Jane. Jane wrote literary notices for the thrice-weekly Belfast *Northern Whig*, while Frank prepared to take over the proprietorship of that paper from his ailing father. Father Finlay was a one-time printer's apprentice from County Down, who in 1824 founded the *Northern Whig*. Because the paper advocated the emancipation of the Catholics in Protestant Ulster, it at first had a stormy existence. In 1826 Finlay had to halt publication in order to serve a three-month prison sentence for libelling a landlord. Arraigned for libel again three years later, Irish leader Daniel O'Connell came to his defense and the charges were dropped.

Unlike O'Connell, Finlay did not support the Repeal agitation of the 1840s, but he shared O'Connell's misgivings about the Young Ireland movement that followed.[7] With the Liberator, he held ultraconservative opinions about property, and he objected to rebellion under any guise. By 1856 he had made the *Northern Whig* a respectable critic of the establishment in Ireland, a liberal, but not radical, paper that young Godkin could identify with at no cost to his principles.

In April, barely two weeks after Godkin arrived in Belfast, he accepted a position as a contributing editor to the *Northern Whig* at a salary of twenty-five pounds per month.[8] Disdaining office labor, he forwarded his contributions from his lodgings in Holywood, a middle-class residential town four miles east of Belfast. When an acquaintance asked him what he did for the paper, Godkin laconically replied that he was in the religious department, his way of saying that he spent much of his time attacking the Ulster Protestants.[9] Contemptuous of the narrow-mindedness of the Presbyterians who bulwarked the truculent Orange faction in Ulster, Godkin was known to his acquaintances for his free thinking. "I hope Mrs. Godkin has more orthodox views, about church going and such matters, than *you* have, and will make you alter your life in that respect," admonished one of his former Belfast friends in 1884, congratulating him on his second marriage.[10]

Six months passed, and the impatient Godkin began to chafe; he was winning neither fame nor money. Jane Finlay was fond of him; he hoped in a year or two to have the editorship of the *Northern Whig*. But conducting a provincial newspaper held no attraction for him. If he had had the patience to stay on the paper for a few years, he might have emulated the feat of Frank H. Hill. Hill, an Englishman of lesser talents than Godkin, after some vicissitudes following his graduation from college, in 1861 became editor of the *Northern Whig* and married Jane Finlay. Then on the recommendation of Jane's brother he became assistant editor and then editor of the *Daily News*, during which time Godkin was still serving that London paper as a special correspondent.[11] *Sic transit fortuna.* The next time Godkin saw Jane Finlay Hill was more than thirty years later. She was to him still as sharp witted as ever but "old, wrinkled and has a wig." Their reunion had been sparked by an exchange of letters in which she appealed to his vanity by alluding to his handsomeness when they were friends in Belfast, and she expressed the wish to see him and "make you and my husband acquainted, otherwise than by [letter]."[12]

In September 1856 Godkin was nearing twenty-five, and his qualms about his future were growing. When he consulted his friends, Neill offered to aid him in a voyage to the United States, pointing out that his brother-in-law Brace and Olmsted would help him in New York. It was arranged that the traveller would meet his expenses by touring the south to supply the firm of Neill Brothers with information at New Orleans on cotton prices and by supplying the *Daily News* with American correspondence.

On 19 October 1856, shortly after his twenty-fifth birthday, Godkin resigned his post on the *Northern Whig* and set sail for the United States. Was he an ungrateful "assisted immigrant," as later opponents among the New York press alleged because of a falling-out between him and Neill in 1857? The evidence is inconclusive, but Godkin's papers reveal no association with Neill after that date.[13]

The young traveller arrived in New York on the eve of a heated presidential election. The recently organized Republican party, under its free-soil candidate John C. Fremont, was challenging the Democratic candidacy of James Buchanan. The evening of Godkin's arrival on 1 November he attended a Republican rally at the Academy of Music. His reaction, while patronizing, was more tolerant than that of the usual British traveller. He was astonished by the extravagance of the speakers, but he was gratified to find the auditorium "fitted up with boxes and stalls, pit and gallery, just as if it were admitted in this country that all men were not equal. . . ." He concluded that American democracy was more theory than fact:

> The theory of social equality so rigidly carried out in railway travelling here, and which at least has the inconvenience of occasionally bringing one into unpleasantly close contact with excellent citizens of dirty habits, seems to be recognized nowhere else. The custom which prevails of some people living in finer houses than their neighbours brings down no special reprobation, and the much more galling distinction of places in the theatre seems to meet with as large an amount of approval as in the most aristocratic country of the Old World. The rich man goes to the boxes and the poor man to the pit, and nobody grumbles. So much for theories.[14]

With the extravagance that was one of his trademarks as a publicist, Godkin discerned that "nobody" in the United States grumbled over the gulf between rich and poor. And when Buchanan emerged the victor in the election, he appealed to the Hibernophobia of his *Daily News* audience. He asserted that the Republicans lost partly because they were too honest to buy the Irish vote; hence the Irish immigrants followed their usual practice of voting the " 'riglar dimocratic ticket'; wherefore they cannot tell; but so their 'lathers' ordain." With measured irony, Godkin censured his Irish Catholic countrymen:

> No wonder ... the "patriots" of the Emerald Isle were disgusted by the conscientious severity of Colonel Fremont's supporters, and shrank in horror from allying themselves with the evangelical party of the Union, the friends of missions and Bible societies, the sober and intelligent citizens, who still cherish a hearty love and sympathy for England and her institutions.[15]

On his arrival in New York Godkin called on Olmsted, lately returned from his second European trip. The bachelor agriculturalist, nine years Godkin's senior, was brooding over the impending failure of a publishing house in which he had taken a partnership, but he invited his young caller to stay at his south side Staten Island farm. Godkin's arrangements required him to be in the south within two weeks, but he eagerly welcomed the chance to spend time with Olmsted and to hear about his southern travels. Olmsted, drawn by the continuing wanderlust that prompted the walking trip of Europe which had brought him and Brace to Belfast in 1850, made two long journeys through the south in 1852 and 1853 that he described in a series of letters to the New York *Times,* beginning in February 1853. His acuteness of observation and seeming detachment of judgment at a time when southern fireaters and northern abolitionists were arousing sectional passions to fever proportions made him a minor New York literary celebrity, and he was now publishing the letters, after editing and revising them, in book form.[16] As Godkin recalled it:

> The New York *Times* had lately been started, as a sort of "via media," to suit the numerous moderate or timid people who were coming over to the Republican Party from both the Whigs and the Democrats, but were as yet unequal to the strong anti-slavery drink of the *Tribune.* The *Times* had signalized itself by publishing Frederick Law Olmsted's letters from the South, since more widely known in book form. These

I read with intense interest, all the greater because I was
contemplating a journey of two or three months on horseback
in the South that winter myself.[17]

What the instinctive aristocrat, Olmsted, told Godkin of
his personal feelings toward slavery is not known, but his
southern letters do not dwell on the morality of the "peculiar institution." Instead he finds flaws in it on economic
grounds. It was not that Olmsted was insensitive to the
immorality of holding men and women in bondage; for him,
as for Lincoln and many other Northerners, slavery was a
lesser evil than disunion. But for Godkin and British Liberals
accustomed to thinking of the survival of their own union as
a mere parliamentary question, the American mystique of
"the Union" had no attraction.[18] Most of what Godkin and his
British contemporaries knew about the United States they
had imbibed from Alexis de Tocqueville. From de Tocqueville Godkin gleaned that whatever sectional character differences existed in the United States were grounded in
slavery.[19] Unlike the pragmatic Olmsted, Godkin looked upon
slavery as a brutalizing institution.

Taking with him copies of Olmsted's letters for a guide,
Godkin entrained for Wilmington, Delaware, to begin his
southern trip. By rail he made his way to Augusta, Georgia.
Here he discovered that the gentler sex of the white south
was even more proslavery than the men. "I found men who
saw some of the evils of slavery," he reported, "and would
hear them discussed; I never met a woman who did not turn
white with rage at the mere mention of its injustice or
inexpediency."[20]

Besides the insensibility to cruelty that Godkin encountered in white Southern women, he found them physically
unattractive, "nearly as pale as death, besides being excessively thin."[21]

From Augusta Godkin crossed Alabama by way of Montgomery and Selma; he reached Mississippi, the focus of his
journey, late in November 1856. Introducing himself as "an
Englishman travelling for commercial purposes," he acquired
a saddle horse and picked his way through the state for the
next several weeks, gathering information on the cotton crop
and observing the white population.[22] The picture he drew of

Godkin returned to New York from New Orleans early in January 1857, undecided about his future.[42] Whether or not to terminate his travels and return to the British Isles hinged on his hopes for his professional future. Despite his encomiums during the Crimean War to the "glory" of the newspaper press, he was sadly aware of the low social status of journalists. Without the means to become a newspaper proprietor in his own right, the Fourth Estate in America offered no more attractions than the British. But the legal profession in New York City carried undeniable social advantages. Why not remain there and resume his law studies? He obtained a letter of introduction to the internationally known New York lawyer David Dudley Field and began to read law in his office at 82 Broadway.[43] The Americanization of Godkin had begun.

Sensible that writing had impaired his legal studies at Lincoln's Inn, Godkin put down his pen and except for infrequent letters to the *Daily News* for the next year and a half he studied law. In 1858 he passed the New York bar examinations and the next year was admitted to practice.[44] But it was quickly evident that he had chosen the wrong profession. He was temperamentally unsuited for courtroom and office routine. He did not win clients, and the publicist in him hungered for action.

There were only three daily newspapers in New York in 1858 for which Godkin cared to write. Like all the city's dailies, they were clamorously partisan, but in behalf of objectives that occasionally suited Godkin's prejudices. The most famous was Horace Greeley's *Tribune*, which by 1858 had become an American institution. Greeley, a bluff, self-taught man who rose from rural poverty to walk with seven-league boots through the halls of the mighty, had assembled on his staff some of the most learned journalists of the day. He welcomed talent of any sex and persuasion, stipulating only that the *Tribune* act on his notion of principle. Quite opposite to the *New York Herald*, which under the Scottish immigrant James Gordon Bennett was garnering profits by pandering to a sensation-seeking multitude, the *Tribune* accomplished the feat of keeping both its circulation and its standards relatively high.[45]

The second New York newspaper that caught Godkin's eye was *The Evening Post*. Its genteel proprietor, William Cullen Bryant, shared Greeley's antislavery convictions, but temperamentally and editorially the two had little else in common. The aging rural poet, with his cultivated partner John Bigelow, gave the *Evening Post* an air of "hors concour" that to Godkin made up for its lack of circulation.

Lastly there was the *New York Times*, under the tutelage of New York politician Henry Raymond and his business partner George Jones. The *Times*, after three lean years since its birth in 1851, was now paying its expenses. Like the *Evening Post*, the *Times* sought to reach an informed, relatively well-to-do readership. Politically moderate, even though its proprietors were opposed to slavery, its circulation exceeded that of the *Evening Post*. The *Times's* chief drawback in Godkin's eyes was that its editorial independence was impaired by the need to support Raymond's political ambitions.

If young Godkin, with his open disdain for "editors on horseback" and for the details of editorial management, hoped to obtain an editorial post on any of these three papers, he was slated for disappointment. But all was not lost. The *New York Times* consented to publish one or two of his pieces each week; the *Daily News* engaged him as its regular New York correspondent; and the *Evening Post* accepted several of his pieces on European affairs.[46] In addition, *The Knickerbocker*, a well-regarded New York literary monthly now falling on evil days, accepted some of his historical articles. These articles, though reasonably informed, did not attract attention in literary circles, and it was evident to Godkin that it was as a political and social commentator that he would make his mark. His writings of the period, like the "via media" of Raymond's *New York Times*, take up an ideological position somewhere between Whiggish conservatism and the Radicalism of Leicester Square, London. Practically this meant that on some issues he would incline one way with his American audience, another way with his British audience. His *Knickerbocker* essays, for example, soft-pedal his criticisms of democracy.[47] Writing eulogistically in 1858 of the death of the old East

India Company, he offered his American readers a nostalgic backward look at British imperialism, combined with a sentimentalized view of democracy:

> On the morning on which Clive threw down his pen, and buckled on the sword, a new light burst on the English people, and a new world was opened to them. A state of things, in which a friendless clerk could, by the aid of a clear head and stout heart, push his way, in half a year, into the front rank of generals and statesmen, was something they had not seen for many a long year. . . . Here, at least, was a field in which birth and position were of no account. . . . The democratic spirit which led its first founders to declare even to Queen Elizabeth, that "they desired not to employ any *gentlemen* in any place of charge," characterized it to the last.[48]

But to his English audience in the *Daily News* Godkin offered a disheartening portrait of American democracy in action. In an 1857 letter he described the political condition of New York City, which "furnishes a curious and rather instructive illustration of the working of universal suffrage in a large commercial community." Because the best people did not take part in politics, the Common Council was composed mainly of "low Irishmen of intemperate habits, who have been unable or unwilling to gain a livelihood in any honest calling." He elaborated:

> . . . if you can suppose a series of meetings to be convened by the leading publicans and prize-fighters in St. Giles's, Whitechapel, and Mile-end, and attended by their customers, by pawnbrokers' clerks, cabmen, and costermongers, and candidates to be then and there put in nomination for the various city offices . . . to be elected by the votes of the male denizens of the worst portions of the east end, to meet under the presidency of a fraudulent bankrupt . . . if you can suppose the police to be selected from amongst the most turbulent Irishmen from the alleys . . . and the inspectors to be chosen from amongst the keepers of the best-known sporting public houses, some of them having been guilty of gouging and biting off noses . . . you would have a tolerably accurate, though probably a still somewhat defective notion of the state of affairs in New York at the present moment.[49]

"There certainly could hardly be a more curious illustration of the oddities of democracy," Godkin told his British readers, in an attack on orator Edward Everett, "than the respect in which Everett, in spite of the weakness of his character, his vacillation, his ridiculous affectation, and his subserviency throughout his whole life to the party in power, is held throughout the country."[50]

When a boxing contest between two Irish fighters was billed as an "American championship" contest, Godkin excoriated it as further evidence of the weakness of popular government. The puerility of elevating "a pounding match between two blackguards" to the level of "an important public event . . . is a fact which no admirer of democratic institutions can afford to overlook."[51] Constantly he fretted at the growing "backwoods element" in Congress, whose "grossness of habits and demeanor" were overcoming "the small modicum of civilization and refinement contributed by the states on the Atlantic."[52] And when in May 1858 three able senators bowed to an inflamed public opinion and denounced the British for boarding some American vessels in the Caribbean, Godkin minced no words; the three legislators "raved against England, and shrieked for war with an absurdity of which nobody but schoolboys should be guilty . . . the whole thing is a singular striking illustration of the inability of the strongest natures to bear up against the crushing influence of a powerful democracy."[53]

Like many publicists of his day, Godkin held racist notions that influenced his attitude toward democracy. Confidently he predicted the march of the "Anglo-Saxon race" into Central America and the development of a great Anglo-Saxon Australian empire spanning the Pacific, while paradoxically he pondered the wisdom of the United States acquiring Mexico and Central America because of the "mongrel" nature of their populations.[54]

Like Goldwin Smith, who styled himself an antiimperialist while simultaneously holding the British empire in India to be the "noblest the world has seen," Godkin was persuaded of the uniqueness of the Anglo-Saxon "race." To his American audience he predictably praised the revolt of the colonists in 1775 against British rule, whereas to his English audience he extolled the British use of repressive measures toward dissident native populations in the east.[55] During the 1857 sepoy rebellion in India he, with characteristic extravagance, attacked an Irish-American mass meeting held in

New York to express sympathy with the sepoy cause, and he extolled Anglo-Saxon imperialism. As he wrote:

> Not a man of any standing in the city attended the meeting except the reporters of the press. It was a contemptible affair altogether. . . . The interest felt in events now occurring in the East is growing deeper in the United States every day. The feeling is becoming general that England is now engaged in a great struggle for a common humanity and a common Christianity. She is now pre-eminently fighting the battles of civilisation against heathenism and barbarity, and God nerve her arm for the glorious work.[56]

But if Godkin showed insensitivity toward the plight of native peoples under the yoke of imperialism, he demonstrated more concern for freedom in his treatment of the slavery issue in the United States. John Brown's raid in 1859 at Harper's Ferry at first made little impression on him, but as its significance began to unfold in the press, he notified the *Daily News* of the "profound consternation" it had created in the slave states. For Brown's raid, believed Godkin, there could be no defense: "If the condition of the blacks is ever to be really improved," it must be brought about "peacefully and gradually," yet

> in spite of all this, no one can see a grayheaded man, who has lost five sons in the cause of freedom, step in, with the last survivor of his family by his side, between the slave and his master, and with his thirteen other companions bid defiance to a whole state in the name of the Lord of Hosts, without more or less admiration.

There was "something grand in the old fellow's madness," concluded Godkin, "and those here at the North who most condemn him, acknowledge him to be well worthy, if not of a better, of a more hopeful cause, and of a happier fate than that which now awaits him."[57]

Godkin was still going through the motions of visiting his law office, but he was earning his living principally from writing. At *The Knickerbocker* he was in established company with R. H. Stoddard, George W. Curtis, and Thomas Bailey Aldrich, and, at the *Daily News*, with Harriet Martineau. He had now formed what would be a lifetime habit of allocating about four hours a day to writing. After sketching out in a notebook, or in his mind, what he wanted to say, he wrote rapidly in a barely legible scrawl. When finished, he made numerous changes in the text of his article and then paid a copyist to put it into legible form.[58] His spelling was less than perfect and his punctuation was worse, but he was evolving a polemical style that combined caustic invective and witty sarcasm with reasoned argument. Even critics agreed that, whatever the temperamental Anglo-Irishman's faults, he was a brilliant writer.

Meanwhile, Godkin, as James Ford Rhodes recounted, was "seeing socially the best people" in New York. He contrived invitations to evening receptions of the *Tribune's* managing editor, Charles A. Dana, the "darling," he cynically noted, "of those who would remake the world." With the help of his patrons, Brace and Olmsted, he obtained introductions to Curtis, Bigelow, Raymond, and the legendary George Ripley, the literary editor of the *Tribune* whose overflowing heart, the unsentimental Godkin thought, "was too much for his brains." He cemented friendly relations with George E. Waring, Jr., a young scientific farmer who had written a textbook on farming and now rented Olmsted's Staten Island farm.[59] Waring shortly would break ground for the construction of Central Park.

Another early acquaintance was the budding landscape architect Calvert Vaux, a disciple of Andrew Jackson Downing, who had formed a partnership with Olmsted to carry out the construction of Central Park. Through Brace, Godkin wangled invitations to evening gatherings at the Dobbs Ferry home of the aged Colonel James A. Hamilton, a son of Alexander Hamilton whom Andrew Jackson had appointed district attorney, and Hamilton's daughter and her husband, the G. L. Schuylers. And to the old frolicking grounds of Brace and Olmsted, New Haven, he carried from them a letter of introduction to President Theodore Woolsey of Yale.[60]

It was at Dr. Woolsey's home one day in 1857 that Godkin met the statuesquely attractive twenty-two-year-old Frances Elizabeth Foote. "Fanny," whose cousins included Harriet Beecher Stowe and Henry Ward Beecher, was the daughter of Samuel E. Foote of Cincinnati and New Haven. The Footes sprang from an illustrious Connecticut family that traced its American lineage back to 1635. Among them were the Sena-

tor Samuel A. Foot—he insisted on dropping the "e"—who
offered the "Foot resolution" that sparked the Webster-
Hayne Debates of 1830 and Foot's son, the later Civil War
naval hero, Andrew H. Foote.[61]

Fanny's father, now seventy, had early been a sea captain,
who at the age of forty married a second cousin and, together with other Foote relatives and his brother-in-law Lyman Beecher, migrated to Cincinnati. It was while his niece
Harriet Beecher was preparing to marry Professor Stowe of
Cincinnati's Lane Theological Seminary that in 1835 Fanny
was born. As Fanny grew up, family acquaintances commented on her looks and demeanor, especially on her close
resemblance to her mother, a tall woman of "great beauty of
countenance and an exceedingly clever brain."[62]

About 1850 Sam Foote, who made his fortune in Cincinnati
as president of the Ohio Life Insurance and Trust Company,
retired from active labor and brought his family to New
Haven to live. At his home, Windy Knowe, he created a
congenial environment for the discussion of public issues.
The Foote home became a gathering place for antislavery
men in New Haven, yet the proslavery publicist George
Fitzhugh was hospitably entertained there in 1855 when,
chiefly at Foote's instance, he came to New Haven and
lectured at the Lyceum.[63]

But the talk at Windy Knowe that summer of 1857 was not
of slavery but of the collapse of the Ohio Life and Trust and
the severe financial panic that it brought with it.[64] Sam Foote
never recovered from the blow, and the next year he died,
leaving behind a neurotic, semiinvalid wife and four unmarried children. Godkin could hardly have picked a less
favorable time to court one of the daughters. But Foote's
estate was settled and, after waiting for a few months while
Mrs. Foote became accustomed to her new circumstances,
on 27 July 1859 Godkin and Fanny were married in Trinity
Church, New Haven. They went to New York to live.

No one can say precisely how much Godkin's marriage
changed the course of his life—though, undeniably, it
changed Fanny's. On the one hand the marriage brought to
the young immigrant the social position and the financial
security he craved. On the other it brought unaccustomed

responsibilities and what he regarded as excessive female frivolity. However much Godkin liked creature comforts and drawing-room manners, he equally liked the freedom of the out-of-doors. Although he disdained natural—which is to say uncleared—surroundings, he took great delight in horseback riding, together with an occasional mountain climb with his peers. Especially irritating to him was the impudent artificiality and newness of New York City, where, as Charles Eliot Norton told James Russell Lowell in 1861, "The only old things . . . are yesterday's newspapers." A country gentleman at heart who loathed spending the entire year in the city, Godkin once pondered the advantages of keeping a milk farm on Staten Island.[65]

Fanny, on the other hand, looked upon horseback trails and carefully groomed countryside as mere scenery, and she irritated "Mr. Godkin" (as all were prompted to call him) with her incessant opera-going.[66] Given the excessive nineteenth-century gallantry of men toward women, it is not possible confidently to assess Fanny Godkin. Years later Godkin inexplicably expressed to his second wife distaste for what he called "the Fannie-kind of woman," but such evidence as there is does not support the theory that he lacked respect for his first wife. Henry James, Sr., gallantly informed Fanny in 1875 that he did not find her frivolous, and Godkin himself testified that, although not suited to rustic living, she would "behave like a brick" if asked to go and live in a rustic setting. Whatever the full truth, although Godkin did not accept all of Fanny's habits, he loved her.[67]

Like most marriages, that of the Godkins had its ups and downs from the start. The first winter was a difficult time. Godkin's law practice was going nowhere, and he had not made the editorial connection he wanted. His neurotic, though well-disposed, mother-in-law was alternately fussing with herself and with others over Godkin's management of her finances, as well as fretting over two unmarried daughters and a future invalid teenage son. Her brother Charles Elliott, an acquaintance of Brace and Olmsted, chronically irritated Godkin.[68] Finally in March 1860, with Fanny pregnant, Godkin lost what would apparently be his final law case.[69] Persuading himself that he was having an emotional collapse and suffering from a recurrence of his eastern fever, he waited throughout May for Fanny to have their baby and then sailed off for Ireland alone.

Chapter Four
The Civil War Years

I am not popular in my manners and
could never become so.

Leaving Fanny and the baby at his mother-in-law's in New Haven, Godkin went first to Ireland for a brief family reunion, then proceeded in leisurely fashion to London and afterwards to Paris. In the fall Fanny joined him with baby Lawrence, and Mrs. Foote came afterward to look after the child.

For two years Godkin and Fanny lived a life of leisure; winters in Paris, spring in London, and summers in Switzerland. Aside from their sorties to the theaters of Paris and to Alpine resorts, there is little in Godkin's life between 1860 and 1862 for the biographer to record. Outwardly it was a period of idleness, but underneath it was one of nagging self-doubt. Govone, in the letter of introduction that he gave Godkin to show his friends in Turin, had called him "un buon diavalo, allegro, que ha spiritu e parla poco," but beneath Godkin's abrupt yet confident exterior, he was a brooding, dissatisfied person.[1] He didn't fancy journalism as a full-time career; he had failed at law; he was too impetuous for the discipline of scholarship; politics was out, for he had no oratorical ability and he rejected "getting close to the people"; he was drawn to a leisurely rural existence, but not to rural people.[2]

Meanwhile, the Civil War had begun in the United States. While Godkin and Fanny were trying out a new summer hotel at the Bel Alp in Switzerland, his American friends were joining the Northern war effort. Olmsted had taken leave of absence from his post as the landscape architect of Central Park and with his lieutenant, special relief agent Frederick N. Knapp, was industriously helping the Reverend Dr. Henry W. Bellows organize the Sanitary Commission, the

medical and service organization for Union volunteers
created in the summer of 1861. George Waring was off for
the Virginia front as a major of New York volunteers. In
New Haven, Fanny's friend Sarah Woolsey was preparing to
serve as a volunteer nurse to Union casualties in the New
Haven hospital, while Sarah's New York cousin Abby Woolsey labored at gathering clothing and supplies for Union
volunteers through the Women's Central Association of Relief.[3] Together with Abby's sisters, they would all be involved with Olmsted in his labors as general secretary of the
Sanitary Commission during the first half of the war.

Like all Union sympathizers living in Europe, Godkin was
disturbed by the critical attitude of the foreign press at the
start of the war, especially that of The Times of London.[4] A
largely unspoken reason for the British hostility to the North
was middle and upper-class fear of the spread of democracy
in England. This fear, fueled by John Bright's pro-Northern
speeches before London trades unions, within a year helped
transform traditionally antislavery English public opinion
into widespread sympathy with the "peculiar institution."
Southern officers, reported Godkin, were believed to be
"some sort of aristocracy and their cause that of the landed
interest, while the Northern army was made up of foreign
mercenaries and low people of various sordid occupations."[5]

Yet not all of the foreign press was unfriendly to the
North. In Paris the liberal journals the Revue des Deux
Mondes and the Journal Des Débats were friendly, God-
kin especially admiring the pro-Northern writing of August
Laugel. And in London the Daily News, under editor Thomas
Walker, with his abolitionist leader writers Harriet Mar-
tineau and John R. Robinson, lent its support to the North, as
did the Morning Star, the struggling Radical organ edited by
John Bright's brother-in-law Samuel Lucas.[6] Of the weeklies
aimed at the educated classes, the Spectator supported the
North in the face of strong internal pressure, aided by the
Westminster Review and William Jerold's popular, penny
Lloyd's Weekly. And in the provinces the Liverpool Daily
Post, the Manchester Examiner and Times, and Godkin's old
journal, the Belfast Northern Whig, were all under pro-
Northern editorial direction. Still, these friendly voices were

sometimes drowned out by the others. In Paris, Godkin could find little being said favorable to the Union, except that it was "une bonne cause mal soutenue."[7]

Godkin, who was just turning thirty as the first year of the Civil War came to a close, had not lifted his pen for a year. Then occurred the *Trent* crisis with England. The captain of a United States naval vessel halted the British steamer *Trent* on the high seas and seized two Confederate commissioners, James Mason and John Slidell, as they were on their way to England. While an indignant British government demanded the release of the two men, a delighted Congress voted Captain Wilkes the thanks of the nation for his unauthorized exploit. At first, part of the British press took a cautious view of the incident, conceding that Wilkes had acted in accordance with earlier English precedents. But the next week *The Times*, with the rest of the London press following suit, launched a scathing attack on the United States.[8] Thereupon Godkin broke his long literary silence and began from Paris firing letters to the editor of the *Daily News*.

Godkin was convinced that Captain Wilkes had acted in accordance with international law. "There is no point of public law half as well settled," he informed the *Daily News*, "as that a belligerent cruiser may stop any neutral ship on the high seas and make any inspection that may be necessary to satisfy himself that she is really neutral, and there is no contraband on board. . . ." Challenging the claim of the *Daily News* that the seizure of persons "stands on a different footing" from the seizure of contraband goods, Godkin argued that Mason and Slidell were "officers" of the Confederacy, hence equally contraband of war as a cargo of "Confederate generals" or a cargo of ammunition. "There is nothing I would consider more deplorable than a conflict between Great Britain and the United States, but I am satisfied that Americans are neither so weak nor so base as to allow England to set aside all the decisions of her own courts because they do not now happen to suit her altered convenience."[9]

The next week Godkin returned to the attack, in another letter to the editor of the *Daily News*, accusing the London press of ignoring international law. "A tippling politician in an Illinois bar-room, expatiating on 'manifest destiny', could not display greater contempt for musty precedents," he maintained.[10] In a third letter he accused the British government of warlike intentions toward the United States. "The most perverse ingenuity could not have devised better means of tempting the Americans not to surrender Mason and Slidell than asking for them at the very outset at the cannon's mouth. . . ."[11]

As he found himself once again sounding the charge, Godkin felt his bristling self-confidence return. Quickly he sent off a fourth letter to the editor and then wrote Brace — whose letters, along with those of Olmsted, had lain unanswered on his writing table since summer — to tell him of his recovery. In the somewhat peremptory tone which he often employed with his friends, he urged Brace to woo newspaper friends into quieting the Anglophobia of the American press. He told Brace:

> I want you, as far as your means go, to urge on the newspaper men in New York attention to the fact that there is a large party in England composed of dissenters, democrats, reformers of all shades . . . who strongly sympathize not only with Northern anti-slavery principles but Northern theories of government, whose feelings of nationality the North ought to menager. The abuse of England has been so indiscriminate that these have all been driven over to the Tory side. . . . The Southerners have beaten us hollow in the management of public opinion on this side of the water. You know how much more of the work of diplomacy is done in social intercourse than by note writing; and yet no member of the legation here speaks one word of French. . . .
>
> There are signs of a political revival [in France] and men are getting over the shock of 1848, and the example of Italy is begetting a return of admiration for self-government. Louis Napoleon is really a great man, wise as well as shrewd. Weed has been denouncing you over here for saying Seward wanted to escape from the Southern imbroglio by a war with England. I was not present, and so did not knock him down.[12]

Despite his revived spirits, Godkin continued to guard his leisure. Contrary to the account of Allan Nevins, who inexplicably finds him at work in Paris in 1862 providing the New York Evening Post with the "shrewdest and clearest view of French opinion published in any American news-

paper," Godkin wrote nothing, aside from the letters to the
Daily News, during his two-year stay in Europe.[13] Early in
1862 he tried to arrange a reunion in Italy with Govone,
now an Italian general of brigade. Failing, he elected to
spend the spring of that year in London. From London he
wrote another letter to the editor of the *Daily News,* this
time challenging the authority of Liverpool merchant James
Spence, whose pro-Confederate editorials were appearing in
The Times and whose partisan book, *American Union,* was
running through several successive editions.[14]

As spring drew to a close, Godkin decided to return briefly
to Paris and then, in the fall, to sail to the United States
to serve again as the *Daily News* special correspondent in
New York. In June he broke his long silence to Olmsted,
bidding Olmsted send him another long letter on the war,
"but mind and write on thin paper. Your last was on a modi-
fication of stout bandbox paper." He hinted to Olmsted that
his stay in London had altered his thinking about the war;
especially was he ambivalent toward emancipation. He informed Olmsted that

> the total absence [in the South] of any appearance of Union
> feeling as the Northern army advances, has confirmed the
> vast majority of people in France and England, including those
> most friendly to you, that a reconstruction of the Union is
> impossible, supposing resistance in the field were at an end
> tomorrow. To hold the South down by military force, will it
> is also said, be either physically impossible or can only be
> achieved by the sacrifice of your own liberties. . . . How long,
> I should also like to know, will slavery be held more sacred
> than everything else in America?[15]

After summering once more in Switzerland, Godkin went
again for a short visit to Ireland and then sailed with Fanny
and Lawrence for New York. They arrived home in the
fall of 1862 at a critical time in the war. Lincoln had just
issued his Preliminary Emancipation Proclamation, which
was incurring Democratic opposition in the North. The inactivity of the Army of the Potomac under General George B.
McClellan "weighed like a nightmare on everybody's mind,"
reported Godkin to the *Daily News,* and he and the public
had begun to have doubts about Lincoln.[16] "Nobody doubts
his zeal or honesty, but he is accused loudly, and it seems

to me, justly accused, of great want of firmness, and discretion, and discrimination in the choice and management of his subordinates."[17] With two-thirds of the generals "at loggerheads," alleged Godkin, the president was doing nothing in the crisis to "enforce harmony" among them. "He seems to have a delicacy in dealing with individual shortcomings which is nothing short of weakness; and weakness which entails the failure of combinations and the loss of battles is just now little short of crime."[18]

As the weeks wore on, Godkin's criticisms of Lincoln grew more edged.[19] On the surface he supported the Emancipation Proclamation; inwardly he was suffering doubts. As the January first date for the implementation of the Proclamation approached, he accorded a respectful hearing to Democratic claims that Emancipation would result in the Africanization of the South. As he wrote in the *Daily News:*

> It does not follow, it is true, that if the negroes were emancipated tomorrow they should at once share in the political privileges of the whites. But every one feels that their exclusion could not last very long, in an atmosphere so charged with democracy; and then timid men not unnaturally ask, what would be the effect of the addition of this mass of ignorance, passion, and credulity to our electoral body? We have already suffered severely from the influx of Irish and Germans, unfitted by previous training for the exercise of the suffrage. . . . Would not four or five millions of citizens, with the marks of the whip still on their backs, who are impulsive beyond any civilised race, and whom we cannot absorb, furnish demagogues with a most tremendous weapon for the destruction or degradation of the nation?[20]

"These fears may be visionary," concluded Godkin, "but they cannot be overlooked in the discussion of this tremendous problem."

By December 1862 Godkin was convinced that Lincoln and his cabinet were incompetent. He did not oppose the president's assumption of dictatorial powers; he approved his suspension of the writ of *habeas corpus* and the jailing of Southern sympathizers, but he condemned Lincoln's "mischievous meddling" in military matters and his sacrifice of the army "to what he considers 'the exigencies of politics.'"[21] The Union disaster at Fredericksburg in December severely tested Godkin's faith in an ultimate Union victory. Somewhat extravagantly he labelled the Fredericksburg reverse "unparalleled in the annals of military blundering," due wholly to the "incurable incapacity of the President and his cabinet."[22] With finality he concluded: "That Mr. Lincoln is utterly unequal to the responsibility the crisis has imposed on him is now demonstrated beyond question in the opinion of everybody of all parties."[23]

Late in November Godkin journeyed to Washington, D.C. for ten days, where he received dinner invitations from Secretary of State Seward, who was an acquaintance of Brace, and another member of the cabinet. At Seward's he met Lincoln, whom, unbeknownst to the assembled guests, he was now severely criticizing in the Daily News.[24]

Peering through the mists of thirty-five years, Godkin in 1896 remembered the circumstances quite differently:

> Of all the mistakes made by [the North's] enemies, none was so great as their estimate of Lincoln's character and capacity. . . . And I do not think I exaggerate when I say that the greatest glory of the Daily News in its fiftieth anniversary is its having understood him from the beginning. I saw and spoke with him but once, at a dinner at Mr. Seward's, in the winter of 1862-63, and then perceived the injustice done by his photographs to that wonderful face of his. . . . Since William the Silent, probably no man ever bore more distinctly the burden of a nation's sorrow, and none ever showed more clearly in feature and expression that he was fit to bear it."[25]

But if, in truth, Godkin in that dark fall and winter of 1862-63 failed to appreciate Lincoln, he was not alone. A wave of pessimism was sweeping the North, and Godkin, pessimistic by nature, could hardly be expected to rise above the tide.[26] In his letters to the Daily News he began edging toward the camp of the Republican Radicals. While Olmsted nervously warned him that the army was "violently" opposed to black troops, in the Daily News Godkin advocated arming the slaves.[27]

When the Democrats nominated Horatio Seymour as their candidate for governor of New York, Godkin called him a "secessionist candidate" and accused the Democrats of fostering an accommodation with the South through which New England would be expelled from the Union. He defended General Benjamin Butler's military rule of New Orleans, including Butler's hanging of a Confederate sympathizer and his much criticized order concerning the treatment of women who had insulted Union soldiers.[28] He found Southern women lacking in character, while he praised New England women for their willingness to lay their sons on the altar of freedom: "They are not all as Mrs. Putnam, of Boston, made of such heroic will as to talk with pride and delight of the fate of an only son in one of the bloodiest and most purposeless affairs of the war, that of Ball's Bluff; but they are profoundly convinced that the cause is good, and that their sacrifices in its behalf find favour in heaven."[29]

Faintly suggestive of the leftward turn in Godkin's thinking early in 1863 was his expressed concern for the future welfare of the slaves about to be freed by the Emancipation Proclamation. When Lincoln issued his preliminary proclamation in the fall of 1862, the indefatigable Olmsted drafted a measure—which he persuaded several United States senators to sponsor—to create, on the model of the English poor law, a federal emancipation bureau to care for the liberated slaves and their families until they found employment. The bill passed the Senate but died in the House of Representatives when the Treasury Department objected to its cost. In the *Daily News* Godkin expressed the fear that unless the government acted soon, "the fate of these unfortunates will leave a stain on the cabinet which will do much to dim the lustre of its anti-slavery policy."[30]

Yet one must not exaggerate the concern of Godkin—who employed the word "humanitarian" in a pejorative sense and believed that caring for social unfortunates was not a concern of the public—for the blacks.[31] An "expediency" man, he could not ignore the fact that many of his associates, such as Olmsted, thought the exslaves had a legitimate claim on the nation. Freedmen's rights was a fashionable cause in the genteel liberal circles in which Edwin and Fanny moved in New Haven and New York, besides being a deeply held conviction with some radicals of their set.

Godkin now was receiving detailed letters on the conduct of the war from Olmsted, with the suggestion that he print some of the military observations Olmsted had made while moving around as general secretary of the Sanitary Commission. Godkin obliged by incorporating some of this material into his *Daily News* letters, giving as his source "a friend of mine."[32]

Although Godkin objected to the scolding tone of the Northern press toward England, he did not hesitate to chastise John Bull himself when appropriate. His target for one trenchant sally in 1863 was Foreign Secretary Earl Russell, whom he branded abysmally ignorant of the South:

> I see by the last mail that Earl Russell, in the debate on the Queen's speech, said he should witness the subjugation of the South with regret, because amongst other things "it must put an end to a free press and destroy the right of free discussion at the South." It would be hard to put into one sentence stronger evidence of the complete ignorance of the social and political condition of the South during the last forty years than this sentence contains. There has been no such thing as free discussion known at the South since the invention of the cotton gin.[33]

Godkin was now writing with his old diligence. Besides his detailed, twice-weekly letters to the *Daily News*, he had resumed writing one or two pieces a week for the *New York Times*.[34] He could probably have had an editorial post on that paper or on some other morning paper, except that he detested night work, and none of the evening papers—such as the *Evening Post*—had room for his services.[35] Early in 1863 he and Olmsted discussed starting an independent national weekly in New York. From the St. Louis headquarters of the Western Sanitary Commission, Olmsted in the spring wrote Godkin: "I am ready to go into a paper with you at a month's notice." But Godkin, who had recently passed up an opportunity to buy into the *New York Times*, was reluctant to risk his money in a publishing venture. Thereupon Olmsted set about the project on his own.[36]

On a warm June evening in 1863, not long before the battle of Gettysburg, Olmsted strode into New York's Union League Club. There were fifty or sixty members present, including several of Olmsted's fellow officers in the Sanitary Commission, its President Bellows, Treasurer Dr. George T. Strong, and Actuary Dr. Benjamin Gould of Cambridge. With these and half a dozen others, Olmsted repaired to a third-story room where they discussed his "dream of an honest weekly paper." "What vast good such a paper might do," Strong told his diary that night, "if honest and able men could be found in sufficient number to form an editorial staff."[37] The next day Olmsted and Strong met with New York businessman Howard Potter, and together they drew up a list of persons who might be willing to subscribe $500 or more toward a working capital of $30,000 for the paper. A few days later a five-man committee was named to solicit funds, and it was settled that Olmsted would have full proprietorship over the paper, the investors "to know nothing of the editing or who edits it."[38]

Olmsted, whose first publishing venture as a partner with George W. Curtis and others in *Putnam's Magazine* had ended in 1857 in bankruptcy, had long dreamed of his own journal, one that would equal in quality such British weeklies as the *Spectator* and the *Saturday Review*.[39] During the summer that followed, he devoted much of his spare time to the project, occasionally discussing it with Godkin. He printed and distributed a prospectus, urged friends to nominate contributors, and consulted a respected authority, Charles A. Dana, for his opinion of the scheme. "I don't believe it will succeed—but I'm not sure," Dana replied. "I'll be glad to have it tried."[40] In quest of a name for his weekly, Olmsted collected forty-five suggestions, including one of Godkin's that he and Dana rejected—"The Week."

July fled. Sanitary Commission affairs consumed Olmsted's time, and the bloody New York draft riots that summer prevented anything being done by the fund-raising committee. Olmsted instructed his lieutenant, Knapp, to go to Boston and apply to acquaintances there for funds for the proposed weekly. Then suddenly the project faced collapse; Olmsted was offered the alluring prospect of a partnership in a California mining venture. He explained the situation to Godkin, who eagerly agreed to carry on the newspaper project in Olmsted's absence. Meanwhile Olmsted reasoned, "If there is one man in Boston who can help us, it is Charles E. Norton." He gave Godkin a letter of introduction to Norton and left without delay for California, forgetting to mail Norton the covering letter he wrote to him about Godkin.[41]

The thirty-six-year-old Charles Eliot Norton was, like Olmsted, a man of unselfish zeal. As secretary of the New England Loyal Publication Society, he had edited the society's papers and had blanketed the northeast with cogent appeals for the Union. He had helped to found the *Atlantic Monthly*, and as Lowell's coeditor he would now infuse new vigor into the moribund *North American Review*. Norton, a frail aristocrat with a genius for the friendship of the world's great in the field of letters, was not a literary giant himself, but he was ever ready to help those who were.[42]

Godkin arrived in Boston with his letter of introduction late in September 1863. He looked more than his thirty-two years. Already his dark brown hair was flecked with grey, and his bearded face and squat frame were taking on the settled look that John Fiske four years later saw as that of "a stout old Englishman." He took care not to divulge his Irish background. Norton was impressed with his impeccably attired visitor, and he invited Francis Parkman and Edward Everett Hale to meet him. Thus commenced between Parkman and Godkin a lasting acquaintance.[43]

Hale was on a committee of the Examiner Club to weigh the prospects of launching a literary review, and he found Godkin "an agreeable person, the least possible slow perhaps."[44] Married to a relative of Fanny Godkin, Hale later would vigorously question Godkin's probity.[45] Norton offered to help Godkin—who now was describing the scheme that Olmsted had fathered as "my newspaper project," which he called "The Week"—in every way except to lend him money, but others tentatively offered financial help. Godkin tardily reported to an impatient Olmsted in California, "I came away assured of $5,000, or thereabouts, if New York would do her share."[46]

Returning to New York, Godkin tried to re-enlist the help of Bellows and Strong; but as with Olmsted's earlier efforts, they seemed "to forget all about" the fund-raising project when Godkin's back was turned. Then as a final blow a similar journal, the *Round Table*, announced that it would soon begin publication in New York—"the very thing," sighed Godkin to Olmsted, "I had in my mind." Discouraged, he shelved "The Week" and accepted Dr. Bellows's offer of the editorship of the fortnightly *Sanitary Commission Bulletin*.[47]

A further discouragement for Godkin was that Olmsted's departure for California had left him bereft of his closest friend. Olmsted and Brace had been his only firm patrons since coming to the United States — and even with them he was not on a first name basis — and Brace was now moving from the "amorous" stage of life to the "acquisitive" stage, Godkin facetiously told Olmsted, and preoccupied with getting rich. True, Godkin did not lack for friendly acquaintances, such as Colonel Waring, Dr. Bellows, Vaux and Green of the Central Park, the Schuylers, the Woolsey sisters, and Mrs. Foote's brothers, Charles and Henry Elliott. Nor was he shy about seeking introductions to strangers. Yet except for a summer and early fall spent with Fanny in New Haven and Sharon Springs, Godkin's life in 1864 was uneventful. Evenings Fanny haunted the operas with her friends, while Edwin called on acquaintances or frequented the Century Club, the exclusive New York club to which Olmsted had sponsored him the year before.

It was in this period that publisher Henry Holt first laid eyes on Godkin. As Holt recalled it:

> I think I first saw him at a church . . . on Fortieth Street [where the Reverend O. B. Frothingham] used to dispense to more or less "brainy" people . . . Unitarianism. In the congregation, my attention was attracted to a rather thick-set man of about thirty-five with dark hair, mustache, and imperial, who was accompanied by a tall, brown-haired singularly elegant and beautiful woman. . . . I soon came to know them well as Mr. and Mrs. Godkin.[48]

For nearly a year Godkin edited the *Sanitary Commission Bulletin*, also continuing to write twice a week for the *Daily News* and the *New York Times*. That his anonymous labors for the *Daily News* were appreciated by its proprietors is attested to by several editorial mentions of him in that paper.[49] He found the editorial work of the *Sanitary Commission Bulletin* easy but disagreeable — merely the task every ten days of gathering together accumulated articles and commission reports — and the one hundred dollars a month pay was welcome. He had now boosted his income from his own labors to about three thousand dollars a year, which he augmented with dividends of about 8 percent on four or five thousand dollars of western railroad and other stocks that Fanny had brought into their marriage.[50] Moreover Mrs. Foote provided them with a home. Thus the erstwhile Irish "assisted immigrant" and his wife were financially comfortable.

Godkin had not overcome his aversion to office work, and, though he spent little time at the office of the *Sanitary Commission*, he was not outwardly displeased when, late in 1864, the *Bulletin* was moved to Philadelphia and handed over to a new editor. (Aside from the sheer boredom of the job, Bellows's "rampant Republicanism" irritated Godkin because it was bringing down on the Sanitary Commission the censure of the Democratic press, as well as a rival service organization, the Christian Commission, whose agents, averred Godkin to Olmsted, "abuse the Sanitary wherever they go all over the country, and lie like sinners of the lowest grade. They find at last that spiritual consolation is not much needed by wounded men on the battlefield, so they are working might and main to get hold of the supplies as well.")[51]

In October Godkin received a note from Goldwin Smith, visiting in Toronto, who had been reading Godkin's *Daily News* letters, that he was coming to New Haven for a visit. Smith, Regius professor of modern history at Oxford University, had been doing yeoman work in England as a publicist for the North, and Northern scholars were anxious to meet him and listen to him lecture. Godkin, who had now returned from New Haven to New York for the winter, sent word by Norton to Smith that it was imperative that Smith, because of the impending November elections, come without delay to New York City, where "the horrors of Yankee life at such periods, may be witnessed in greater perfection . . . than in New England."[52]

After a triumphal course through New England, including time spent at Harvard, Goldwin Smith arrived in New York, where he was honored with a public banquet and dined and spent an evening with Godkin.[53] Each enjoyed their exchange of views, and in time Smith would preside over a

Canadian Mugwump replica of Godkin's soon-to-be-established New York *Nation*—although their frequent agreement would not prevent them later from getting into a protracted public dispute over Irish Home Rule. Godkin especially enjoyed counteracting for Smith the "humbuggery" he contended foreign guests routinely suffered at Harvard. Godkin did not wholly share the optimism of Lowell, Norton, and some of their Harvard friends about democracy, for example. Their differing outlooks were highlighted about this time by an exchange of letters by him and Norton with Olmsted. In one Norton apprised Olmsted of his satisfaction over the way an informed public opinion was being brought to bear on the legislative process:

> Every day convinces me more and more of the soundness of the main principles on which our nationality is founded. The war has been the most useful of commentaries on our democratic institutions. This country is the only one where democratic principles are fairly understood, or where a science of ideal politics can be really studied with a view of applying its conclusions to actual conditions.[54]

Godkin was less sanguine about the future of democracy. For one, his illusions about Republican Party virtue, he wrote Olmsted, had been shattered. "I am sorry to say I [am] perfectly satisfied the leading republican politicians are worse than the democrats, inasmuch as they are fully as corrupt while making far more pretensions to honesty." Public affairs, Godkin conceded, looked well in 1864, but he had no faith in the country's leaders in financial matters. "If this government avoids bankruptcy, and meets all its liabilities honestly, it will in my opinion, be due [exclusively] to the outstanding resources of the country. . . ." American politicians, unlike those of other countries, knew nothing of the "laws" of "political economy" and learned everything from costly experience, as Americans "learn nearly everything."[55]

Olmsted's problems were more intimate. His resignation as general secretary of the Sanitary Commission and his hasty move to California had been impelled partly by overwork. Now he was again overdoing, especially at night, and was suffering emotional stress. Writing particularly became

an agony, "a single sheet entirely upsets my digestion, sets
my brain throbbing, and my ears singing and half suffocates
me—also my eyes twitch."[56] Abandoning his projected history of civilization in the United States, Olmsted stuffed his
notes and drafts into a pigeon hole of his desk with orders to
give them to Godkin in the event of his death.[57] Godkin
sought to reassure his friend by challenging the opinion that
he suffered from a heart condition. "I have had every symp-
tom you describe," he told Olmsted, "with palpitation so
violent as to keep me awake at night. . . . There never was
anything the matter with my heart except functional derangement caused by the state of my nerves."[58]

Bored by his intellectual isolation in Bear Valley, Olmsted
came up with a scheme for planting a colony of easterners
there, and he proposed that Godkin, with his wife and four-
year-old son, join the colony. Godkin's answer shows something of his state of mind in 1864. He replied that he found
the invitation tempting:

> In the first place, my present employment leads to nothing,
> and I have a good many rather sad half hours—between our-
> selves—in the reflection that I am slowly frittering my best
> years away in what is for the writer certainly the most un-
> profitable of all literary labour. I am winning neither fame nor
> money. . . . Something may turn up in the newspaper line that
> may suit me, such as an opening in the Ev[ening] Post, or some
> other evening paper; but for the moment I see no sign of
> anything. Consequently my prospects are by no means so
> brilliant as they seemed when I first determined to settle in
> this country. My illness has knocked me off the track, and if
> I were not now sincerely attached to the country, and deeply
> interested in its future, married and so forth, I would go back
> to England.[59]

Godkin also cited, as an inducement to migrate, his lack of
friends in the east; in California he and Olmsted "could grow
old, and grumble over the ways of the world together." He
pointed to the call of the outdoors, conceding that he lacked
the "literary temperament" and was "by nature and temperament rather fitted for an outdoor than an indoor life." But
against this, he told Olmsted, he was too fastidious for
western living, especially the people he would encounter
there. "I am not popular in my manners and could never

become so."[60] Besides he was dubious of being able to make a quick fortune in California, "so as to secure me at an early period, what I have always longed for—leisure and liberty to choose my own work."[61]

In point of truth, Godkin never gave serious thought to joining Olmsted in his isolation. Throughout 1864 he redoubled his efforts, with the help of his patrons, to find an editorial post on one of the eastern papers. One evening in February 1864 Vaux encountered him at Brace's, another guest being John Swinton of the editorial staff of the *New York Times*. Fanny was at the opera for the third time that week, so Vaux accompanied Godkin home from Brace's and they smoked a cigar together in Godkin's extension and talked about the delays in the construction of Central Park and other matters. Godkin was handling some of Olmsted's funds and serving as unofficial legal adviser to him and Vaux.[62] Godkin asked Vaux to introduce him to Samuel Bowles, the proprietor of the influential *Springfield Republican*, which Olmsted thought the best paper in the United States, and Vaux agreed to a meeting at his home.[63]

For several months Godkin had been procrastinating on an invitation from Charles Norton to write for the *North American Review*.[64] The *Review's* rate of pay—two dollars a page—did not attract him, but in the *Review* he would reach an intellectual New England audience not unlike his English audience in the *Daily News*. Accordingly, in the spring of 1864, he bestirred himself and sent Norton his first offering, a thirty-page analysis of what he deemed to be the defects in the United States Constitution.[65] It was the first of fifteen essays that he would ultimately write for the *Review*.

In the meantime the military fortunes of the North had taken an upswing when Ulysses S. Grant assumed supreme command. But to Norton Godkin proposed that they temper their optimism: "Lee, I am confident will 'die game.' He is the only man in the Confederacy whose fate I should regret if they were all at the bottom of the James river."[66] He was not confident, he told Olmsted, that there would be a Southern military surrender. After organized opposition was crushed, the Confederates would likely "fight as guerillas and then assassinate; until they are gradually improved off the face of the earth, and their places taken by northern settlers, a process which I expect to see lasting a great portion of my lifetime."[67]

Godkin's essays for the *North American Review*, like his *Knickerbocker* essays, reflect his obsession with material forces as determinants of human behavior. His second, and most important, essay for the *Review*, "Aristocratic Opinions of Democracy," provocatively explores the role of the frontier in shaping American democracy.[68] Had Godkin given the essay a more felicitous title, it might have escaped the dust bin of forgotten theories of government. Taking as his working assumption the postulate that historian Frederick Jackson Turner a generation later would elaborate as the "frontier thesis" of American history, Godkin argued that the flaws which foreigners detect in American society are not flaws inherent in democracy but are a result of the ever-repeating movement of populations from the settled regions of the country into the wilderness frontier.[69] Godkin argued it this way:

> The agency which, in our opinion, gave democracy its first great impulse in the United States, which has promoted its spread ever since, and has contributed most powerfully to the production of those phenomena in American society which hostile critics set down as peculiarly democratic, was neither the origin of the Colonists, nor the circumstances under which they came to the country, nor their religious belief; but the great change in the distribution of the population, which began soon after the Revolution, and which continues its operation up to the present time.[70]

Although Turner was a staunch believer in democracy and in the strength of the American character, Godkin at his optimistic best was only guardedly so. Yet Godkin might have set down in 1865, in almost the same words, what Turner below wrote nearly thirty years later in his essay, "The Significance of the Frontier in American History":

> To the frontier the American intellect owes its striking characteristics. That coarseness and strength combined with acuteness and inquisitiveness; that practical, inventive turn of mind, quick to find expedients; that masterful grasp of material things, lacking in the artistic but powerful to effect great ends; that restless, nervous energy; that dominant individualism, working for good and for evil, and withal that buoyancy

and exuberance that comes with freedom—these are traits
of the frontier, or traits called out elsewhere because of the
existence of the frontier.[71]

As he published his essay "Aristocratic Opinions of Democracy," Godkin sensed that he had elaborated an important theory, and he set about trying to give it currency. In
San Francisco, Olmsted—who had helped Godkin formulate
the theory—was unconcerned when a copy of the essay that
Godkin sent him was lost in the mail. A self-educated man
of extraordinary, though diffused, talents, Olmsted seems
not to have resented Godkin's talent for listening to the
thoughts of others and setting them down in writing as his
own.[72] Olmsted had bounced back from his mental dis-
quietude of the previous year and was once more filled with
schemes—one for a book on the influence of pioneer life and
democracy.[73]

To the great English utilitarian, John Stuart Mill, Godkin
sent a copy of his essay asking for Mill's comments. Their
correspondence is worth reproducing:

37 East 19th St., New York
April 1 [1865]

Sir:

I took the liberty of forwarding you a week ago, a copy of
the *North American Review* for January last, containing an
article by me, on "Aristocratic Opinions of Democracy."

The explanation there offered of some of those defects of
American society and government, which European observers
commonly ascribe to the working of democratic institutions,
and you yourself, if I am not mistaken, to the growth of the
commercial spirit—is, so far as I know, novel. I should be very
much flattered by learning that you had discovered in it any
other merit than that of originality, and shall venture to hope
that you will, at all events, deem the article worthy of your
perusal.[74]

I am, Sir,
Your obedient,
faithful servant

J. S. Mill, Esq.   Edwin L. Godkin

Mill, writing in the belief that Godkin was a New Eng-
lander, replied:

Avignon, May 24, 1865

Dear Sir:

I thank you very sincerely for your article in the *North American Review;* not merely for sending it to me, but for writing it. I consider it a very important contribution to the philosophy of the subject; a correction, from one point of view, of what was excessive in Tocqueville's theory of democracy, as my review of him was from another. You have fully made out that the peculiar character of society in the Western States —the mental type formed by the position and habits of the pioneers—is at least in part accountable for many American phenomena which have been ascribed to democracy. This is a most consoling belief, as it refers the unfavorable side of American social existence (which you set forth with a fulness of candor that ought to shame the detractors of American literature and thought) to causes naturally declining, rather than to one which always tends to increase.

But if any encouragement were required by those who hope the best from American institutions, the New England States, as they now are, would be encouragement enough. If Tocqueville had lived to know what these States have become thirty years after he saw them, he would, I think, have acknowledged that much of the unfavorable part of his anticipation had not been realized. Democracy has been no leveller there, as to intellect and education, or respect for true personal superiority. Nor has it stereotyped a particular cast of thought, as is proved by so many really original writers, yourself being one. Finally, New England has now the immortal glory of having destroyed slavery. . . .

It is a happiness to have lived to see such a termination of the greatest and most corrupting of all social iniquities which, more than all other causes together, lowered the tone of the national and especially the political mind of the United States. It now rests with the intellect and high aspirations of the Eastern States, and the energy and straightforward honesty of the Western, to make the best use of the occasion, and I have no misgiving as to the result.

Do not trouble yourself to send me the *North American Review,* as I already subscribe to it. But I shall always be glad to be informed of any article in it which is of your writing, and to know your opinion on any American question.[75]

I am, dear Sir,
Yours very sincerely,
Edwin L. Godkin, Esq.   J. S. Mill

Despite Mill's polite invitation to further correspondence, Godkin—who did not subscribe to Mill's later democratic theory—never wrote him again.

It was in his third essay for the North American Review, a companion piece to "Aristocratic Opinions of Democracy," that Godkin had his first disagreement with the editors of that journal. For months he had been bothered by the uncritical support cultured New Englanders were giving to the enfranchisement of the freedmen. To his English audience in the Daily News, he complained that Americans confuse citizenship with voting—oblivious to the fact that, whereas the first is a right, the second is a privilege—a distinction "which the democratic tide here has nearly effaced."[76] Throughout 1864 Godkin had been vacillating in the Daily News between supporting the radicals and, conversely, the moderates on Reconstruction; but Lincoln had now risen in his esteem and, for the moment, he was back in the moderate camp. He was especially irritated by the point of view of the leading abolitionists, such as that expressed by young Wendell Phillips Garrison, son of the abolitionist William Lloyd Garrison, when he proposed privately in a letter to his brother a mass meeting of abolitionists and blacks to protest Lincoln's Reconstruction policy.[77]

Godkin now determined to carry his opposition to Negro suffrage into the territory of the black man's friends. In February 1865, warning Norton that his opinions would "sound shocking to a good many people, if not to you," he sent him a long essay for the North American Review postulating black inequality.[78] Norton declined to publish it without change, and a debate between them ensued, Norton clinging to Lowell's position that natural rights are indefeasible; therefore morality dictates giving the blacks the vote. Godkin responded by denying that there is such a thing as a natural right to vote; the "precise form of government" that a country adopts has nothing to do with morality—it is "purely a question of expediency." Already the electoral process of the United States was reeling from an "enormous influx of ignorant foreigners"; why add to them a million of liberated slaves "in the lowest state of ignorance and degradation?"[79]

Godkin emphasized that he did not oppose enfranchising those blacks who could prove their fitness by "a moral as well as an educational test." But Americans, he contended, talked too much about natural rights; it was time they asserted "the value of education, and the authority of training and culture" in government.[80] Unconvinced, Norton proposed that Godkin change his essay to conform to Lowell's views and to concede that morality, in addition to expediency, carries weight in human affairs. In addition he requested Godkin to tone down his language. "Anything like exaggeration . . . injures a good cause."[81] Godkin politely retorted that he disagreed with Lowell. Then, unexpectedly, he capitulated and on 10 April wrote Norton: "I shall recast all I have said about the negroes, and put it in a shape which will not clash with your own opinions and those of the *Review.*"[82]

Godkin's amended essay appeared in the July 1865 *North American Review* just as the country was turning to the problems of postwar reconstruction.[83] The Anglo-Irish immigrant had lost his first skirmish against giving blacks the ballot, but in time—through iteration—he would bring Norton, Lowell, and many of their friends over to his way of thinking.

Chapter Five
Founding the *Nation*

*The NATION, now in course of pub-
lication in New York, is without exception the best newspaper we have
yet seen from America.*
Trübner's American and
Oriental Literary Record (London)

"I was under the impression," Godkin brusquely answered
an encyclopedia compiler in 1871, "that you were sufficiently
familiar with the history of the *Nation* to make it unneces-
sary for me to say anything about it." With this remark, the
fiery first editor of the New York weekly launched into an
account of some of the journal's early struggles. "It was
established in 1865, by a joint stock company," he began.
"Owing [to] internal dissensions . . . the company was dis-
solved in 1866, and the paper sold to myself and two other
persons, Fred[erick] Law Olmsted and J. M. McKim."[1]

The war-spawned *Nation* found itself engulfed in dissen-
sion at the start because editorially it breathed controversy.
Few readers in the charged atmosphere of post-Appomattox
America were able to lay aside the opinionated weekly without instant opinions of their own as to its worth. Goldwin
Smith flattered Norton that the weekly represented in its
way "the first fruits of the regeneration which a great moral
struggle was sure to produce." The new weekly, deduced
one of its contributors, Arthur G. Sedgwick, was truly "a
continuation and completion of the work of moulding opinion
which had its beginning in the Loyal Publication Society."[2]

But many American subscribers to the *Nation* in the summer of 1865, including some of its founders, did not share
these sentiments. The hostility of some toward the journal
stemmed from what they charged was Godkin's breach of the
terms of its founding. Many of the financial backers of the

75

Nation were abolitionists who had invested in the idea that it would be an organ of the freedmen's associations. To fulfill one of the goals stated in the prospectus of the *Nation*—"the removal of all artificial distinctions between [the black] and the rest of the population"[3]—Boston abolitionists led by George L. Stearns invested more than $20,000 of their own money, as well as $16,000 of the funds of a committee formed for the recruiting of black soldiers. Freedmen's Aid men gave nearly all of the $25,000 pledged to the *Nation* in Philadelphia and Baltimore, and the erstwhile headquarters of the American Freedmen's Aid Union in New York became the *Nation's* first home. But the Radical cause in 1865 was hampered by divisions; the *Nation* became a microcosm of the sectarianism that had disrupted the American Anti-Slavery Society and would now similarly afflict the American Freedmen's Aid Union.

To return to early 1865; more than a year had passed since Godkin gave up the scheme for a weekly paper that Olmsted had hatched, and the war was drawing to a conclusion. From San Francisco Olmsted wrote Godkin that he was thinking of returning east and resuming his scheme. Meanwhile the New England Unionist zealot John M. Forbes was in Washington proposing Olmsted to head the Freedmen's Bureau; but Olmsted, who already was reflecting signs of the mental disturbance that later would wholly disable him, stayed put in San Francisco.[4]

Meanwhile in Boston and Philadelphia the abolitionist former clergyman James M. McKim was pushing plans for a national weekly to succeed the *Anti-Slavery Standard* and the *Liberator*. McKim, the soft-spoken Quaker ally of William Lloyd Garrison who had gone to Harper's Ferry with Mrs. John Brown to bring back her husband's body, envisioned himself as the proprietor of a new journal "devoted to the national questions and interests involved in the condition and position of the black race on a broader ground than that of the old papers."[5] McKim meant to create editorial positions on the paper for himself and his new son-in-law, Wendell Phillips Garrison, third son of the abolitionist. The hardworking, self-effacing young Garrison, fresh out of Harvard, was already gaining editorial experience under Theodore

Tilton on Henry C. Bowen's Brooklyn antislavery weekly, *The Independent*.[6]

By April 1865 McKim's scheme had the blessing of prominent Freedmen's Aid men and members of the Loyal Publication Society.[7] In Boston Norton, John Greenleaf Whittier, and Francis J. Child offered support, and in Baltimore Judge Hugh L. Bond was enlisted. In Philadelphia McKim's fellow members in the Pennsylvania Freedmen's Relief Association pledged their support.[8]

With this encouragement McKim began a search for a publisher. His son-in-law, young Garrison, was enjoying satisfactory relations on *The Independent* with an able young brother-in-law of Tilton, Joseph H. Richards, and in mid-April McKim offered Richards the post of publisher. Before accepting, Richards laid down a set of conditions. Foremost, he did not intend to hand down his "name from *The Independent* and hoist it at the masthead of a sinking ship. . . ." McKim must give him written assurance that the editorial end of the paper would be adequately manned, "as, for instance, yourself and Mr. Garrison, laboring with as much zeal and ambition as you expect of myself. . . ." Moreover representatives of the various freedmen's organizations must give the paper "substantial help," and the soon-to-expire *Anti-Slavery Standard* and the *Liberator*—as well as the executive committee of the American Anti-Slavery Society—must recognize the paper as "in some sense" to be their heir.[9] With these conditions more or less met, Richards consented to become publisher.

McKim and his friends had now given the weekly a name —the *Nation*—and they set about to raise $50,000 to finance it. At this point a backer appeared in Major Stearns of Medford, Massachusetts. This antislavery valiant of Whittier's elegy, who "forgot his own soul for others," numbered Emerson, Charles Sumner, and Wendell Phillips among his friends. Proud of having supplied John Brown with the weapons the old man and his companions used at Harper's Ferry, Stearns performed yeoman labors during the war organizing the recruitment of black troops.[10] A man of boundless energy in raising funds and distributing abolitionist tracts, Stearns was the principal figure in the founding of a Boston antislavery weekly, the *Commonwealth*. Earnest, dedicated, and — as Emerson and Whittier testified — possessing admirable qualities, Stearns, as an anti-Garrisonian with deep sympathies for the black, would find himself too uncompromising for what now lay ahead for the *Nation*. "Such men as Sumner, Stearns, Hallowell, etc.," Norton assured Godkin, "presume on the virtue of their motives and can conceive of nothing better than themselves."[11]

It was now April, and the founders of the *Nation* were hoping for a 1 July publication date. Norton, Stearns, and the others tactfully persuaded McKim that he and young Garrison lacked experience for the overall editorial direction of the weekly, and a search was begun for an editor-in-chief. George W. Curtis and Whitelaw Reid were the first to receive consideration. Norton's and Stearns' choice, with McKim in assent, was the New England-born Curtis, once a boarder at Brook Farm and a friend of Olmsted, now earning $10,000 a year as editor of *Harper's Weekly*. But after a day's deliberation, Curtis turned the offer down. "I doubt if $50,000 is capital enough to start such a paper," he told Norton, stressing as his objection that the *Nation* was too lofty to appeal to the public at large and would be read only by those "who need no conversion."[12] Thereupon the choice for editor-in-chief turned to Stearns' young friend of wartime Washington days, Whitelaw Reid, a choice John Murray Forbes warmly seconded. But although Reid held antislavery views, he lacked the zeal of the New England "come outers" and, occupied with a cotton speculation in the south, he declined.[13] In a few years he would succeed Horace Greeley as proprietor of the *New York Tribune*.

While the search for an editor continued, Olmsted was still in California and Godkin in New York, each ignorant of the paper being promoted in Boston. Godkin was writing for the London *Daily News* and the *New York Times* and was now toying with joining Olmsted in a newspaper enterprise in San Francisco. The only hint Godkin received of the *Nation* came in March, when Norton casually mentioned McKim's venture to him and suggested he offer his services as a contributor.[14] When the search for an editor-in-chief got under way, Norton did not mention Godkin. Aside from

Godkin's inexperience, an obvious reason was Norton's awareness that the attitude of Godkin toward the black man differed from that of the *Nation*'s backers. Since February Norton and Godkin had been locked in their debate over Negro suffrage in connection with the article Godkin had submitted for the *North American Review*. But when in April Godkin capitulated and agreed to change his position, Norton considered tendering him the editorship of the *Nation*.

Up to this point neither Stearns nor McKim had heard of Godkin. Hurried conferences ensued, in which, without mentioning their debate over Negro suffrage, Norton described Godkin to the satisfaction of the others as an "Englishman" schooled in British liberal journalism. Stearns in particular was pleased to learn that Godkin in his youth had written a book praising Kossuth. At the end of April Norton and Stearns met with Godkin in New York and formally offered him the editorship.[15] An elated Godkin wrote Olmsted in San Francisco that "there is a strong probability—almost a certainty that I shall start the weekly paper on the 1st of July. . . ." He assured the older man that the paper would be "substantially the same as that which we had projected," to which Olmsted replied, "I immediately declared a holiday and we went up the mountain and drank success to your enterprise in good Rhine wine."[16]

Godkin stipulated to the *Nation*'s sponsors that he enjoy absolute editorial freedom, to which they agreed with the condition that he raise in New York $25,000 of the paper's total capitalization—in accordance with Curtis's advice—of $100,000. Stearns and Norton agreed to raise $50,000 in Boston, and McKim promised to get the remaining $25,000 in Philadelphia and Baltimore.

McKim, Norton, and Stearns had hired in Godkin a man of modest editorial experience but of undeniable talent and positive views, intent on controlling the *Nation*. McKim, although he had his own prospectus for the paper and was counting to the last on an editorial post, accepted the prospectus that Godkin now drew up and good-naturedly bowed out, after reiterating his promise to raise funds in Philadelphia. The terms of Godkin's employment were the same as those of publisher Richards—a salary of $5,000 a year, plus 12½ percent of the annual profits remaining after the payment of a 6 percent dividend to the stockholders. Godkin and Richards each consented to take a token interest in the Nation. On Stearns' motion it was informally agreed that each man would be employed for a trial period of from one to two years.[17]

By this time Stearns had displaced McKim as the principal backer of the Nation, and without delay he sought out Godkin for a conference. Warily Godkin hedged in his conversations with the abolitionist. After several meetings between the two in New York during May, Stearns invited one of his sons and Wendell Phillips to be present with them for lunch at the Brevoort House. Young Stearns afterwards recalled that the conversation "was chiefly concerning the reconstruction of the Southern states and the political position of the Negro race there, and Mr. Godkin assented to everything which Mr. Stearns proposed." Phillips, although he would decline to take stock in the Nation, endorsed Stearns' favorable impression of Godkin, whereupon Stearns approved the condition that Godkin have "autocratic control" over the paper.[18]

With the Nation now moved to New York, setbacks occurred in Boston. Emerson had been dubious of the project from the start, and his negative attitude deepened when a foreigner was named editor-in-chief. George Bancroft took an active dislike to Godkin, and antislavery leaders Charles Sumner, William Lloyd Garrison, and Benjamin F. Butler joined Phillips in according a cool reception to the editor's wooing.[19] "In New York one Herald is enough for one city," Butler explained to Edward Pierce, "One [James Gordon] Bennett for an Age."[20] Later Butler recalled:

> When Godkin was starting his pernicious weekly, he went around to all the old Abolitionists to get subscriptions to his stock. He came to me, for one. He told me he intended to publish a journal for the education and elevation of the emancipated and enfranchised slaves.[21]

But Stearns, still confident of Godkin, was undisturbed by the doubts of the others. The Nation had enough capital within reach, he inferred to Senator Sumner, to begin with a circulation of 40,000. "I am glad that the good work is proceeding," a possibly unconvinced Sumner replied. "A strong paper is needed."[22]

The *Nation* was only one of the propaganda schemes of the Radicals in the spring of 1865, as John Forbes pointed out to N. M. Beckwith in June:

> We are trying to form an association to mould public opinion. . . . Perhaps we shall do it through the Loyal Pub.; perhaps in various other ways. The L. P. has been, we think, a great success, reaching about a million of readers a week.
>
> We have also started a new weekly in New York, "The Nation," under Godkin, into which I have put some money as a proprietor, and to which you ought to subscribe. . . . Then we are going to establish a free press in Delaware, under [Charles] Nordhoff, now working editor of the "Evening Post," in the hope of saving to freedom the two senators from that little half-alive nest of slavery.[23]

To Forbes Norton proposed that Olmsted, whose Mariposa mining venture had collapsed, be lured home to head the propaganda association. After conferring with Godkin, Norton offered his plan: the Loyal Publication Society and the *Nation* jointly would employ Olmsted. But McKim, now embarked on his new duties as secretary of the American Freedmen's Aid Union, had a better idea. He contrived to have Olmsted appointed general secretary of the American Freedmen's Aid Union, with part of his duties being to write for the *Nation*. But Olmsted steadfastly remained in California.[24]

The *Nation* office, meanwhile, opened at the vacated New York headquarters of the American Freedmen's Aid Union at 130 Nassau Street, and Richards, Godkin, and Wendell Garrison set to work preparing for the 1 July publishing date. Godkin was gratified to find Garrison industrious and with "that foundation of all usefulness, a willingness to obey 'lawful orders.' "[25] Garrison set about to design the letterhead of the *Nation* stationery, mail out advertising circulars, write book notices, and recruit literary contributors. Richards, Godkin also found a "very good man," although periodically he would reverse his estimate of the publisher. The two decided to print the *Nation* expensively in leaded *bourgeois* type on thirty-four pages of the size of the *American Artizan*. Thinking that capital was no problem, Richards and Godkin agreed on a temporary half-of-cost subscription

rate of three dollars a year "to get an audience at the outset."
Norton's notion that this rate was too low was confirmed at
the end of the year when the *Nation* found itself losing
$4,000 a month and had to double its rates.[26]

In devising the content of the *Nation*, Godkin determined
to avoid "dosing the public" with freedmen's rights. And he
did not forget the name he had meant to give Olmsted's
paper—"The Week." To writer Charles C. Hazewell he described his intention of creating a feature called "The Week"
as the lead department of the *Nation*: "I propose to have in
the *Nation* about three pages of paragraphs, somewhat in the
style of the London *Spectator*, containing not news but comments on anything and everything of interest." Godkin requested Hazewell to write each week a half page to a full
page of leader paragraphs with "force or brilliancy or both,"
for which he would pay him ten dollars a page.[27]

Having made arrangements of this kind, Godkin turned the
direction of "The Week" over to Garrison.[28] (Some writers
have assumed that Godkin wrote "The Week," but although
he contributed regularly to it, it was the work of the entire
staff, including J. R. Dennett, Garrison, Hazewell, William
Dean Howells, Arthur G. Sedgwick, and even Norton. Godkin's only stipulation was that the paragraphs be clever and
not clash with his own views.) Since the overworked Garrison
could not do everything, Godkin at the last minute ceased
contributing to the *New York Times*.[29] But he continued to
write regularly for the London *Daily News*, and for the next
year and a half he wrote as much for that paper as for the
Nation.

Godkin had never known office routine, had always done
his writing at home, and fled the city in summer. Thus he
was fretful of the prospect of having to keep regular hours.
At Stearns' suggestion he asked through Norton for the help
of Charles Nordhoff during the coming summer. In declining,
Nordhoff counselled Norton, "I think Mr. Godkin will find no
difficulty in getting someone to do what he really needs to
have done—to superintend, namely, the mere routine of the
paper. For the rest, I have no fear but that he will get
through it, if he sets his own shoulders to it, and makes
proper use of his friends here and in Boston."[30] Godkin did

not need the final hint. McKim visited the office regularly and was helpful and considerate. "The freedmen department of the paper, of course, fills [McKim's] head so much that he does not seem to think much of the critical portion," Godkin reported to Norton, but his fears that the older man would insist on the *Nation* being "swamped by freedmen documents" did not materialize.[31] Godkin instructed Olmsted to help by "fishing up contributors, writing yourself, or getting subscriptions." In New Haven, where Godkin had lived with his bride, the editor set Professor Daniel Coit Gilman to recruiting contributors at Yale College.[32]

The most energetic of Godkin's unpaid helpers was Norton, without whose unselfish aid the *Nation* could not have been born. Throughout May and June 1865 Norton recruited contributors, raised money, mailed manuscripts to Godkin, fended off critics of the irascible editor, and faithfully responded to Godkin's sometimes daily letters.[33] Still fearful of the competition of the *Round Table,* Godkin asked Norton to help him draw up an advertising prospectus listing future contributors to the *Nation.* For promotional purposes they agreed that the list need not be accurate. Norton's thinking was illustrated by a letter he sent Godkin on 9 May:

> I will see [Professor H. W.] Torrey and [Asa] Gray in a day or two. Edmund Quincy who has been long one of the editors of the *A[nti]-S[lavery] Standard* had better be engaged. McKim has already spoken to him, and he is interested in the journal, and expects to write for it. His name will be of value with the A[nti] S[lavery] people. . . . Wendell Holmes I am weary to death of. . . . But he is still popular and his name might be of some use. . . . It would be well perhaps to add Emerson, I rather think his name would help. And perhaps (more doubtfully) other names like Mrs. [Lydia Maria] Child and Miss [Louisa May] Alcott, and T. W. Higginson might be added. Whittier of course—and indeed it could do no harm to assume that all promises made to McKim are still binding.[34]

Godkin went a step further. Without directly consulting either man, he added the names of William Lloyd Garrison and Theodore Tilton. "I do not think they will repel anybody," he told Norton, "and they are certain to attract a good many."[35] Neither man would ever write for the *Nation.*

Late in May Godkin went to Boston to see Norton and

Stearns and to recruit more contributors, staying overnight
at Shady Hill, Norton's home in Cambridge. Norton gave a
party for him, during which bickering between protectionists and free traders among the investors in the Nation
surfaced. Speaking for the Philadelphia manufacturers, Mc-
Kim asked for assurance that the Nation would not become a
free-trade journal. Fearful that a refusal would lose the
journal its Philadelphia support, Godkin dictated to McKim a
pledge to the Philadelphia investors to avoid the tariff issue.

The next day, as rain fell in Cambridge, Godkin borrowed
Norton's umbrella and crossed the Charles River to Stearns'
house in Boston. After some amicable conversation with the
Nation's principal stockholder, he made his farewell, leaving
Stearns with Norton's umbrella but innocent of knowledge of
the "Philadelphia pledge."[36] The explosion that would greet
the exposure of Godkin's agreement did not come until after
the Nation's birth, when in July Godkin declined to publish a
free-trade article by Boston stockholder Edward Atkinson.[37]

Before departing from Boston, Godkin stopped at Ashbur-
ton Place to see a young protegé of Norton, Henry James,
to ask him to contribute to the first number of the Nation.
"I . . . was to find myself," the novelist recalled, ". . . invited
to the high glory, as I felt it, of aiding to launch, though on
the obscurer side of the enterprise, a weekly journal which
. . . was soon to enjoy a fortune and achieve an authority
and a dignity of which neither newspaper nor critical review
among us had hitherto so much as hinted."[38]

Godkin was working with greater-than-usual diligence,
but he was little known, and it was through Norton's help
that half of the contributors to the first number of the Nation
were enlisted. Similarly it was on the recommendation of
Norton that some of the early editorial employees of the
Nation were hired. One was the talented young Harvard
graduate John R. Dennett, whom Godkin hired in June at a
salary of $150 a month and traveling expenses to go south
and write a weekly description of conditions in the former
Confederacy. Dennett was unwell, but arming himself with
medicines to ward off chills and fever, he set out from
Boston late in June 1865. Before he left, Stearns asked him
to distribute on his tour copies of Stearns' Negro pamphlets.

"I . . . told him," Dennett reported to Norton, "I was entirely in the hands of Mr. Godkin to whom I looked for instructions, and that I would do nothing tending to injure me in my capacity as correspondent."[39] Dennett's "The South As It Is" series ran in the *Nation* for six months. Godkin's practice of keeping *Nation* contributors anonymous later caused historian A. B. Hart inaccurately to publish a segment of "The South As It Is" as the work of Godkin.[40]

According to the investors' agreement, the *Nation* could not start publication until the entire $100,000 capital had been raised, and May saw a concerted effort to reach that goal. In New York Godkin was secretly experiencing fundraising difficulty, although Howard Potter was working with sporadic zeal to help him with that city's quota. In Philadelphia McKim was conducting a well-organized campaign for funds with the aid of manufacturers Samuel S. White and John Sellers, Jr. Ultimately twelve persons in the Philadelphia-Baltimore area, chiefly members of the Freedmen's Aid Union, made pledges. The chief support of the *Nation* was in the Boston area. There Stearns, its biggest backer, promised $10,000 which he increased to $12,000 when Boston fell short of its quota in June. In addition about $16,000 was pledged from the treasury of the Committee for Recruiting Negro Troops, a fund-raising organization that Stearns had been active in forming in Boston in 1863 and to which many of the Boston investors in the *Nation* belonged. The pledge of the "Negro Committee" was made with the stipulation that the *Nation* be "devoted to the *equal rights of all men,* in connection with various Freedmen's Aid Societies."

Other substantial backers of the venture in the Boston area were Forbes, Martin Brimmer, Edward Philbrick, and Oakes Ames, of subsequent congressional notoriety. Smaller pledges came from the Negro Recruiting Fund treasurer Richard P. Hallowell, Norton, Atkinson, J. W. Field, Samuel G. Ward, Charles Beck, and William Endicott, Jr.[41]

Because many made their pledges to the *Nation* as an investment in a worthy cause rather than a financial speculation, there were qualms in Boston about personal liability in case of the journal's failure. This fear led Forbes to direct that his $5,000 be pledged in Norton's name. "I understand your trust," he emphasized to Norton, "to be to use the amount for carrying on the *Nation* but not to incur any liability beyond that."[42] With effective control of the paper now in the hands of Godkin in New York, other Bostonians followed suit. Edward Austin and Henry Bowditch jointly sent Norton $1,000 "provided that we do not appear as stockholders or have any liability beyond that sum." In order partially to free the investors from liability, Stearns proposed an agreement among Richards, Godkin, and the yet-to-be-chosen trustees of the *Nation* Association: the entire capital would be surrendered to the trustees, who each January thereafter would furnish an annual report of the financial affairs of the company to the county clerk.[43]

During May Godkin began effecting the legal organization of the *Nation* Association. The largest bloc of the *Nation's* nearly forty investors and over half of its capital were in Massachusetts, but according to New York law joint-stock companies chartered in that state had to be controlled by New York citizens. Thereupon Godkin decreed that control of the company be vested in five trustees from New York, two from Boston, and two from Philadelphia. Lest the Boston group have other ideas, Godkin informed Norton that the meetings of the trustees would be held in New York. In preparation for the first meeting, the three groups of investors now met and selected their trustees. The Boston group chose Stearns and Norton; McKim and White were the choice of the Philadelphia group; and Christian E. Detmold, George C. Ward, Robert B. Minturn, and Cannon represented New York. William F. Blodgett, a would-be New York trustee, had gone to Europe for the summer.[44]

The first meeting of the trustees was held in New York on 31 May 1865, with Stearns absent. Detmold was elected president of the *Nation* Association, McKim was named secretary, and George C. Ward volunteered to serve as treasurer. After authorizing the bylaws and the preparation of stock certificates, the trustees took two controversial actions: first, they voted to disband as an effective body in favor of a three-man executive committee consisting of Norton, Detmold, and McKim; and second, they directed that the pledges to the *Nation* be paid in cash without delay.

Although more than $85,000 had thus far been pledged, little cash had been paid over. Yet Godkin, bristling with confidence, reported to Gilman in New Haven: "We have completed our organization and the first number will appear about the 6th of July." Equally misleadingly, McKim told Maria Chapman, "*The Nation* will start under the most favorable of auspices," and he added, "Now that its establishment is an accomplished fact my connection with it ceases."[45]

Norton returned to Boston on 4 June, and that afternoon he reported to Stearns the actions taken by the trustees. Distress signals went up as word spread in Boston that the pledges must be paid all at once and in cash. Charles Beck, who had subscribed with the understanding that he could pay in installments, withdrew his pledge. The rumor flew that Stearns, influenced by Wendell Phillips, was cancelling his investment in the *Nation* and meant to prevent it from using the Negro Recruiting Fund. After talking with Stearns, Forbes nervously informed Norton that he was withholding his $5,000 until "you tell me the capital is secure by good reliable parties."[46]

The displeasure of Stearns stemmed from Norton's report of the meeting of the trustees. Stearns seemed satisfied with the report until Norton mentioned the three-man executive committee, whereupon the folly of having excluded the *Nation*'s principal stockholder from the committee dawned on Norton. Stearns' complaint, Norton reported to Godkin, was that the abolitionist and his friends were unrepresented; the executive committee "was not as radical a committee as a new member [Stearns] of the new Executive Council of the new American Anti-Slavery Society would have liked. . . ."[47] Nonetheless Norton was encouraged that Stearns was still good-natured, and he told Godkin he thought the older man would "come out all right." Other investors were not sure. "I have always regretted that Mr. Stearns should represent so large an interest in the stock," Atkinson advised Norton, "and I think it would be best to let him off easily, trusting to our control of the . . . Recruiting Committee [funds], of which I think there are nearly $10,000 [beyond the $15,000 now pledged to the *Nation*] not yet appropriated." When Norton responded that Stearns had apparently regained his com-

posure, Atkinson replied, "I am very glad that Stearns has
come to his senses, but as he may not retain them long I
should be quite content to substitute the remainder of the
Rec[ruiting] Fund for his subs[cription]."[48]

Meanwhile Stearns was writing Godkin, intimating that he
would not pay his pledge if the executive committee remained as constituted. Godkin rushed to Boston and, in the
presence of Norton, urged Stearns to rescind his objections.
Stearns agreed to do so if Godkin would allow him to reduce
his pledge to $3,000, but Godkin demurred, saying this
"would break up the project," and he reminded Stearns that
the latter had guaranteed the Boston subscription of $50,000.
Stearns thereupon paid over his capital and that of the Recruiting Fund, which he and Hallowell had been holding.[49]
By late June 1865 most of the Boston subscription and all of
the Philadelphia subscription were in the hands of treasurer
Ward.

The remaining financial hurdle was New York, where
Godkin's efforts thus far had brought in only $3,000. More-
over as the July date of publication neared, disagreements
multiplied among the stockholders. Forbes vented his irritation at the bickering among the antislavery people. "It
amazes me highly to see your Radicals fighting each other,"
he told Norton, "Wendell Phillips Samson being on the conservative wing in the case of John Brown and Bravero McKim
—while I one of the Chief Workers am appealed to by the
Radical element as being *of them*."[50]

As the first number of the *Nation* went to press on 30 June,
numerous problems remained. Less than $85,000 of the re-
quired capital had been raised, most of the shortage being in
Godkin's New York quota. The "delay weighs on my spirits,"
Godkin told Norton, though he did not reveal to the other
man the full extent of the shortage.[51] Richards, too, was
discouraged; news agents were warning him that the public
would not buy a journal as "heavy" as the *Nation*.

Then suddenly on 5 July the pains of birth ended. "Number
one," announced a relieved Godkin to Norton, was in the
newstands, "and the tranquility which still reigns in this
city, under the circumstances I confess amazes me."[52]

The *Nation* was afloat.

Chapter Six
The Weekly "Day of Judgment"

*Speak what you think today in words
as hard as cannon balls, and tomor-
row, speak what you think in words
just as hard though you contradict
everything you said today.*

Ralph Waldo Emerson

Although the Nation had been launched, how long it
would stay afloat was a subject of conjecture. Among the
initial reactions to the new high-brow weekly was a ridicule-
punctuated editorial in the New York Times, from whose
ranks of contributors Godkin had just retired with the well-
wishes of its proprietor.[1] A Richmond, Virginia, paper specu-
lated, to Godkin's amusement, that Wendell Phillips was at
the bottom of the enterprise.[2] And in the hallowed precincts
of New England abolitionism, friends of the black man read
on page one of the Nation, with varying disapproval, what
William Lloyd Garrison called the Nation's "objectionable
paragraph":

> The negro's success in assuming a prominent position in the
> political arena, seems to be in the inverse ratio of the earnest-
> ness with which it is sought to suppress him, and put him out
> of sight. Everybody is heartily tired of discussing his condition,
> and his rights, and yet little else is talked about, and none
> talk about him so much as those who are most convinced of
> his insignificance.[3]

The next several numbers of the Nation put the fat in the
fire. Although in outward essentials Godkin obeyed the bidding of his stockholders and formally supported the Radical
cause, he could not resist criticizing Radical leaders like
Senator Sumner, Phillips, and Ben Butler, and he equivocated on black rights. The result was a declaration of war for
control of the Nation. Although Wendell Garrison acknowledged Godkin guilty of a breech of trust, he, Norton, and

McKim stood by him, while Stearns and Hallowell led a small band of stockholders in demanding that the editor honor the objective of Negro equality stated in the *Nation's* prospectus. To General Butler a Boston Radical complained: "A few of us some months ago met to start a paper especially for the freedmen. Others joined who doubted the policy of such a limited objective and the result was a merely literary and political paper. It is not therefore *our* paper. . . ."[4]

When it became clear that Stearns had no influence over editorial policy, Sumner advised him to stop the *Nation:* "It does more hurt than good. . . . An argument to show that Equality is not essential to the Republican idea is in the worst vein of copper-headism. How long? Oh! How long?"[5] (Years later, Godkin recalled to an acquaintance how the Radicals vilified him for being too soft on reconstruction, while the southern press berated him for being too harsh.)[6]

When Wendell Phillips raised his stentorian voice against the *Nation* before a Boston antislavery meeting, Godkin, with a posture of injured innocence, declared: "I expect no quarter hereafter from the Stearns and Wendell Phillips set. They are, I think, bent on my destruction. . . ."[7] He was right. Stearns was now sending stockholders printed circulars calling for the editor's dismissal, and privately he excoriated Godkin as an Irishman misrepresenting himself as an Englishman. With equal extravagance, Godkin shot back that Stearns was a professional liar and a "low-bred" man.[8]

It must have taken some soul-searching for McKim—who was up to his ears in his own troubles trying to control the Freedmen's Aid Union—and Wendell Garrison to come to Godkin's defense against opposition from the antislaveryites, but the gentle Quaker and his son-in-law saw no other course. "The *Nation* is not the organ of the Freedmen's movement," McKim rebuffed a Boston complainant. "It is established and is to be conducted in the interest of all virtue. Therefore we Freedmens men—who are also more than Freedmens men—favor and support it."[9]

In this fashion McKim and Garrison confessed their failure to found a weekly that would battle for equal rights for the blacks. After some vacillation by Forbes and Atkinson— whose objections to Godkin were aside from the question of black rights—the stockholders, with the exception of Hallo-well, joined McKim and Norton in supporting Godkin. Out-numbered, Stearns vainly tried to withdraw his investment in the Nation; then he gave up the effort and late in 1865 established another paper in Boston, the Right Way, to push for the rights of the freedmen.[10]

The radicals, in losing their fight to control the editorial policy of the Nation, had suffered a major defeat. But God-kin in victory had been discredited in some eyes, and bick-ering among stockholders continued. Atkinson was not yet reconciled to the editor's edict that the Nation would avoid the tariff issue; and in Baltimore Judge Bond sought to speak for antislavery stockholders when he demanded that the Nation take a more affirmative position on black rights. Then opposition developed from a new quarter, as Godkin reported to Norton in December, 1865:

> You remember young Dodge,—one of the Trustees—very rich, good, a rigid blue Presbyterian, wife ditto . . . very narrow in every way. Dodge was active and kind in helping to get the paper up, and I have never had a hint of dissatisfaction from him since, except with regard to a criticism on [Albert] Bierstadt. It appears, however, that he and his wife have been suffering awfully in secret. They had Olmsted to dinner yes-terday, and were very violent in their denunciations of the paper, she for its "vulgarity," and "slanginess"(!!) and he for its generally "sensational" tone. . . . Most of the abuse I have received hitherto has been for our "ridiculous dignity," and "heaviness," and didactic tone, so this has the merit of pro-ducing in my breast a very novel sensation. All of this of course proves more clearly than ever the necessity of getting out of reach of the Stockholders.[11]

The happy thought occurred to Godkin that Olmsted, who had just returned from California and was not involved in the Stearns dispute, might be a way out of the Nation's dilemma. In a final gesture toward stockholder harmony, he brought Olmsted into the Nation Association as associate editor.[12] This failing to heal the breech, Godkin offered to refund to the stockholders the unspent portion of the capi-tal, fired Richards, and liquidated the Nation Association. Financed by money that McKim and other stockholders con-sented to leave behind, he took principal control of the Nation in 1866 under the name of E. L. Godkin and Company.

Henceforward the *Nation*—the "weekly Day of Judgment" as Charles Dudley Warner dubbed it—would be what Godkin wanted it to be.[13]

That Godkin had carried off a coup with other people's money, few would deny. The measure of his future reputation would be how well he justified the trust that McKim, Olmsted, and other investors were now placing in him to produce a weekly of high standard. Demean Godkin's stature as one will, thought William Roscoe Thayer, "posterity will get at the truth of the chief public affairs in America between 1865 and 1881, in the *Nation* better than in any other contemporary source."[14] It was logical for cultured Victorians—Thayer graduated from Harvard in the same class as Godkin's son—to be drawn to Godkin's Olympian journal, for the *Nation* was read only by the "best men."

"May the Pudding leave their *Nations,* and neglect their recitations," facetiously intoned class poet George Pellew at an 1880 Harvard Hasty Pudding shindig, decreeing a moratorium on undergraduate enthusiasm. Andrew C. McLaughlin, though not as eminent an historian as Worthington C. Ford or Henry Adams—each of them stockholders in the company that owned the *Nation* after 1881—spoke for many historians when he declared that no one produced "abler discussions or keener analyses of problems presented by the political and social life of America" than Godkin. Small wonder that Harvard offered the editor a professorship in history and gave him an honorary degree and other honors.[15]

Self-congratulatory by nature—what lesser pretension would befit the prophet of the "New Jerusalem"?—Godkin seldom admitted that omniscience has its limits. But with commendable intuition he spared his readers his occasional spare-time versification, though a single bit of his unpublished doggerel conveys as succinctly as all his editorials what he meant to say to his generation:

> Rapine, avarice, expense
> This is idolatry; and these we adore;
> Plain living and high thinking are no more;
> The homely beauty of the good old cause
> Is gone.[16]

In the *Nation* Godkin set about to emulate the best features of the *Saturday Review* and the *Spectator.* In its literary criticism Godkin's paper came close to equalling the Tory *Saturday Review* during that weekly's palmy days, and the *Nation's* editorial leaders, though more cynical and less even-tempered, rivaled those of the *Spectator* of R. H. Hutton and Meredith Townsend. Matthew Arnold and James Bryce thought the *Nation* the best weekly in the United States and possibly in the world.[17] For this Godkin rightly is given credit, but without the volunteer help of Norton and the Spartan office labors of Garrison, the *Nation* would have failed at the outset.

Contrary to legend, Godkin did not write most of the *Nation,* although he sometimes contributed as many as four pages to a number. The lead political article was usually his, and with other contributors he wrote leader editorial paragraphs for "The Week." The literary side he left to John Dennett and Garrison. Dennett, a talented but unsentimental Nova Scotian with a compulsion to carp, excited as much reader animosity as Godkin. "They are very thin skinned people at *The Nation,*" Thomas Bailey Aldrich told E. C. Stedman, "and though they are fond of being saucy, they can't stand the least roughing themselves." "If six or seven of us younger fellows were to systematically rap Dennet [*sic*] across the knucks whenever we got the opportunity, it wouldn't make him courteous but it might teach him decency."[18]

When it seemed the *Nation* might perish for lack of readers, Godkin set about with indifferent success to lighten its fare. "The cultivated class we have with us," he noted to Norton, "but the class next below, do not quite know what to make of us, and are suspicious or hostile."[19]

The strongest unbroken influence on Godkin's weekly from the start was English political economy. Some thoughtful men, who in their youth had embraced Ricardo and James Mill, were now disillusioned by the worker misery that attended Mill's Economic Man in action. Not so Godkin, who without ceremony wedded the *Nation* to the tenets of Manchester economics. The *Nation* announced in its prospectus that it would have as one of its objectives the gathering of information "as to the condition and prospects of the Southern

States, the openings they offer to capital, and the supply and kind of labor which can be obtained in them."[20]

In his hard-hitting political and social articles, Godkin directed his fire impartially at anyone who violated the "laws of trade" as well as his elevated notions of culture. He deplored Irish-American politicians, labor reformers, the "Western type of man," evangelical clergymen, the growing "servant problem," the eight-hour day, the failure of Americans to dress for dinner, "sentiment," untutored immigrants, universal manhood suffrage, popular journalists, noisy patriots, reactionaries, and reformers of all hue.

A subscriber to the devil theory of politics, Godkin was much criticized for his resort to personalities. "My dear Sir," he retorted to an acquaintance, "rascals in all ages have objected to personalities!"[21] When the City Club announced its finding that New York's municipal corruption was traceable not to individuals but to a "system," he shot back: "This city is badly governed owing to the bad conduct of certain men, and owing to nothing else under heaven."[22] As someone rightly observed, it was not sin that Godkin attacked but sinners.

A more intimate reason for disliking Godkin was his manner. His uncivility sent more than one caller away from his office an enemy for life. Yet underneath Godkin's brusque exterior lay a hearty appreciation of the ridiculous in man's affairs. Although not a learned man, when he was at his best, none could match the force and humor, as well as the common sense, of his editorials.[23] This earned the *Nation* an admiration among nineteenth-century scholars unrivalled by any other paper in the United States. "The *Nation* . . . was my first love," testified Worthington C. Ford, "and it has served as a weekly inspiration and counsellor for more than thirty years, and the longer I live the more do I hold to the political ideals it has maintained." In like vein, brother historian Frederick Bancroft wrote: "In twenty-five years, I doubt if I have failed to read three numbers of the *Nation*. . . ."[24] Woodrow Wilson kept detailed notes from Godkin's editorials in his notebooks while a graduate student at Princeton, and in Emporia, Kansas, young William Allen White learned from one of his professors that Godkin's weekly was a model of literary and political excellence.[25]

Besides Bancroft, Ford, and Wilson, a distinguished array of later nineteenth-century American historians either wrote for the *Nation* or were disciples of its proprietor, such as Henry Adams—who later soured on Godkin—James Ford Rhodes, Francis Parkman, Moses Coit Tyler, James Schouler, John Fiske, Andrew C. McLaughlin, and that "Godkinite hangover" of the twentieth century, Ellis Oberholtzer. Parkman, Rhodes, and Schouler contributed to fund-raising drives by the *Nation*.[26]

In the British Isles William Lecky and James Bryce were *Nation aficionados*. Lecky's observations on American matters were "ludicrous," the Godkinophobic Theodore Roosevelt told John Morley, "partly because they were largely derived from Godkin and the *Nation*."[27] Bryce's great *American Commonwealth* is, in some of its passages, pure *Nation*. But Bryce purposely omitted Godkin from the acknowledgments in his first edition because, as he somewhat guiltily explained, he feared for the book's acceptance. He would have liked to dedicate the book to Godkin, he told him, but, "if I had said what I owed to you in the Preface, you being the head and front of the Mugwumps and Reformers, those who are attacked in the book . . . would at once have said, 'this is an utterance of the Mugwumps; the Mugwumps have put up an Englishman to say this and that'. . . ."[28]

Of Godkin's American disciples none was more slavish than historian Ellis P. Oberholtzer. To him the editor represented perfection, "such personal courage, such learning, combined with such talent for expression." One could hardly "appraise too highly the services of this able and fearless monitor of the American republic." Enthusiastically Oberholtzer endorsed the well-known condolence of William James to Godkin's widow that her husband "was certainly the towering influence in all thought concerning public affairs," and in his *History of the United States Since the Civil War* Oberholtzer used, and misused, the *Nation* more than three hundred times.[29]

Scarcely a less ardent Godkinite was historian James Ford Rhodes, who began reading the *Nation* after the war while a student at the University of Chicago; "of which since that time I have hardly missed a number." Rhodes congratulated Charles Francis Adams, Jr., on their agreement in historical questions. "Like you, I have been profoundly influenced by the Nation."[30] In an appreciation of Godkin six years after the publicist's death, Rhodes testified that the Nation (1) converted him to tariff reform and civil service reform; (2) gave him his "correct" views on the currency question; (3) helped shape his attitudes toward international copyright, the problems of municipal government, and "negro-carpetbag rule in the South."[31] When Theodore Roosevelt read Volume VI of Rhodes' History of the United States from the Compromise of 1850, he lectured the historian at the White House about his jaundiced view of Reconstruction, stridently giving Rhodes his opinion of Godkin's unreliability.[32]

From Rhodes' history—Volumes VI and VII of which cite the Nation almost exclusively—is but a short step to William A. Dunning's controversial volume on Reconstruction in the American Nation Series, which bears a prefatory acknowledgment of Dunning's debt to Rhodes, and, subsequently, to Claude G. Bowers's lurid The Tragic Era and Paul H. Buck's jaundiced The Road to Reunion, 1865-1900, each of which appreciatively cites the Nation.

To the historian tackling the yellowing pages of the Godkin Nation today, that weekly's extravagances loom as legion. Why, then, did mugwump historians attach such weight to it? The answer is that many of the Nation's extravagances arose from prejudices sacred to the intelligentsia of Godkin's day, prejudices that, served up in the editor's witty and incisive editorial style, could not fail to gain endorsement. And if the Nation was often inaccurate, it was more perceptive than many contemporary journals. One reason why professors followed Godkin is suggested by this trenchant 1883 editorial in which he scolded business men for operating colleges on the theory that "anyone can teach":

> The general result of this state of mind on the part of college trustees is that, in founding or endowing a university, their main interest is given to buildings and material equipment. The professors are treated as subordinate accessories, on which economy can most readily be practiced. When a pinch comes, for instance, the reduction of their salaries is apt to be the first way of saving that is thought of. How far astray

trustees are in all this must be inferred from the fact—which
we hold to be indisputable—that a university consists of the
professors, that all other things are but accessories, and that
you might have a great and successful university, in which
the thirst for knowledge would be very eager, and the stim-
ulus applied to those seeking it very powerful, in a barn or a
large tent.[33]

One way of perceiving Godkin is as a reformer crusading
against major flaws in American democracy; another is to
see him, as did historians Charles and Mary Beard, as a
Brahmin "mainly pleading for good manners."[34] Neither description adequately characterizes the Nation between 1865
and 1900, but the latter contains an important kernel of the
truth. Godkin, as his private letters reveal, was a veritable
snob who cavilled to a fault about "the democratic plan of
doing everything" in the United States.[35]

No one who knew Godkin doubted that the Nation was a
faithful mirror of his prejudices. Progressives disliked him
because instinctively he was a conservative; reactionaries
rejected him "for such liberalism as he showed." Inacces-
sible to subordinates, abrupt toward persons seeking his
counsel, he could nonetheless be charming with women and
witty and engaging in the company of those whom he considered his social equals. The young William Dean Howells
saw him as a congenial employer, mainly because Godkin
found in the Howells of 1866 the social graces he admired,
but Lincoln Steffens and George Edward Woodberry found
him unpleasant to work for.[36] Sensitive persons he easily
wounded, no doubt because he disliked people. "I am not
sympathetic," he admitted to Olmsted in 1864, "and I am too
old to change now."[37]

Godkin intended for the Nation to wear the look of sober,
cultivated reason; but like all editors with large egos, he did
not shrink from giving the weekly strident voice to his prejudices. His disdain for New Yorkers and his liking for Bos-
tonians was his chief excuse for wanting to be a Harvard
professor and the reason why someone found the Nation the
"best New York paper edited in New England." Boston,
Godkin believed, was "the one place in America where
wealth and the knowledge of how to use it were apt to
coincide."[38] Interestingly, this point of view was not wholly

shared by his Boston friend William James, who told his brother Henry, "Give me a human race with some guts in them, no matter if they do belch at you now and then."[39]

The pages of the early *Nation* reveal a somewhat ambivalent attitude toward the democratic process. But stripped of their liberal rhetoric, the *Nation's* reflections about democracy suggest only the traditional mistrust of the conservative for popular government. This mistrust mounted as the genteel tradition declined.[40] Readers during the late 1860s learned that American civilization was trembling in the balance because the country had not solved the Servant Problem.[41] Once Godkin reached the conclusion that good valets were vanishing, there was no place for him to turn but to pessimism. "The time is not far distant," the *Nation* gloomily prophesied in 1865, "when all things will be in common and grass grow in Broadway."[42]

It was not Godkin's intention to extend democracy but to "purify" it. As the *Nation* put it in 1869:

> Democracy, in so far as it means equality, may be said to have at last conquered the world. Privileges and privileged classes are gone; society is hereafter to exist for the benefit of the many, and not of the few. But it sometimes looks as if in warring against them a spirit of disbelief in the value of things old, and of belief in the capacity of each generation to work out for itself all problems that may be presented to it, of whatever nature, had been developed, which if not resisted now at the outset, would assuredly carry us into some strange regions.[43]

"That Godkin, by intellectual descent hardly a conservative at all, should have been the most respectable opponent of innovation in the Gilded Age," suggests Russell Kirk, "is evidence sufficient of the dismal fatigue that American conservatism suffered during those hard years."[44] Godkin's mistrust of democracy was linked to his utilitarianism. To him popular government was an experiment whose usefulness hinged on whether or not it provided a favorable climate for the growth of virtue and culture. And almost everywhere Godkin looked after 1865 he saw virtue and culture crumbling. "This experiment in democratic government," he assured Joseph B. Bishop toward the end of his career, "is practically sure to fail. The trouble is I'm afraid I shan't be here to see it fail."[45]

True, Godkin was not consistent. The British belief that "a minority is more apt to be right," he averred to Norton, is foolish; "an ass in a minority remains still an ass."[46] But elsewhere in his writings one encounters well-reasoned defenses of hereditary monarchy. Ignoring his inconsistencies, one may generalize that Godkin found popular government attractive only in theory. Not only did he wobble on Negro suffrage—holding that blacks are intellectually and morally inferior to whites—he opposed woman suffrage on the argument that it would permit servant girls to outvote their mistresses.[47] He called for a halt to immigration of peoples from southern and eastern Europe, and he demanded literacy and intelligence tests—and in the case of blacks a moral test as well—for voting. He urged naturalization laws that would bar immigrants from the ballot, and he proposed that the wealthy receive extra votes. He never lent his support to the direct election of the United States senators.

From the start contributions to the Nation were unsigned, and the weekly's views became so identified with its editor that readers fell into the habit of saying "Godkin says" rather than "the Nation says."[48] Typical was the flattery that Lowell directed to the editor: "Every Friday morning, when the Nation comes, I fill my pipe and read it from beginning to end. Do you do it all yourself? Or are there really so many clever men in the country?"[49] To contributor Moses Coit Tyler, Godkin explained his policy of anonymity: "Lest you should think that our failure to annex your name to your articles, is due to any desire to rob an able man of his due credit and appropriate it to ourselves, let me say [that this is the only way] a periodical can be kept up to a really high standard." He continued:

> The publication of names, of writers, by shifting the responsibility as to quality from the editor's shoulders makes him careless as to quality, and in part converts his paper into a dumping ground in which "celebrities" shuck their rubbish. Moreover, it makes writers careless, too, because "names," have acquired such a potency, that in the existing state of culture in America, a good many men, are enabled under cover of them to palm off trash on the reader—Witness [Edward] Everett's balderdash in the New York Ledger. Then also, if

you publish one man's name, you have to publish all, and
publishing all, any week you are not able to get some distinguished body to "scratch off" something for you, people
think the number a poor one.[50]

Of the early contributors to the Nation, the name of Norton
properly graces the head of the list. This weekly became his
vehicle for lamentations about American tastes and manners,
while in the North American Review paradoxically he kept
alive his optimism about democracy. A biographer bares
his torment: "America had no hereditary lower class—
and no distinguished higher class; snobbery was absent
in America—and so were 'good manners'; in America every
man had 'a chance' to become wealthy—and after obtaining
wealth, to squander it in tasteless, barbaric extravagance."[51]

An equally prolific early Nation contributor was the acerbic Dennett.[52] Called by W.C. Brownell "the most remarkable talent New York journalism has ever had," Dennett
was a staff member for nearly seven years and Godkin's
second-in-command during part of that time. It was in the
Nation that Dennett introduced to the literary world the
expression "Knickerbocker Literature."[53] Arthur Sedgwick
pointed out that Dennett wrote "enormous quantities" of the
Nation, including political editorials and paragraphs in "The
Week" that many supposed were the work of Godkin. In addition Dennett did book reviews which, though punctuated
with ridicule and sarcasm, were of "remarkable originality."[54]
Sedgwick's own productivity hardly suffers by comparison.
Recruited for the Nation by his brother-in-law, Norton, and
becoming a staff member in 1872, Sedgwick wrote hundreds
of political editorials, social and legal articles, literary notices and book reviews, besides contributing regularly to
"The Week."[55]

Lodging in New York in 1865 with a relative at 441 West
47th Street was young William Dean Howells, recently returned from his Italian stay, during which he wrote a number
of Venetian sketches for the Nation. In December Howells
happily wrote his wife: "Today Mr. Godkin engaged me to
write for the Nation at a salary of $40 a week. This leaves me
free to write for all other papers except the Round Table;
and does not include articles on Italian subjects, and poems,

which will be paid for extra. . . ."[56] For a few months Godkin
and Howells occupied adjacent desks in the *Nation* office,
Godkin coming to have a deep affection for the younger man
because "he is by far the best man I have met for my purpose
—social experience seems so rare."[57] When an editorial position became vacant the next year on the *Atlantic Monthly,*
Howells departed from the *Nation* with Godkin's blessing.

The work horse of the *Nation* from the beginning was
Wendell Garrison. It was a fortunate nepotism that had
brought him, at the insistence of father-in-law McKim, to the
weekly. After Dennett's untimely death in 1872 of tubercu-
losis, Garrison for the next twenty-five years functioned,
against the opposition of the Garrison family, as Godkin's
loyal right arm and alter ego.[58]"If anything goes wrong with
you," Godkin informed him during one editorial crisis, "I will
retire into a monastery." The volatile editor was frequently
subjected to libel suits and arrest for slander; Garrison, with
his pedantic attention to detail, was the dike keeper who
sometimes prevented the "mighty flood" of Godkin's invective from overflowing its banks.[59]

First as subeditor, then as Richard's successor as publisher, and finally as managing editor, Garrison ran the
Nation office during Godkin's frequent absences and gave
painstaking direction to its battery of contributors. Somewhat defensively to his mother he described his role in
editorial policy: "I don't write any of the editorials in the
Nation. I contribute something to the *Week* generally, and
regularly write the greater part of the *Literary Notes;* more
rarely book reviews nowadays, for which I have not the
time."[60] Garrison's life, as James M. McPherson points out,
"was the *Nation* and the *Nation* was his life." He ruined his
health in its service, "often arising before dawn to read
proof; he took few vacations, and found time to relax only on
his occasional walking tours of the New Jersey countryside
or his salt baths at the Battery in Manhattan."

> He was an ideal editorial assistant, but he would have been
> a failure as editor-in-chief. He had few original ideas, and
> seemed to reflect the ideas and style of the stronger minds
> and personalities with whom he was associated. . . . After
> 1865 he came under the sway of Godkin, and was to a con-
> siderable extent molded into the genteel, elitest mugwump

> image for which Godkin was famous. . . . Like Godkin, he was
> indifferent to or ignorant of the poverty of the masses who
> crowded into urban slums, and largely hostile to the cause
> of organized labor. . . . He was thin-skinned about criticism,
> quick to bring the artillery of his pedantic knowledge to bear
> in a counter-attack on critics.[61]

The roster of occasional contributors to the *Nation* was
an impressive one. Young Henry James wrote often for the
weekly, as did his brother William. The presumed influence
of Godkin on the development of Henry James as a writer
has been noted by others.[62] Another frequent contributor
was Charles Sanders Peirce, the pragmatist forerunner of
William James and John Dewey. Peirce's wife's un-Victorian
tastes ran to writing passionate love letters to the uncon-
ventional English author George Eliot, but her husband's
interest lay in formulating theories of the logic of relatives.
For twenty years Peirce's facile mind ranged over a variety
of scientific and philosophical questions in the *Nation*. When
Godkin, who was fearful of novelties, overcame his suspicion
of evolution, Asa Gray and others used the columns of the
Nation to praise the evolutionary theories of Darwin, Wallace, and Spencer.[63]

Godkin's mistrust of the new, shared by Dennett and Garrison, extended to innovation in literature—such as that
espoused in New York's literary Bohemia of the sixties—
and the *Nation's* literary reviews reflected the strait-laced
canons of the ruling New England genteel set. Walt Whit-
man, Bret Harte, Thomas Bailey Aldrich, Mark Twain, and
Sidney Lanier never wrote for the *Nation*. To Gibson Peacock
Lanier proposed that Peacock do a satirical reproduction in
the Philadelphia *Evening Bulletin* of "one of those tranquilly
stupid political editorials in the *Nation* which seem as mas-
sive as the walls of Troy and are really nothing but conden-
sations of arrogant breath."[64] A friend of E. C. Stedman and
other denizens of New York's literary Bohemia, Aldrich
hoped "to live to see the day when not a single American
publisher will send either book or advertisement to those
Nation blackguards." Aldrich ached, he told James R. Osgood, to wage a "war of extermination on Misther Godkin
and his little tribe of Celts and English-plated Americans."[65]

The poetry critic of the *Nation* for many years was Thomas

Wentworth Higginson, who bought stock in the weekly even though he disagreed with some of Godkin's conservative social views. When Garrison directed Higginson to review his own (Higginson's) poetry, the modest poet responded by giving it only passing mention, whereupon Garrison assigned the task of poetry critic to George Edward Woodberry, who had held a staff job on the *Nation* until an altercation with Godkin ended his services.[66] Godkin lacked feeling for poetry, and after printing a few verses by Lowell, Helen Hunt Jackson, and Stedman, he virtually eliminated it from the *Nation*. "I think the *Nation* would pay $10 or $12 for three verses," Howells in 1866 advised Aldrich, "as much for good as for bad ones; but Godkin regards 'fresh poetry as a luxury'."[67]

The task of reviewing novels was assigned to Boston Brahmin Thomas Sergeant Perry, until an altercation with Godkin ended his services. Rasmus B. Anderson was the *Nation's* authority on philology. Brander Matthews was an occasional literary contributor, and Charles C. Nott, Michael Heilprin, and Professors Thomas R. Lounsbury and W. D. Whitney of Yale wrote often on a variety of topics.[68]

In its foreign correspondence the *Nation* was without a rival among American weeklies. James Bryce wrote on English politics, while August Laugel for forty years served as Paris correspondent, and Jesse White Mario served for an equal period as Italian correspondent. International law received occasional attention from John Pomeroy.

Men of affairs were well represented in the *Nation*. Until his 1884 falling-out with Godkin, Henry Cabot Lodge wrote infrequently on domestic affairs, and from abroad Goldwin Smith, Herman E. von Holst, Albert Dicey, and Friedrich Kapp wrote on international affairs. When Henry Adams, who made the acquaintance of Godkin in New York in 1868 on his way to Washington, D. C., ceased supplying the *Nation* with letters from the capital, Senator Carl Schurz consented to serve without pay as the weekly's secret Washington correspondent. Charles Francis Adams, Jr., contributed articles on the railroads, and David A. Wells, former special commissioner of the revenue, wrote on the internal revenue and the powers of the secretary of the treasury.

J. C. Ropes and Jacob Dolson Cox, after Grant forced him to
resign from his cabinet, were the *Nation*'s authorities on
military matters.[69]

Godkin's writers regarded the *Nation* as a paper "written
by gentlemen for gentlemen." A major complaint that gentlemen had against the press of 1865 was its clamorous partisanship. Editors, thought James Russell Lowell, were either
"beggars on horseback" or *parvenus*. The politically independent journal did not exist, a situation that Godkin intended
to correct. In 1869, eulogizing Henry J. Raymond's services to
journalism, he offered his opinion of the contemporary press.
Under Raymond the New York *Times* "encouraged truthful-
ness—the reproduction of facts uncolored by the necessities
of 'a cause' or by the editor's personal feelings. . . ." In so
doing, the *Times* helped to abate the "greatest nuisance of
the age, the coarseness, violence, calumny, which does so
much to drive sensible and high-minded and competent men
out of public life or keep them from entering it."[70]

Godkin scoffed at the idea that young men aspiring to a
career in journalism ought to have special training in the
mechanics of the Fourth Estate; all they needed was a good
university grounding in such areas as history, "legislative
science," and political economy; in brief, the fields "which
every man pretending to be educated ought to cultivate."[71]

But to assert that Godkin was an independent editor is not
the same, of course, as saying that he was an unbiased
editor, which he precisely was not. By 1866 he had veered
the *Nation* so far from the reformist objectives envisioned for
it by some of its sponsors that he jocularly remarked that he
was "afraid to visit Boston this winter, lest the stockholders
of the *Nation* should lynch me."[72] To Norton he explained
his impatience with radical reformers: "I have come to the
conclusion that the narrowest of all human beings are your
'progressive radicals.' They 'progress' as I have seen many
mules progress, by a succession of kicks and squeals which
make travelling on the same road with them perilous and
disagreeable work."[73]

A characteristic example of Godkin's emerging conservatism was his growing hard line against black rights. In 1868
Anna Dickinson angrily lectured the *Nation* for its attitude

toward the freedmen:

> A certain paper which shall be nameless here, which the
> Tribune designates as an obscure literary weekly, but which
> accounts itself a power in the land . . . begs us to hold our
> peace on this vexed question of negro equality until certain
> wise and learned men shall determine precisely the status of
> the negro . . . whether he is a cross between an ape and a
> man or not! . . . What is the negro to do while these savants
> are settling their dispute? Is nothing to be done to elevate
> him in the scale of the races at least, and is he to be left
> without protection?[74]

For a time, Godkin—in line with the Radical objectives of
the Nation's founders—permitted the weekly to advocate
severe treatment of the defeated South; then he changed
course and asserted his intention of steering a middle path
between President Johnson's Reconstruction policy and that
of the Radicals in Congress. But as was characteristic of the
temperamental editor, at no time was the editorial position
of the Nation well defined. One example of this was the
Johnson impeachment proceeding. At first Godkin opposed
impeachment; then he became scarcely less vehement than
the Radical New York Tribune in demanding the president's
ouster. But when the acquittal came, he pronounced it a
vindication of the law, significant at a time when "we are
adding to our voting population a vast body of persons on
whom the great laws of morality sit only lightly. . . ."[75]

As the seventies opened, Godkin broke wholly with the
Radicals and began to assail carpetbaggers and to call for
the restoration of civil government in the south.[76] "Many
persons who have been Radicals all their lives are in doubt
whether to be Radical any longer," he told the Nation's
readers in 1871.[77] In an 1874 editorial he found the average
intelligence of blacks "so low that they are slightly above
the level of animals."[78] With Richard Watson Gilder in The
Century, Godkin looked upon the return of the southern conservatives to power in 1877 with satisfaction. As he told a
now receptive Norton, "I do not see . . . how the negro is
ever to be worked into a system of government for which you
and I would have much respect."[79]

Godkin was convinced that southern whites realized that
slavery had been an economic curse to their section, and in

the *Nation* he ridiculed northern fears that southern whites were conspiring in 1877 to reenslave the blacks:

> Their minds are really occupied with making money . . . and their designs on the negro are confined to getting him to work for low wages. His wages are low—forty cents a day and rations, which cost ten cents—but he is content with it. . . . On one [Virginia plantation] there were, before the war, about one hundred and fifty slaves of all ages. The owner, at emancipation, put them in wagons and deposited them in Ohio. His successor now works the plantation with twelve hired men. . . . He laughs when you ask him if he regrets slavery. Nothing would induce him to take care of one hundred fifty men, women, and children, furnishing perhaps thirty able bodied men, littering the house with a swarm of lazy servants, and making heavy drafts on the meat-house and corn-crib, and running up doctor's bills.[80]

Godkin, "in shifting his concern from the manners of Jay Gould to the 'universal suffrage which gives an air of menace to many of the things civilized men hold most dear,'" asserts Gabriel Kolko, was representative of the movement that began in 1877 to articulate "major American anti-democratic ideologies relevant to an industrial society." In like vein, Allan P. Grimes finds Godkin to be one of the leading anticipators of such twentieth century anti-democratic theorists as Paul Elmer More, Irving Babbitt, and Ralph Adams Cram.[81]

Godkin on his return from the Crimea. The sword was given to him by a group of Hungarians as a testimonial to his History of Hungary. From a daguerreotype made in 1855 or 1856.

Godkin at age 39

Frederick L. Olmsted in 1893

Wendell P. Garrison in 1891

Charles Eliot Norton

Horace White

Henry Villard

Carl Schurz c. 1880

Godkin in an 1898 Cory cartoon

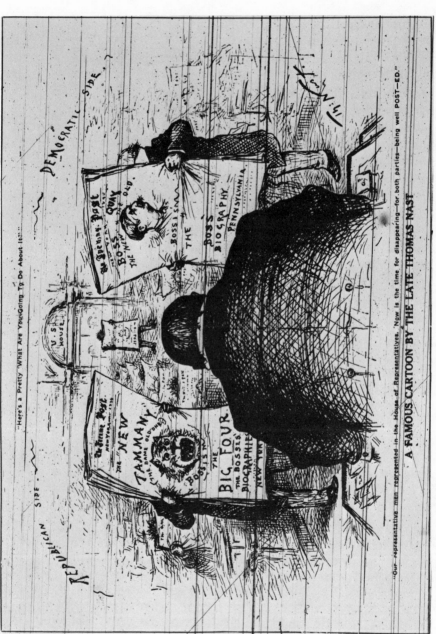

Nast cartoon depicting the Evening Post and its attack on bossism in both parties

Silver loving cup presented to Godkin in 1894 by a gathering of New York civic women

Henry and William James c. 1900

Chapter Seven
"Annexation Fever" and Immigration Folly

> *Every interest of our society calls for*
> *more condensation of our people and*
> *less expansion of our territory.*

The world was rapidly drawing together in the last half of the nineteenth century. Few American editors grasped this as readily as Godkin, and the foreign coverage of the *Nation* from the start rivalled that of any American paper. But just as with his competitors, Godkin's information was often unreliable; moreover because of the slowness of news in arriving from Europe, the *Nation* found itself resorting to speculation. Small wonder that the attempt to lay an Atlantic cable in the summer of 1865 found Godkin an interested, though not always approving, onlooker.[1] One advantage he saw in the cable was the opportunity it gave for commercial growth, but he was fearful of other forms of expansionism —especially territorial expansion.

Godkin in 1865 had reason for his fears that the United States was embarking on renewed territorial expansion, for not all of the energies of the American people between 1861 and 1865 were harnessed to the prosecution of the Civil War. The westward expansion had continued throughout the conflict; certain events of the war had rekindled interest in the annexation of Canada; and there was an undeniable expansionist undercurrent in the American hostility to the French intervention in Mexico.[2] With Appomattox the stage was set for a full-dress revival of manifest destiny.

In 1867 Secretary of State William H. Seward seized an opportunity to buy Alaska from Russia for $7,200,000. Although the purchase met with a degree of popular favor, the *Nation* editorially lampooned Seward's "chimerical project of saddling us with a frozen desert of a colony." Godkin, sharing a popular misconception about the temperate climate of

Iceland, sarcastically likened Alaska to that Danish possession. For some months the Nation continued periodically
to criticize Alaska and the "mania for buying territory,"
although by 1874 Godkin had decided the Alaska purchase
"is very likely to prove a piece of good luck for us, and
perhaps in after years will redound to the credit of Mr.
Seward's statesmanship."[3]

Godkin's arguments against what he called "the annexation fever" were economic, racial, and cultural. His economic objection was that of political economy; colonialism,
the Manchesterites taught him, was inconsonant with political economy because it was incompatible with free trade.
Racially, he opposed bringing "inferior" peoples under American jurisdiction. Culturally, he objected to expansionism on
the grounds—mirrored in his dislike of western Americans—
that civilized society flourishes in compactly settled areas.
He began early to warn Americans against adding a "vast
extent of wilderness to our already enormous area." As the
Nation put it in 1866:

> Our government and society are now suffering greatly from
> the too rapid and too wide diffusion of our population. Civili-
> zation, religion, education, and manners are all injured by the
> inordinate increase of "frontier life" amongst us. Every inter-
> est of our society calls for more condensation of our people
> and less expansion of our territory.[4]

An exception was Canada; like the English Liberals Richard Cobden, John Bright, and Goldwin Smith, Godkin had
no racial objection to American annexation.[5] Indeed most
"informed" men, he asserted in 1865, favored Canadian-
American union so long as it was achieved "on its own
merits" instead of as the price of a settlement of the American claims in the Alabama controversy.[6] That Canada was
meant to be such a pawn in a British-American settlement
was apparent throughout 1869 in speeches of Senators
Chandler and Trumbull, Chairman Sumner of the Senate
Foreign Relations Committee, Chairman Banks of the House
Committee on Foreign Affairs, the prominent lobbyist Robert
F. Walker, and frequent editorials in Harper's Weekly, the
New York Tribune, the New York Herald, and the New York
Times. Contemplating the rhetorical outpouring below the

border, the tory Montreal *Gazette* exclaimed: "It seemed to be taken for granted that the people of the dominion could be bartered like so many sheep, if Great Britain and the United States would agree to it."[7] In the *Nation* Godkin noted that the United States, in substance, was saying to Great Britain about her recent posture of assistance to the Confederacy:

> Your conduct has been villainous and depraved beyond description . . . and therefore we shall not allow you even to attempt to pay damages. We should give you a good thrashing if we were not otherwise occupied just now, but our intention is to give you one at some future day, when we find you in a fix. However, if you make us a present of Canada—which we shall take from you by force if you don't—we shall look upon it as full satisfaction for all the wrongs we have suffered at your hands. . . .[8]

The achievement of Canadian confederation in 1871 dashed American hopes of annexation, but not before a scare had been thrown into the British empire by the activities between 1866 and 1870 of the Fenian Brotherhood. In 1866 this militant Irish independence organization claimed support from 750,000 American voters, a sympathetic faction in Congress, and the blessing of several New York newspapers.[9]

In May an ex-Union general led several hundred green-shirted American Fenians in an abortive attempt to invade Canada that only prompt action by President Johnson saved from becoming an international incident. Four years later occurred another attempted invasion that, like its predecessors, was a fiasco. After two comic-opera-like encounters with the enemy that alienated the normally sympathetic *World* and the *Tribune,* the Fenian commander was ignominiously taken into custody by a United States marshal. The disillusioned New York press took turns belatedly denouncing the authors of the project, while Godkin gloated over the presses' discomfiture. He especially chided the *World,* which had dwelt on the absurdity of the Fenian commander's entrenching his green-shirted force ten minutes after it crossed the Canadian border:

> [The Fenian Commander] we are quite sure, knew just as well as the *World* the objections to allowing [his] invading army to squat down and throw up clay ten minutes after entering

the enemy's country. But then, if he were to speak his whole
mind, he would tell the World that it must not look at him as
the head of an army intent on reaching Montreal, but as the
head of a mob, which had got into a very bad scrape, and
which the soldiers were coming to disperse.[10]

A scanning of the Nation during the late 1860s shows that
the Irish question rivalled redemption of the currency, the
blacks, and the politics of Reconstruction as a topic of discussion. But Godkin did not take Fenianism, or Irish independence, seriously. He echoed official British allegations,
charging that Fenianism was a swindle perpetrated by a
"gang of impudent and impecunious" impostors to raise
money for their personal use. No intelligent American, he
declared in 1866, paid any attention to Irish revolutionary
leaders or "would give five cents for their opinion on any
other subject under heaven."[11] "Ireland as a nation is as
dead as Naples or Hanover"; Irish independence was a "wild
dream" which could "never be realized for even a month
except by the overthrow of the British Empire."[12]

In Godkin's view, Ireland should renounce the independence notions of its local "rum-soaked criminal adventurers"
and its overseas "blatherskites" planning the conquest of
Canada "safely behind dry goods counters in the Bowery"
and seek home rule through the "cordial cooperation" of
English gentlemen. No unaided Irish efforts would succeed,
predicted Godkin, and if the Fenians found a European ally
foolhardy enough to invade the British Isles, the help the
Fenians would give them "would be of a kind that would in
three weeks either drive a French general mad or cause him
to try his Chassepot rifles upon them."[13]

American Fenianism proved to be only a transient expression of the revival of manifest destiny. But elsewhere as the
1860s closed Godkin found the virus of expansionism very
much alive. Westward in the Pacific was the proposed reciprocity treaty with Hawaii, "a noble-looking thing on paper,"
he commented in 1869, gotten up by a handful of self-serving
American planters. Northward was Seward's as yet unfor-
given purchase of Alaska, consummated by Russian bribery.
"Who was not paid, that ever opened his mouth on the
subject?" Southward was the "ludicrous" proposal to send
a United States battleship to "protect" Santo Domingo.[14]

(Unknown to Godkin, there was already afoot an administration plan to annex Santo Domingo.)

What lay behind this expanionist spirit? It was part of a
scheme by "politicians," "speculators," and the "criminal
element," replied Godkin, to mushroom the functions of the
federal government in order to create more spoils. There
was "hardly a scheme before Congress, however innocent
in appearance, which involves the outlay of money by the
Government, at the bottom of which a speculator is not lying
hid."[15] Voters, seduced by postwar prosperity, abetted the
plunder by standing indifferent to public corruption, looking
the other way while judges sold justice, thieves went un-
whipped, and a "fourth of the public revenues is stolen by
knaves and adventurers." Territorial expansion would only
"stimulate the rapacity and increase the power" of these
elements.[16] Godkin warned his readers:

> Now, all attempts to increase [the Federal bureaucracy] or, in
> other words, to increase the number of duties the Government
> has to discharge, all attempts to annex or "protect" or pur-
> chase territory, or to send out propagandist missions for the
> spread of "seminal ideas," or to spread American influence in
> any way, except through the force of American example, the
> public may set down unhesitatingly as attempts on the part of
> a "ring" to make money.[17]

Another way in which Americans meddled in the affairs of
other nations, noted Godkin in 1870, was by forming cheer-
ing sections for conflicts "in which the United States has no
immediate material interest."[18] In the Nation he deplored the
extent to which the voters were influenced by "sentiment,"
"sympathy," and "enthusiasm" for other people's causes.
The public "went nearly crazy over the Hungarians, and,
indeed, over one [Kossuth] party of the Hungarians which
Hungary has since rejected." Similarly, south of the Rio
Grande "the patriots who Maximilian kept from establishing
'truth and justice, religion and piety' in Mexico have been
fêted and caressed" in the United States; and across the
ocean the "bands of Greek robbers and politicians" who "got
up" the Cretan insurrection received "frantic" American
acclaim. The "latest object" of United States "sympathy,"
complained Godkin, was bleeding, dissension-torn Cuba.[19]

But Godkin saw the Franco-Prussian War of 1870 in a

different light, his admiration for the Prussians contrasting sharply with his contempt for his Irish compatriots. The backwardness of Ireland, he explained in the *Nation*, stemmed from its not having "moved on in the general stream of European progress," whereas the glory of Prussia was that there was "no state more 'modern' in the best sense of the word."[20] The Prussian army was "fighting for a free press, a free parliament, popular education," for "the supremacy of reason over brute force, of the citizen over the soldier, of law over imperial 'decrees,' of an armed people over hired armies, of industry over gambling." In brief, argued Godkin, the Prussians were defending "modern civilization against the worst and latest of its enemies."[21]

When the New York *World* contended that Prussia, with its despotic and feudal government, hardly merited favoritism, the *Nation* shot back that the ends legitimatize the means:

> The arrogance of the Prussians there is no denying, and the foreign policy of Bismarck has certainly been thoroughly unscrupulous; but then his unscrupulousness has been displayed in the execution of schemes to which [we] must wish success. . . . Frederick William and his minister will pass away. The work of their hands will last, and the Prussia they have aggrandized must certainly long remain that community of the old world to which those who are interested in the improvement of human character through political action will look with most hope.[22]

In September one of Godkin's editorials praising Prussia was translated and republished in several German newspapers, the king of Prussia pronouncing it "the best article he had read during the war on the war and on the merits of Prussia."[23] Yet no cause was so sacrosanct in the editor's eyes that it should be allowed to challenge the "laws of trade." When the Prussians emitted cries of distress over the traffic in war materials between Britain and France, he addressed to them this curt reminder: "If any country . . . does not choose to keep a navy, or is unable to keep one, we are not obliged to make it up to her, whenever she goes to war and gets her ports blockaded, by selling nothing to her adversary which is likely to help prolong the contest."[24]

While Godkin was giving rein to prophecies about the Irish and German political futures, there was growing an

American expansionist interest in the Caribbean area. The Spanish-held island of Cuba, vibrating with unrest, was one object of American interest. But it would be another generation before public opinion would support a war to drive Spain from her last major outpost in the Caribbean. In the meantime there were lesser prey. One of Seward's expansionist projects to which Ulysses S. Grant fell a willing heir as president was the Santo Domingo annexation scheme. The little island republic, with its spacious and strategically located Samaná Bay, had for twenty years been an object of interest among the United States military men and expansionists generally.[25] In July 1869 Grant, his interest whetted by reports of the willingness of the Dominican dictator to hand over for a price his revolution-torn country, sent one of his aides, General Orville E. Babcock, to the island. A treaty of annexation followed.

Grant's inept handling of the project, joined to public antipathy toward expansionism into Latin, Catholic countries of the south, deprived the treaty of much press support and antagonized a vocal segment of the president's own party. In New York *Harper's Weekly* added its voice to the *Nation's* in opposing annexation, while the *Tribune,* the *Times,* and the *World* stressed the dubious character and advantages of such an acquisition. Only the *Sun* and the *Herald* supported it.[26] Despite the powerful support that administration supporters in the Senate gave the treaty, it failed (30 June 1870) to pass that body.

But Grant did not discourage easily. In his annual message to Congress of December 1870, he proposed that a commission be authorized by a joint resolution of Congress to draw up a new Santo Domingo annexation treaty, a device to evade the constitutional requirement of a two-thirds majority.[27] This proved too much even for some of Grant's supporters in Congress, and a compromise was effected by which a commission of investigation was authorized to visit the island and report on conditions there. Godkin reacted in the *Nation:* ". . . we deny the right of Congress to send out any such body even to Santo Domingo till the sense of this country has been distinctly taken on this whole policy of absorbing semi-civilized Catholic states. . . ."[28]

The editor, who had warmly endorsed the candidacy of Grant in 1868, had now developed doubts about the intelligence of the Civil War hero. Grant, he declared, did not understand the "laws of trade"; he had been duped by "some ignorant politician" into believing that "$100,000 of Dominican products, imported into the United States, would do great harm if they came from the 'Republic of Dominica,' but great good if they came from the 'State of Dominica' in the American Union."[29] As Godkin saw it:

> The facts of this St. Domingo affair, we believe, are, that the President—we do not know under what influences—has got it into his head that the United States ought to own half the island of Hayti, and that it is of such serious importance to them to acquire it at once that it is better . . . to buy it, and make citizens of 200,000 ignorant Catholic Spanish negroes, than to wait a minute longer.[30]

Behind the treaty, supposed Godkin, was a band of "operators." But he erred in alleging that the treaty had been concluded without the knowledge of Secretary of State Fish. Babcock's formal instructions came from Fish, who, although apparently a somewhat reluctant participant, was fully informed of the progress of the negotiations.[31]

Senator Charles Sumner had been instrumental in the defeat of the treaty, and in March 1871 Grant succeeded through his followers in the Senate in having him removed as chairman of the Foreign Relations Committee.[32] The removal, in that it dispelled fears that Sumner stood in the way of the settlement of the *Alabama* controversy, may have been useful, but the reasons behind it and the way it was brought about evoked an outcry from Sumner's followers. Godkin, who had not forgiven the Massachusetts lawmaker the reception his *Alabama* claims speech received in England, joined the chorus of disapproval with reluctance.

Godkin viewed Sumner's dismissal as a continuation of the corrupt process that began when President Grant fired Special Commissioner of Revenue David A. Wells at the behest of a "few barefaced monopolists," then drove General Jacob Dolson Cox and E. R. Hoar out of the cabinet.[33] But while the editor conceded that Sumner was well fitted for the chairmanship, he believed the uproar over his ouster uncalled for.

Citing the impeachment of President Johnson as an example of the "frantic absurdity" to which Republicans would go, Godkin urged calmness in the "present crisis." Sumner's loss of the chairmanship was not a national calamity; indeed, he might with propriety have resigned when "he found himself arrayed in open and bitter hostility" to the president. As Godkin put it:

> The main business of the Chairman of the Senate Committee is not to negotiate treaties, but to *discuss* with the Executive such treaties as have been negotiated, and receive from it explanations about them. His first business, therefore, is to be a good organ of communication on his particular class of subjects between the President and the Senate, and nobody can be said to be well fitted for this duty whose personal relations with the President are of an unpleasant nature.[34]

A comparison of the above editorial with a passage in the Pulitzer-Prize-winning biography of Hamilton Fish by Allan Nevins reveals Godkin to be the author of what Nevins offers as his own interpretation of the duties of the chairman of the Senate Foreign Relations Committee.[35] Ironically, the interpretation that Nevins appropriated from the editor differs from one Godkin gave three months earlier. In December 1870 he defended Sumner against demands for his removal, arguing that "the duty of the Chairman of the [Foreign Relations] Committee is to *examine* the President's projects in all that relates to foreign affairs, and hostility to the President is a disqualification for it only when it becomes factious. . . ." It would be a singular step, Godkin added, to drive a well-qualified man from his post simply "as a penalty for disrespectful language to the President."[36]

Meanwhile the committee of investigation had gone to Santo Domingo; in January 1871 it returned and drew up a report favorable to annexation. But senatorial opponents of the scheme were active; Sumner, though shorn of his chairmanship, continued his opposition from his Senate seat, and in April President Grant resignedly transmitted to Congress the committee's report with the recommendation that it be published so that the American people would be informed of the merits of the case. With the whole policy of annexation now in discredit, the Santo Domingo project died.

In 1867 Anson Burlingame, a former congressman turned diplomat, threw up the post of United States minister to China and assumed the leadership of a Chinese treaty mission to the United States and the rest of the powers. Early in 1868 the colorfully garbed delegation set out with circuslike fanfare for the United States. Public reaction was mixed, although most American editors appear to have been taken in by Burlingame's showmanship, Godkin among them. Writing in the *Nation* shortly before the delegation's arrival in the United States, Godkin threw both accuracy and his usual skepticism to the winds:

> The opening of China to the outside world after thirty centuries of seclusion . . . can hardly be over-rated. It is in some respects equivalent to the discovery of a new continent; and that the empire should, on its entry into the family of civilized nations, adopt the United States as its friend and protector, is perhaps as high a compliment as any country has ever received.[37]

As a consequence of Burlingame's efforts, Godkin predicted, San Francisco or New York would ultimately replace London as the western *entrepot* for the far eastern trade. It was an hour of triumph for the United States through the "moral force that lies in the walk and conversation of a single public servant. . . . We have triumphed mainly because we were represented by an able and honest man."[38] In sharp contrast the tory British *Saturday Review* found Burlingame a lackey of New York capitalists intent on capturing far eastern commercial privileges.[39] A treaty ensued.

Godkin was particularly impressed by the provisions of Burlingame's treaty for cheap labor. Cold to the argument that American wages and working standards would suffer from the introduction of coolie labor, Godkin, in a *Nation* editorial entitled "The Coming of the Barbarian," cited two interests that he believed outweighed the "popular prejudice" against the Chinese: first, the irresistible "demand of capital for labor"; and, second, the need of farmers and other Americans for cheap help.[40]

Godkin acknowledged that some would dispute the desirability of importing oriental labor to America, but he was confident that practical people, "those who consider the facts of American life apart from the theories of American progress preached on platforms," saw its value.[41] Whereas the European farmer was a happy and contented peasant with "few desires above those of the ox in [his] plow," and his wife similarly a "robust animal" who thoroughly enjoyed her domestic labors "without a suspicion that she is capable of anything higher or better," the American farmer was trying "to live, while laboring with his hands, as only super-intendents of labor live in other countries."

A tale of equal privation might be told, Godkin went on, of the large class of urban Americans who could not afford a servant, or who "endure the untold and unutterable agony of trying to get intelligent assistance out of one." City dwellers accordingly anticipated the Chinese with "the thrill of de-lighted, eager expectation"; the servant question was "fast becoming a question of civilization itself," with "Marriage, divorce, child bearing, female health, the permanence and purity of homes all . . . affected by it."[42]

In July 1870 the first Chinese workers arrived in New England. Although sardonic in his reaction to the dismay their arrival had created in the hallowed portals of aboli-tionism, Godkin conceded that the Cheap Labor Treaty may have been hastily concluded. But able to offer no remedy, he resorted to characteristic irony in the Nation. "It is too late," he wrote, "to have the Mongolian blood analyzed, and the low condition of Chinese morals exposed." What could be done if the Chinese did, as predicted, pour in and "undersell our laborers by their low standard of living, and debauch our politics by their ignorance and immorality?" Nothing, answered Godkin. The country had gone too far in entrusting such matters to Providence "to go back now and attempt to construct protective machinery."[43]

Besides, believed Godkin, the Chinese might be a bless-ing in disguise for a large nation trying to conduct its affairs on "the model of the town meeting," with "ignorant for-eigners" using their franchise to do political mischief. The "Chinese invasion" might force the hand of defenders of universal suffrage—in particular the Irish and the propo-nents of the Negro vote—who were blocking the road to "electoral reform."[44]

As for the fears of humanitarians that the coolie system would be established in the United States, those "who fear this," Godkin smiled, "can hardly have estimated the keenness of the look-out which is now kept in all parts of the country, by large numbers of gentlemen, for attempts to 'establish caste in America.'"

> Indeed, let the employers be ever so peaceable and long-suffering, we do not doubt that there will spring up what may be called a coolie bar, composed of legal gentlemen entirely devoted to egging on the Chinese to make their masters uncomfortable in innumerable ways. So that we earnestly recommend all persons who are afflicted by the prospects of even a partial revival of slavery amongst us, to hang up their harps and trumpets, and possess their souls in peace.[45]

The Unitarian divine O. B. Frothingham sent Godkin warm congratulations on the above editorial.[46]

Godkin's argument in support of the importation of coolie labor gave way to invective in the *Nation*, as he resumed his periodic attacks on Wendell Phillips. Deriding the social-reforming efforts of the old abolitionist, he taunted Phillips and his fellow "labor reformers" for their scheme to require employers to pay workers a full day's pay for laboring "for eight hours only."[47] This

> pernicious [eight-hour day] nonsense is uttered in the presence and hearing of thousands of ignorant laborers all over the country, who are thirsting for a life without toil, and whose efforts in pursuit of it are disorganizing nearly every branch of industry, are marked by every variety of crime and outrage, and are exercising a markedly deteriorating influence on the arts.[48]

Interestingly the Chinese traffic that Godkin defended arose partly from a violation of the Cheap Labor Treaty. Had the terms of the fifth article of Burlingame's treaty, reprobating involuntary immigration, been enforced, there might have been no great influx of Chinese laborers into the United States. But greedy employers were to be served, and foreign labor contractors in alliance with unscrupulous native officials were not particular in their method of supply. United States Minister to China George F. Seward outlined the problem in a memorandum to Secretary of State Evarts in March 1879. He explained that

> As the law now stands no Chinese can land in this country
> who has not proven before the consul of the United States at
> the port of departure, that he is a voluntary immigrant. But
> this law is a dead letter. Nearly all immigrants come from
> Hong Kong, and the Consul at that port is not provided with a
> sufficient staff of officers to enable him to make the required
> examination.[49]

Meanwhile relations between the races in the western states had taken a difficult turn. As the number of Chinese entrants rose—reaching almost 10 percent of the Pacific Coast population by 1878—discriminatory legislation and outrages by white workers on the Chinese workers multiplied.[50] Opponents of the Cheap Labor Treaty ranged from demagogues, fanning the fires of race prejudice, to responsible trade unionists and humanitarians who charged that the Chinese were being imported into virtual involuntary servitude. Some of Godkin's readers withheld support from his editorial stand in favor of coolie labor. The economist F. W. Taussig, a frequent contributor to the *Nation* after 1880, opposed the importation of Chinese laborers on the ground that a "permanent group of helots is not a healthy constituent in a democratic society."[51]

Meanwhile, the Chinese question had been thrust into the presidential campaign of 1880 with the publication of the Morey letter. In this letter, denounced as a forgery, Republican nominee James A. Garfield was represented as stating that he was opposed to any limitation on Chinese laborers "until our great manufacturing and corporate interests are conserved in the matter of labor." The obvious intent of the Morey letter was to discredit Garfield, but, when a judge arraigned the publishers of the letter for libel, Godkin— although he supported Garfield's candidacy—had the *Nation* voice stern objection: "If it be libelous to say in a canvass that a candidate is in favor of Chinese immigration in order to keep wages down, editors of newspapers ought to know it."[52]

When aroused, Godkin took liberties with the facts. One tactic was to overstate ludicrously his opponent's position, then feign agreement with the caricature he had drawn. This irony succeeded where staying with the facts would have failed, but it had its dangers. During the debates over

Chinese exclusion, the *Nation* sarcastically suggested that Congress pass laws to "authorize the summary slaughter of all Chinamen found within the country after a certain date." An appalled Japanese paper, the *Jiji Shimbun*, hoped editorially that the United States government would not implement this inhuman proposal.[53]

Godkin, asserted Henry Adams, blunted his effectiveness as a critic because he equated virtue with property.[54] Whether Godkin's writings contain liberal or conservative underpinnings is often disputed, but the instances are legion where he wobbled on liberty.[55] It was thus not surprising that when in 1893 Congress moved to renew Chinese exclusion for another ten years Godkin found no "reasonable objection" to it.[56]

In 1891, forgetting his declaration in the Chinese debate that race ought not to be a criterion for admission to the United States, Godkin stridently called for laws to exclude the "Latin race." Inaccurately declaring that in 1889 200,000 Italians entered the United States, he proposed legislation requiring all immigrants to read and write English. This, he explained, "would to a great extent confine immigration to English, Scotch and Irishmen, but why not, if the restriction be really undertaken in the interest of American civilization? We are under no obligation to see that all races and nations enjoy an equal chance of getting here."[57]

To explain these contradictions is not difficult. Godkin, like many contemporaries, believed the hope of civilization lay with the Anglo-Saxon. Although each man would wince at the comparison, Godkin was in step intellectually with his enemy Theodore Roosevelt, who thus praised Chinese exclusion: "Democracy, with the clear instinct of race selfishness, saw the race foe, and kept out the dangerous alien."[58] Racist feelings underlay and girded Godkin's argument even when, on occasion, he was disagreeing with Roosevelt's desire to exclude the Chinese. The Chinese question, in brief, found Godkin's racial and economic interests in conflict. It was not an irreconcilable conflict, for Godkin would argue that race and political economy are not goals in themselves, but means to a great end—civilization. If an influx of Chinese laborers could free their Anglo-Saxon "masters" to get on with the unfinished business of civilizing the United States, that was the end to be desired. Had Godkin been born in South Carolina, he would have been a slaveholder.

What eludes writers who discourse on Godkin's attachment to freedom is the extent to which he prized culture over liberty. Man's allegiance, he held in opposing Negro suffrage, is to civilization and liberty, in that order. An editor should be "above all things loyal to civilization." In the name of civilization, the *Nation* stridently called for increased use of capital punishment and, when legal processes ceased working to its advantage, the assassination of "Boss" Tweed and his confederates. Americans ought not to "be satisfied with 'government of the people, for the people, by the people,' unless that government is a really progressive and improving government," remarked the *Nation* in 1876, a government which makes valuable additions "to the art of living in society." Vernon L. Parrington was correct when he remarked of Godkin that "culture dispossessed liberty in his affections."[59]

Informed by the teachings of classical economy, the *Nation* took as its slogan: "To govern well, govern little." Doctrinaire in this, Godkin tried to be consistent. Since protective tariffs violate the laws of political economy, Protection is "socialistic." Equally, labor standards, old age assistance, and the relief of widows and orphans are "no more the business of the Government than of railroads or banks."[60] The *Nation* began early to oppose the eight-hour day; ultimately it found graduated taxation "socialistic," "inquisitorial," and "a form of violence comparable to brigandage." But like present-day conservative organs, it was spongy enough in its laissez-faire that it could call for state intervention to help corporations quell their labor disputes.[61]

Clinging to a static eighteenth-century liberal view in a nineteenth century bubbling with socioeconomic ferment, the *Nation* became openly reactionary when it contemplated the problems of municipal government. Like George W. Curtis, Godkin was converted to civil service reform when he decided the spoils system no longer worked to the advantage of the men of his class in the community. By reforming the civil service, sermonized the *Nation* in Hamiltonian accents, the

United States could be returned to its earlier rule by the "intelligent and virtuous" classes, and good government would filter downward to the masses. As early as 1866 Godkin identified the municipal problem:

> The purses of the rich cities are everywhere passing into the hands of the ignorant, the vicious, and the depraved, and are being used by them for the spread of political corruption, for the destruction of the popular faith in political purity, for the promotion of debauchery and idleness among young men of the poorer classes, for the destruction of our system of education.[62]

Everyone, continued Godkin, knew the cause of the evil— immigration. "In all our large towns a swarm of foreigners have alighted. . . ."

The hazards of generalizing about Godkin are illustrated by his editorials on immigration. Sometimes, as above, he found immigration to be at the bottom of municipal corruption; sometimes he denied this. In 1896 Henry Cabot Lodge, a one-time *Nation* stockholder now an arch foe of Godkin, elicited from the editor a sharp rebuke when he claimed that immigration was the cause of the municipal difficulty. "As to foreign illiteracy," tartly shot back Godkin, "we affirm that it has not done us a hundredth part of the mischief wrought by native literacy."[63] Yet Godkin, with other genteel publicists of his day, usually found illiteracy the trademark of the immigrant. (With a little research they might have learned that, according to the records of the United States commissioner general of immigration, more than 80 percent of the immigrants entering during the decade of the 1890s could read and write. This compares favorably with the 86.7 percent literacy for the United States population as a whole reported in 1890 by the Bureau of the Census.)

In a strident 1893 editorial, Godkin declared that immigrants were "sacking" the cities in the absence of a naturalization law "to arrest the incessant additions to the voting population by the half civilized newcomers." "In truth," accused he, "there is no corner of our system in which the hastily made and ignorant foreign voter may not be found eating away the political structure, like a white ant, with a group of natives standing over him and encouraging him."[64]

But the immigrant, said he, was only part of the problem; the initial mistake was made during the Jacksonian era when the vote was given to the masses, when the United States embarked on a "government of mere numbers."[65]

In 1867, to Godkin's disappointment, the voters of New York rejected a proposed new state constitution. Angrily, Godkin, who had favored the constitutional convention to obtain an educational test for voting and a special voice in representation for property, complained to his friend Norton of the stand that William Cullen Bryant's *Evening Post*, through its able managing editor Charles Nordhoff, had taken in support of popular government:

> I sent you a scrap of Nordhoff's stuff yesterday. It amazes me to read such immoral trash. An ignorant, unthinking "Red" in charge of an influential newspaper is an unpleasant sight, and I am afraid that is what must be said of it. When he talks of "the people having a right to misgovern," he most probably does not know what he means, and this is perhaps the kindest construction we can put on his balderdash.[66]

Soon after this, the Tweed Ring got control of the state legislature and began helping itself to public funds in New York City. Godkin played no role in the exposure of the ring, but he found in the resulting scandal ammunition with which to attack popular government. To reformers who proposed to avert Tweed scandals by giving "power to the people" the *Nation* replied that the scandal had happened because the people *were* in power. Before municipal offices became elective — before the coming of rings and corrupt legislatures — "the first merchants and lawyers of New York then controlled political meetings and deemed it an honor to hold the office of alderman."[67]

In 1875 Governor Samuel J. Tilden appointed Godkin to a state commission chaired by William M. Evarts to study the "decay of municipal government" and to devise a new plan of municipal government for the State of New York. In 1877 the commission submitted its findings, including an ill-fated proposed constitutional amendment with a controversial provision for the elimination of nonpropertied citizens from voting on municipal money matters.[68] Late that year "Boss" Tweed was brought from jail to testify before a committee of

New York aldermen. His revelations provoked Godkin to declare afresh the need to open the eyes of those who prattle about "natural rights and human brotherhood." New Yorkers have far too long "permitted all the paupers and criminals in the community—those who have no interest whatever in municipal administration beyond fear of the policeman or desire for free soup or city work and wages—to have an equal share in the management of enormous financial interests with those who furnish the money and who alone are likely to desire its economical administration." To bestow the right to disburse money "or of choosing those who are to disburse it, upon one who had had nothing to do with its acquisition . . . will soon, we believe, be looked upon in municipal affairs as the method of madmen, and any attempt to defend it as too irrational to call for serious discussion."[69]

The scathing attacks of Godkin on Tammany Hall during the 1890s, merited in part though they were, overlooked the human side of the organization—the hope that the machine in some degree brought to the huddled populations of New York's tenement house districts. The sins of Tammany were well publicized; less publicized were the corporate frauds and individual peculations of some of the respected Republican opponents of Tammany.[70] Of the men whom the *Nation* singled out for repeated personal attack, Horace Greeley, Wendell Phillips, John Peter Altgeld, William Jennings Bryan, and Richard T. Ely were each striving toward the fulfillment of the American Dream. The truth was that the *Nation* had misgivings about the American Dream.

Almost since the first issue of Godkin's weekly in 1865, the United States had been undergoing the birth pains of a social reform movement, one that rejected the class goals of the *Nation* and some of its mugwump followers. While Godkin was tartly dismissing agrarian protesters as "cranks" and New York's "other half" as those who "choose to herd like pigs in the slums of the Tenth Ward of New York," William Dean Howells, who in 1865 had been tutored in the Brahmin ideals of the *Nation*, was exploring new paths. So was former Godkin subordinate Lincoln Steffens.[71]

How important a reform magazine, therefore, was the Godkin *Nation*? Perhaps the *Nation* in the nineteenth century was not a reform magazine. True, it attacked with spirit the chicanery that was the facade around the Gilded Age; yet it uncompromisingly defended the system underneath. "Though it always pressed for respectable reforms, it resisted every political-economic change that was truly significant. . . ."[72] Dwelling on appearances rather than fundamentals, the *Nation* presented a distorted picture of the Gilded Age, enlarged by the practice of contemporary journals plagiarizing from it, and lending credence to Nevins's contention: "As the greatest role in the leadership of opinion in the generation preceding the Civil War had been played by Horace Greeley, so the greatest single part in the next generation was with little doubt that of E. L. Godkin."[73] Although recent scholarship indicates that Nevins exaggerated the Anglo-Irish editor's stature, further inquiry will show that no one exercised greater influence than Godkin on the writing of the history of the Gilded Age.

Chapter Eight
The Liberal Republican Movement of 1872

> *Dear Mr. Schurz . . . . I do not know
> whether you are aware what a con-
> ceited, ignorant, half cracked, obsti-
> nate old creature [Horace Greeley]
> is; but you must know enough to feel
> that we did at Cincinnati, a most
> serious, and dangerous thing.*

In the late 1860s Charles Francis Adams, Jr. returned to the United States to discover that his country had changed considerably since his wartime absence with his father in England. The postwar period, he reflected in the *North American Review,* had "witnessed some of the most remarkable examples of organized lawlessness, under the forms of law, which mankind has yet had an opportunity to study." Particularly was this true of the men who controlled the railroads. "These modern potentates have declared war, negotiated peace, reduced courts, legislatures, and sovereign States to an unqualified obedience to their will. . . ."[1]

While Adams was writing this, five hundred New York merchants, with the editorial support of Godkin, were petitioning Albany for legislative action to control the railroads.[2] Writing earlier in the *North American Review* in 1868, Godkin found the answer to the dislocations of postwar society in the breakdown of tradition:

> We are, at present, witnessing in the immorality which per-
> vades the commercial world, and taints nearly every branch of
> business, the results of the decline of habit as a social force,
> before mental and moral culture has reached a sufficiently
> advanced stage to take its place. Every man at present may
> be said literally to live by his wits; hardly anybody lives by
> tradition, or authority, or under the dominion of habits ac-
> quired in youth. The result is a kind of moral anarchy. . . .[3]

Yet to approve social injustices that worked to the benefit

of the capitalist classes was a middle-class reflex during the Gilded Age. Were there differences between the hard-shell Baptist John D. Rockefeller—who avowed that God gave him his money—and the liberal Congregationalist Henry Ward Beecher, who cried, "God intended the great to be great and the little to be little . . . the man who cannot live on bread and water is not fit to live"? Or Godkin, who praised the relocation of orphans in the west by Brace's Children's Aid Society, but affirmed that it was neither possible nor desirable to abolish poverty?[4]

The same year, 1868, that Adams returned home and that Godkin was writing in the *North American Review*, Ulysses S. Grant was elected to the presidency. Godkin enthusiastically supported the general during the campaign, not very presciently prophesizing that "he will be sickened by the spectacle of disorder and corruption" in the diplomatic, revenue, and postal services.[5] Later, disappointed by the general's cabinet choices, he was politic enough to permit the *Nation* to say that the cabinet was as good as might be expected.[6]

It will be recalled that in asserting control over the *Nation*, Godkin assumed editorial positions that did not enjoy the backing of all of his stockholders. One such position was his support of civil service reform, a "Prussian" scheme thought one of his critics. Another was tariff reform.[7] The year 1867 saw the founding of the American Free Trade League. Active in it in New York were acquaintances of Godkin such as special commissioner of the revenue David A. Wells, Robert B. Minturn, Jr., Howard Potter, Charles H. Marshall, and Alfred Pell, Sr. A future brother-in-law of Godkin, Mahlon Sands, was executive secretary, and the youthful Henry D. Lloyd, an occasional literary contributor to the *Nation*, was assistant secretary.[8] Linked to the Free Trade League was a dining club called the Round Table, whose genteel members found tariff reform a respectable cause for which they were "ready to dine."[9] The Round Table met regularly at the Knickerbocker Club; besides its principal founder, Godkin, it included Marshall, Pell, and New York lawyer E. Randolph Robinson, a transplanted Virginian descended from John Randolph of Roanoke.

In December 1869 Godkin sent Lloyd to New Haven, armed with a letter of introduction to President Woolsey and Professor Daniel Coit Gilman of Yale which explained that Lloyd was coming to organize a free trade meeting, and he requested their help.[10]

Disenchantment with the Grant administration was starting to set in, and the American Free Trade League was about to become a focus of it. In Illinois in 1870 free trader Horace White enjoyed virtually a free hand in drawing up the tariff reform stand of the Republican Party of that state.[11] Under attack in Grant's cabinet was a staunch champion of civil service reform, Secretary of the Interior Jacob Dolson Cox, and civil service reformers and free traders alike rallied to his defense. Early in October Godkin talked with Cox and came away persuaded that his resignation was imminent.[12] It occurred several days later. The next month Godkin travelled to New Haven to attend a Civil Service reform meeting at Yale College. President Woolsey presided; Godkin made a short speech, and a warm letter of support of Cox was drawn up.[13]

Not all tariff reformers were civil service reformers, and some were averse to breaking with the administration over Cox. But six days after the New Haven civil service reform meeting, Sands sent out invitations from the Free Trade League for a conference on tariff and revenue reform in New York on 22 November 1870 to determine "whether an effort may not, with advantage, be made to control the new House of Representatives by a union of Western Revenue Reform Republicans with Democrats."[14] In the meantime Godkin was dining at the Knickerbocker Club with Sands, Marshall, Robinson, Pell and others, helping to lay plans for the conference.

The conference was a modest success. Besides Godkin and the officers of the Free Trade League, there were about twenty-five in attendance, including William Cullen Bryant and Charles Nordhoff of the *Evening Post*, Wells, Samuel Bowles of the *Springfield Republican*, Colonel William Grosvenor of the St. Louis *Democrat*, Jacob Brinkerhoff, Henry Adams, and his brother Charles F., Jr. "C. F. is growing quite fat and chubby," reported Godkin to Fanny, who was in the Bahamas with her ailing brother, "and looks more comical than ever."[15] No Democrats were invited, and, contrary to some scholars, Cox and Senator Carl Schurz did not attend, although each was apprised of the results of the conference.[16]

At the conference it was revealed that some of the officers of the Free Trade League inclined toward an open rupture with the Republican Party, whereas the representatives of the press, including White, Godkin, and Grosvenor, opposed talk of the "new party" except as a means of prodding the administration. The advisability of working with the civil service reformers was discussed. After joining the tariff question to the civil service question, the conferees voted down a proposal to form a central committee empowered to call a convention if Congress failed to act on their demands.[17] The conference "was very successful," Godkin reported to his wife, "and I was amused by the growing deference with which my opinions are treated. . . . The Lord is delivering the politicians into our hands."[18]

The free trade conference was the opening gun of the Republican anti-Grant movement in the east, but it was not the beginning of the liberal Republican movement, which had got under way several months earlier in Missouri when Grosvenor and Schurz formed a coalition with the Democrats that swept B. Gratz Brown into the governorship. Soon a medley of malcontents joined the movement.[19] Schurz and Cox opposed Grant for his coolness to civil service reform. Wells disliked him for his high tariff position, while Senator Lyman Trumbull rejected his Radical southern policy. Ignatius Donnelly found the president inimical to populist objectives, while the conservative Charles Francis Adams saw him as a barrier to the restoration of New England's power. Influential editors like Horace Greeley, Manton Marble, Godkin, Oswald Ottendorfer, Murat Halstead, Henry Watterson, Parke Godwin, Charles A. Dana, Bryant, White, and Bowles were impatient with the administration for a variety of reasons.[20]

On 23 March 1871 White turned the editorial columns of the *Chicago Tribune* against Grant, while in a letter to Godkin Schurz was underscoring the weaknesses of the admin-

istration:[21] "The Republican party is, as you well know,"
wrote Schurz, "at present controlled in its official capacity
by the office-mongers who go through thick and thin with
the Administration and who find in the Administration their
only rallying points and strength."[22] Schurz concluded that,
for the sake of the "vitality" of the party, Grant must go.
Godkin, disappointed that Schurz and Trumbull found it
inexpedient to back the Free Trade League, agreed with
Schurz about Grant, but he believed that the anti-Grant
forces were dwelling too much on the president's ouster
of Senate Foreign Relations Committee chairman Charles
Sumner. He told Schurz:

> I think the points of attack should be points that are clearly
> vulnerable and at which success is certain. I did not think
> Sumner's removal was of this class. . . . Sumner's faults of
> temper, and especially his vanity and annoyance [sic] are
> well known. You cannot, therefore persuade people that he is
> altogether in the right in any controversy, in which his self
> love is wounded.[23]

Unless a reform party, led by "gentlemen," took possession
of the government soon, prophesied Godkin to Schurz, "we
shall witness some great catastrophe."[24]

The New York Times was one of the New York newspapers actively opposed to the stop-Grant movement. Late in
1869 Godkin resumed writing for the Times on the condition
that his contributions be kept secret. But his critical attitude
toward the administration soon brought a request for an end
to his services. Godkin retaliated with an editorial attack
on the Times in the Nation, to which in March 1872 the
Times responded:

> Mr. E. L. Godkin, who seems to be a man gifted with more
> literary ability than discretion or good sense, has thought
> proper to write a letter to the Tribune, which is marked, we
> must take leave to say, by the bad faith and want of veracity
> too often characteristic of Mr. Godkin.
>   Mr. Godkin's present troubles and anxieties have arisen
> from that passionate temperament which prevents him at
> times from distinguishing between right and wrong. . . .[25]

Godkin was a "quarrelsome and somewhat reckless, though
able man," concluded the Times, who wrote under the cloak
of secrecy while he denounced secrecy in others. The Times

charged—a charge that Godkin denied in a letter to the
Tribune—that by prearrangement with the *Times* Godkin
adopted the pseudonym "James Madison" and wrote letters
to the *Times* over the signature "J. M."[26] The evidence appeared to sustain the *Times*'s charge.

Meanwhile, despite a move to placate the tariff reformers
by giving them control of the House Committee on Ways
and Means, opposition to the Grant administration grew.[27]
Schurz was bent on forming a new party, and Grosvenor took
the initiative. On 24 January 1872, in behalf of the Schurz-
Brown faction, he issued a call for a national convention of
liberal Republicans to meet at Cincinnati in May.

As the convention convened, the Missouri and Illinois politicians, who possessed most of the clout in the heterogeneous
assemblage, intended to nominate one of their own as the
standard bearer of the "new party." But it was soon apparent
that White's candidate, Senator Trumbull, did not command
enough delegates, whereupon the Illinois delegation turned
to another favorite son, Supreme Court Justice David Davis.
Members of the press in attendance, such as White, Godkin,
Bowles, Watterson, and Halstead, were unenthusiastic about
Davis, and his support ebbed in favor of two other candidates, Charles Francis Adams and Horace Greeley.[28] In order
to obtain the high-tariff Greeley's support, White, Schurz,
and Wells agreed not to make the tariff an issue in the campaign, but no one supposed that Greeley would be a contender for the nomination. White, who headed the platform
committee, optimistically informed Trumbull from the convention on 4 May: "We came here to break up two old rotten
political parties. . . . I think we have done *that.*"[29]

Eastern independents, such as Godkin, Wells, Edward
Atkinson, Bryant, and Bowles, wanted the nomination to go
to Charles Francis Adams, but practical politicians in the
Fenton delegation from New York and the McClure delegation from Pennsylvania, Godkin told the *Nation* from the convention, meant to support Davis for president and Greeley
or George W. Curtis for vice president.[30] Prior to the convention, Wells had been locked in nearly all-night sessions
with Grosvenor, Godkin, Atkinson, and the Greeley forces
trying to hammer out a platform "on which all could stand."[31]

But from the convention, Godkin reported that there was no "common ground on which the protectionists and revenue reformers" could reach agreement.[32] Additionally distressing to some, the platform equivocated on the race question; officially the platform supported black suffrage, but its preamble emphasized the restoration of home rule in the south.[33]

When the nomination, to the astonishment of the convention managers, went to Greeley, eastern independents were horrified. "Is there no way out of [this] wretched mess. . .?" Godkin wailed to Schurz.[34] Schurz, who had presided over the convention, agreed that the situation was "perplexing and humiliating in the extreme," and he promised Godkin to "do anything to escape from the necessity of supporting Greeley against Grant." But he added his opinion that it was essential to defeat Grant, "in order to break up that party despotism under which we are suffering. . . ."[35] Privately Schurz had made up his mind—according to Curtis, who was now holding firm for Grant—that "both parties must be destroyed, and Greeley's election is the way to destroy them."[36] Nonetheless Schurz proposed that Godkin come to Washington late in June "with as many of our friends as you can induce to accompany you" to discuss the possibility of selecting another candidate.

Meanwhile Schurz was corresponding with White about Godkin's position. The editor of the *Chicago Tribune* had been to see Greeley and was convinced that he was worthy of support. Godkin demurred, but he consented to arrange a meeting at his home early in June with Atkinson, White, Schurz, Trumbull, and others to "talk matters over."[37] Trumbull and Schurz, along with some erstwhile supporters of Charles Francis Adams, were now swinging over to White's position, and on 15 June White complained of Godkin's attitude to Schurz:

> Godkin in the *Nation* of this week, seems to have committed
> himself to Grant in one of the profoundest *non sequiturs* I
> have ever seen.[38] I am sorry for this, but I fear that it cannot
> be helped. It will be a strange sight to see the *Nation* giving up
> the cause of reform in totidem, while Schurz, Trumbull and
> Sumner do not despair of the Republic.[39]

Schurz now pleaded with Godkin to support Greeley,

telling him, "The influence of the 'Nation' is so great and valuable that it ought not to redound to Grant's benefit. . . ."[40] But Godkin held his ground. "Greeley would have to change his whole nature, at the age of 62," he replied to Schurz, "in order not to deceive and destroy you." He wrote:

> What I seek, is not a sham breakup of parties, such as the Greeley movement proposes, but a real breakup. . . . Bowles, White and the rest are to me preaching the very doctrines now, against which we have been all thundering for three years. They are accepting blindly a grossly unfit candidate at the hands of a bellowing Convention and are going to support him solely because he is "available". . . .[41]

The eastern press was divided over Greeley's nomination. Bowles regretfully stuck by the convention's nominee, telegraphing the *Republican* from Cincinnati, "Support the ticket, but don't gush," but in New York Parke Godwin snapped to Schurz: "The man Greeley is a charlatan from top to bottom. . . . Grant and his crew are bad—but hardly as bad as Greeley and his crew would be."[42] Godkin agreed. Contrary to Professor Dexter Perkins, throughout the campaign he made the *Nation* unflaggingly oppose Greeley. White thought he contributed "more than any other writer" to Greeley's defeat.[43]

In the course of the campaign, *The Penn Monthly* noted Godkin's criticisms of both candidates and took him to task for what it termed his "waspish" resort to personalities:

> We fear that we must class *The Nation* among the very worst of these offenders. The friends of that weekly looked to it for the beginning of a great revolution in the newspaper world, in this very respect, but the animus it displays, at present, is of the worst. We gather from all its expressions, paragraph and article alike, that while it almost despises one candidate, it hates the other most fervently.[44]

As Election Day approached, Godkin became vindictive at the prospect of defeating Greeley. "We shall have our revenge for Cincinnati on Tuesday," he gloated to Atkinson.[45] After the election he resisted overtures from White and Schurz to reunite the tattered forces of the liberal Republican movement, scoffing to White: "The result of the Cincinnati movement has been so unfortunate, that there is at present a slight odor of ridicule hanging around everybody

who had anything to do with getting it up."[46]   White forwarded Godkin's letter to Schurz, who was smarting under
an editorial thrust at him in the Nation. "How cruel you are!"
mourned Schurz to Godkin, "The 'Nation' makes me responsible for the disaster at Cincinnati, because I 'had an opportunity to retrieve it, and missed it.'"[47] He pointed out to
Godkin that all of them had been overconfident of the nomination of Adams on the first ballot. But Schurz ended on
a cordial note, proposing to see Godkin in New York the
following weekend.

This was where matters stood when Grant's second term
began in 1873. The following November, on the heels of
Republican reverses in congressional elections, Charles
Francis Adams, Jr., reopened the idea of a third party to
Wells. He proposed a two-day private conference, to conclude with a public dinner to Schurz. "Once met we must lay
down the future faith boldly and loudly,—show the country
in fact that we yet live."[48] But Godkin and White were now
tilting editorially over the Granger movement, and there was
no assurance that the two could be gotten to the meeting—essential, Schurz and Adams agreed, to its success.[49]
Besides presenting his scheme to Wells and Schurz, Adams
approached new Tribune proprietor Whitelaw Reid, as well
as Cox, Watterson, Halstead, Nordhoff, and William M.
Evarts, hoping to arrange a public demonstration to which
"we can let in all except the political bummers;—every man
of the stripe who ruined us at Cincinnati must be rigorously
excluded."[50] The proposal quickly leaked out to the press.

Godkin and other editors were cool to the proposed demonstration. ". . . unless we can make a respectable show of
new names," Godkin told Schurz, "we shall not make much
impression." He continued:

> For instance, I will say to you confidentially, that I dread
> Grosvenor's appearance in the forefront of the battle. He is
> an able and useful man, but he has no character, or rather
> a very bad one. Everybody looks on him as a charlatan
> and adventurer, of those whom we desire to win over and
> conciliate.[51]

In the meantime Adams fell ill, and his brother Brooks
took charge of the scheme. But he was unable to come up

with a date for a meeting that pleased everyone, and Wells proposed to Godkin as a substitute that "we might . . . issue an address, to people of our way of thinking asking them to hold aloof from present parties, and vote independently and rebukingly, of evil—let the consequences be what they may and so nucleate the independents."[52]

When Adams failed to arrange a meeting of the independents, Godkin determined to hold it at his home. But neither Evarts nor Reid were enthusiastic—Evarts informing Wells, "As to any collective sentiment in reference to politics there seems to me little to encourage it at the moment." The project thereupon collapsed.[53]

For years Godkin had wanted a daily newspaper, and during the late weeks of 1873 he joined Arthur Sedgwick in a scheme for an evening edition of the *Nation*. "His daily *Nation* scheme depends now on one capitalist who is in New York," William James told his brother Henry, "but I mistrust Godkin as editor."[54] In a memorandum to Sedgwick, Godkin pontifically laid down his terms for the proposed daily:

1. That not less than $75,000 capital be raised, no part of which the present Editor of the *Nation* shall be expected to raise or contribute.
2. That a third interest in the new enterprize shall be given to E. L. Godkin and Co. in return for the name and good will, and the labor and attention of the editorial staff and of the business management, as well as office expenses.
3. That the whole sole and supreme editorial control shall be placed in the hands of Mr. E. L. Godkin.[55]

. . . .

Happily Sedgwick's scheme failed to attract backers, for Godkin would have failed as the proprietor of a daily newspaper dependent on subscribers. "Going with the crowd" was not his forte. He won his small band of supporters because he made the *Nation* a repository for the conventional wisdom of a minority of the "best people," which is to repeat that he made it a repository for their prejudices.[56] His objection to Jim Fisk, for example, was less the financier's business morals than that he had begun life as a peddler. The awakened conscience that prompted Helen Hunt Jackson in *A Century of Dishonor* to indict the white man for his treatment of the red man struck no responsive chord in Godkin. Not only are his editorials during the 1870s silent on the "final solution of the Indian Problem," they are also silent toward the anti-Semitism that clouded the vision of many of the intelligentsia of his day.[57]

Since Godkin's family destroyed most of his correspondence with women, it is not possible to appraise closely his relationship with the opposite sex, but he was drawn to women and they to him. While he was a stern moralist in public affairs, he was not a slave to the conventional Victorian sexual code of the day. He complained to James Bryce that "a great many of the religious people . . . seem to make chastity the greatest of virtues."[58] But in 1874 his patience was tried by the Beecher scandal, which arose out of charges by Theodore Tilton that Fanny's cousin, the Reverend Henry Ward Beecher, was having sexual relations with Tilton's wife. "What with the nastiness of it, and the newspaper rhetoric on it, it is absolutely sickening," Godkin told James Russell Lowell; and in the *Nation* he editorially raked the publicity accorded the scandal, giving a name to the age—"Chromo-civilization."[59]

During the Grant years Godkin enlarged his circle of friendly acquaintances to include Lowell, Henry James *père et fils*, Professor Ephraim W. Gurney of Harvard and his wife Ellen, the Ashburner sisters of Stockbridge and Cambridge, Massachusetts, Harvard Professor Francis J. Child, Henry Adams and his wife Clover (Marian), Whitelaw Reid, and Henry Cabot Lodge. Although his cordiality with the last four did not last, his capacity for friendship with persons who could withstand his brusque personality remained substantial.

During these years the circulation of the *Nation* continued to grow—by 1872 it passed 10,000—but the paper was barely paying its expenses. The editorial staff remained, as in the beginning, three persons, Godkin, Garrison, and an editorial assistant. Hired in 1879 to replace George Edward Woodberry, after an altercation with Godkin terminated his services, was W. C. Brownell, recommended to Godkin by E. C. Stedman. Brownell remembered his tutelage under Godkin:

> Mr. Garrison shared the first editorial room with me. Mr. Godkin had the back office. The publications offices were in

front, occupied by the amiable Mr. St. John and his staff,
which included a gentle and aristocratic colored bookkeeper
who resembled an East Indian philosopher—plainly a Garri-
sonian protégé . . . . The quiet was broken only by an occasional interchange of conversation between us, or by the
hearty laugh of Mr. Godkin . . . or by a visit now and then
from Arthur Sedgwick . . . or the appearance of Earl Shinn
with his art or dramatic criticism—both the best written, if
not the best, we have ever had in this country. . . . [60]

During the seventies Godkin made the currency question
a fighting issue in the *Nation*, defending the hard money
position against what he called the "paper money intrigue."
Besides giving new-found attention to civil service reform,
he examined critically the tariff, the Granger Movement, the
labor movement in England, the Paris Commune, and the
manners of the *nouveau riche*. Critical of Latin, as well as
black and Catholic, people, he objected to American expansion into the southern part of the hemisphere, while at home
he noted with approval the return of white supremacy to
the south.

The stature of Godkin had reached the point that Ivy
League colleges were vying for his services as a speaker,
but he was apprehensive of the lecture platform. After accepting invitations to lecture at Yale and Harvard and to give
a commencement address at Cornell, he tardily declined
each appearance, proffering as his excuse "a breakdown in
my eyes," even though there was nothing organically wrong
with his vision.[61]

In April 1873 there commenced a series of personal trag-
edies for Godkin. His young daughter Elizabeth, the apple
of his eye, died after a brief illness. "I wish we only *knew*
that she was in the hands of a heavenly father," the religious skeptic told his clerical acquaintance the Reverend
Henry W. Bellows, "under whose eye she would become all
that I fondly and rashly hoped to see her, one day under
mine . . . [62] Fanny did not recover from the blow of Lizzie's
death, and on 11 April 1875 she fell victim to a lingering
illness. Edwin and Lawrence, the only surviving child of
three born to Fanny—a third, Ralph, having died in early
infancy—were alone.

Shattered, momentarily ruminating on suicide, Godkin

dropped most of his editorial duties and, leaving Garrison in charge of the *Nation* office, bought a home in Cambridge, Massachusetts from former Secretary of the Treasury William A. Richardson.[63] Before long the *Nation*, as Garrison delicately pointed out to his absent chief, began having difficulty meeting its obligations. The death the previous year of Godkin's partner McKim, who held a one-third interest in E. L. Godkin and Company, left his son-in-law Garrison partly responsible for the debts of the company. Godkin held seven-twelfths of the stock, and Sedgwick and advertising agent Condit one-twelfth each, acquired when Olmsted quit the concern. By this time all but one of the forty initial stockholders in the *Nation* had departed, most of them acceding to Godkin's suggestion that they donate their stock to the company in recognition of the financial distress of the weekly and of his labors in getting it started. By 1877, with the *Nation* less than half its original size and its circulation again under 7,000, Godkin controlled most of the stock and was utilizing various expedients to keep the paper alive without putting money of his own into it. In the end everyone connected with the financing of the *Nation* lost money except Godkin.[64]

During the Gilded Age the maiden sisters Anne and Grace Ashburner, English-born aunts of Arthur Sedgwick, were popular hostesses to gatherings in their Cambridge home adjacent to that of Professor Child on Kirkland Street, near Godkin's Kirkland Street home. Along with Child's, Lowell's, Longfellow's, and Norton's, "Miss Ashburner's"—for the dominant of the two sisters, Anne—was, in the unpublished testimony of William Dean Howells, where one expected to meet "whoever was most interesting or distinguished in Cambridge society."[65] Godkin, forgiving Miss Ashburner her Tory politics, spent many pleasant hours with the two sisters and their guests during the later 1870s. Young Lawrence was attending Harvard, and the editor saw no reason to return to New York. Where but in Cambridge could he bask in the adulation of the Gurneys, Lowell, "Stubby" Child, Arthur Sedgwick, and Arthur's maiden sister, Theodora?

In 1876, the scandals of the second Grant administration fresh before him, Godkin only supported Rutherford B. Hayes, the Republican nominee to succeed Grant, against

Samuel J. Tilden with many reservations. Moreover the circumstances of that disputed election led him to question Hayes's moral right to accept the presidency. The *Nation* went so far as to propose that a Massachusetts elector, presumably James Russell Lowell, defect from Hayes and cast his ballot for a third candidate, a proposal that caused Lowell to exclaim, "Godkin seems to have lost his head." The editor's course, courageous though it was, cost the *Nation* thousands of subscribers and seriously damaged his relations with Olmsted and Norton.[66] When he returned to New York to live several years later, his ego had been reinflated by his Cambridge circle, but the *Nation* was in serious financial trouble and its influence had waned. For several years Godkin vainly tried to find a buyer for it. The great days of the *Nation* were over.

Chapter Nine
Too Many Mules in the Pasture

*If that tricephalic combination don't
kill the POST within three years, I'll
sign the 39 Articles. . . .*
W. H. Huntington to John Bigelow

By inheritance Godkin, of course, was Irish, bourgeois and combative, but by taste he was English, aristocratic, and "sober." He was predictable only in his combativeness, a trait that occasionally made victims of friends as well as foes. Carl Schurz was one such friend. When in 1902 Godkin's widow and his son set about to obtain his personal letters for publication, they carefully avoided one major source, Schurz. And when Rollo Ogden's authorized *Life and Letters of Edwin Lawrence Godkin* appeared, it contained no mention of the long association between Godkin and Schurz. Godkin's daughter-in-law told Oswald Garrison Villard why: Godkin's papers contained material on the Schurz controversy that the Godkin family "always refused to have made public."[1]

This conspiracy of silence—the Schurz family also abetted it—about the checkered events of Schurz's career as editor of the New York *Evening Post* from 1881 to 1883 has led scholars to misgauge their significance. Allan Nevins in his *History of the Evening Post* copies the version of Bancroft and Dunning in their *Reminiscences of Carl Schurz*, that the ill feeling that occurred between Schurz and Godkin disappeared and their friendship continued. Schurz's biographer C. M. Fuess also adopts the Bancroft and Dunning version and adds this additional misstatement: "Although *no open rupture is mentioned between Godkin and Schurz, they were at odds from the beginning as to the proper policies for the Evening Post to follow.*"[2] Most writers accept Godkin's and Wendell Garrison's assertions of the unfitness of Schurz for newspaper work.

The acquaintanceship that Schurz's biographer misinterpreted and that Godkin's biographer ignored was a long one. It began in 1870, one year after Schurz entered the United States Senate. Godkin described his first meeting with Schurz in a journal entry of 12 November 1870: "Went to the office in the P. M. and while there received a visit from Carl Schurz, the German Senator from Missouri; a tall gaunt man but very pleasant. Like so many others profuse in his comment about the *Nation*." Soon afterward their detailed correspondence began, with both, as has been noted, enlisted in the movement to block Grant's renomination in 1872.

In the meantime, Schurz had begun to contribute unpaid political articles to the *Nation*, stressing to Godkin the importance of keeping his authorship a secret.[3] The two men continued their association through the rest of Schurz's term in the Senate, the tactless Godkin sometimes giving Schurz unsought personal advice on which Schurz occasionally acted. In 1877 the erstwhile German immigrant became secretary of the interior under President Hayes. He had been instrumental during the campaign in bringing Godkin, albeit lukewarmly, behind the Hayes ticket, and the proprietor of the *Nation* was consulted in the cabinet choices. The association between the two men continued throughout Hayes's term, Godkin sometimes writing Schurz in rebuttal to Schurz's concern over the *Nation*'s treatment of the administration, sometimes to criticize administration policy or to obtain a government job for a friend.[4] Whenever Schurz came to New York or Cambridge, he usually made it a point to call on the younger man, although their cordiality never ripened into close friendship.

On the expiration of Hayes's term in 1881, Schurz retired from the public service with the intention of restoring his depleted personal funds. Newspaper work beckoned. He was no stranger to the profession, having been editor of the Detroit *Post* in 1866-1867 and subsequently editor and still part-owner of the *Westliche Post* in St. Louis.

It is at this point that Henry Villard and Horace White reenter the story. Villard, a German immigrant and journalist now turned financier, and White, the former editor of the *Chicago Tribune*, both had been associated with Schurz and Godkin in the liberal Republican movement in 1872. Except for White, all were immigrants to the United States. By 1879 White and Godkin were speculating in Villard's enterprises. Besides their common financial dealings, Villard, Schurz, White and Godkin shared intellectual interests not always found in journalists.

In 1881 the New York *Evening Post* was for sale; Schurz, White, and Godkin were each interested in editing it, and it was in the "editorship of all the talents" that they would now pool their talents to make their fortunes. Behind the purchase stood Villard, flushed with confidence from his recent proxy fight to gain control of the Northern Pacific Railroad and intent on acquiring a newspaper to represent his growing interests. But the financial titan was at pains to conceal his purchase of the *Evening Post* with funds he had transferred to his wife's name. "I see by the newspapers the *Evening Post* is sold . . . to Schurz, White, and Godkin," mused newspaperman W. H. Huntington from Paris to John Bigelow in June 1881, predicting that the triumvirate would destroy the paper.[5] Godkin, writing in confidence to Olmsted, with whom he was once again on good terms, gave a more accurate explanation of the transaction:

> The *Evening Post* . . . has been bought by Villard and Horace White. *This is strictly confidential.* Schurz is to be the new editor in chief—possession 21st of May. . . . They ask me to join, on the same terms pecuniarily as Schurz, but as "associate editor," offer to buy out the *Nation* if I choose, and annex it to the *Post* as a weekly edition like [the] *Pall Mall Budget*.[6]

Godkin at first agreed to, and then balked at, selling the *Nation* to the *Evening Post* for Villard's price, $40,000, less than the paper's capitalized worth of $60,000. But after unsuccessful efforts throughout May to sell the weekly to Henry Cabot Lodge, Parke Godwin, and others, he reluctantly accepted Villard's terms. The *Nation's* stockholders—among them Lodge, Thomas Wentworth Higginson, and Brander Mathews—lost approximately a third of their investment.[7]

Official announcement of the sale of the *Evening Post*

appeared in that paper on 25 May and promptly elicited comment from newspapers around the country. All of them accepted the paper's statement that Schurz, White (who was now an official in Villard's enterprises), and Godkin were the purchasers. In general the papers agreed with the Boston *Herald*, which observed that the *Evening Post* "has always maintained a high character for political independence and literary ability, and its audience today is one of the most select in the country. . . . Under its new ownership and management it will enter upon an important era. . . . Mr. Schurz is a man of the broadest and clearest views and a master of expression."[8]

Schurz was besieged with congratulatory letters. Privately to the New York *Tribune's* honeymooning editor Whitelaw Reid, Reid's replacement John Hay noncommittally wrote, "Schurz begins his editorial work on the *Post* today with a long, serious leader on Civil Service reform."[9]

By agreement with Villard and White, Schurz and Godkin were each expected to take a one-tenth interest in the *Evening Post* syndicate—$100,000—and to receive $8,000 in annual salary plus a guaranteed 4 percent annual dividend on their stock. White was to be associate editor with Godkin and president of the company. As the largest stockholder besides Mrs. Villard, White would direct the paper's financial pages and see to it that its editorial rudder pointed where Villard intended.[10] Disciples of Godkin were prominent in the new organization. The faithful Wendell Garrison, who was Villard's brother-in-law, became treasurer of the *Evening Post* company and titular editor of the *Nation*—although Godkin did not relinquish control—in its new role as the weekly edition of the *Evening Post*.[11] Godkin's friend and colleague, Arthur Sedgwick, who had lately been serving as assistant editor of the *Post*, was retained in that capacity.

Godkin disciples were also in evidence among the stockholders of the new company. Their replies to Godkin's solicitations are suggestive. Frederick Sheldon told him, "If you wish more shares taken by your friends, Cadwalader told me he would take 10 and I could dispose of 10 more here to one of my family—who *would vote with me probably.* . . ."[12] To Henry

Cabot Lodge Godkin wrote: "I wish very much you would [take stock in the company] as I want to have as much of the stock as possible held by my friends."[13] But the perceptive Henry Adams cautiously qualified to Godkin the intent of his investment. "Put me down for $20,000," he told him, "if it suits your interests to do so (and by you, I mean not only you but Schurz and White and the E. P. inclusive)."[14]

While Godkin was thus active in his own interest, Schurz was living quietly, seeing few people except for an occasional meal, once for dinner with John Hay and Clarence King and once for breakfast with Godkin at the Knickerbocker Club. When on 23 May 1881 Schurz called his first editorial meeting, naming an afternoon hour, Godkin—who already had expressed to Olmsted and Norton misgivings that "after sixteen years of absolute power I shall have to work with and defer to another man"—demurred and suggested instead an evening hour. Schurz took no offense; yet, in the light of what followed, the question presents itself: did Godkin from the outset nurse the intention of seizing control of the Evening Post? For years he had aspired to the proprietorship of a daily newspaper; as early as 1872 he had given thought to establishing a daily Nation.[15] And by 1881 the instinct of personal gain was stronger in him than ever.

But if there were any lowering clouds on the horizon, Schurz did not notice them. Although he was unaccustomedly nervous in the face of his new responsibilities, he reported with his old self-confidence on 22 June to his brother-in-law in Germany that the Evening Post was in excellent condition with several thousand new subscribers.[16] And on the surface his confidence was justified. Schurz and his associates were united in their affection for the eighty-year-old Post, which under William Cullen.Bryant's long leadership had set an enviable record of literary excellence and editorial independence.

A trust arrangement was devised by which David A. Wells, Frederick Sheldon, and former Secretary of the Treasury Benjamin Bristow were induced to serve as Evening Post trustees. The plan, which was Villard's, was intended to shield him from the charge that he had bought a newspaper to represent his financial interests, but contrary to

Allan Nevins and other students of the *Evening Post* it did not prevent him from taking an active concern in *Post* policy.[17] Happily Schurz and Godkin concurred in most respects with Villard and White on policy; they were resolved to support "a low tariff, a hard currency, Civil Service Reform, 'independency' in politics, and international peace," and to fight "imperialism and loose spending and corruption in government."[18]

One thing Godkin hoped to change was the *Evening Post's* reputation for heaviness. Henry Adams agreed. "Tell Schurz," he admonished Godkin, "to lighten it all he can. It will always seem hefty, even though Mark Twain and Bret Harte alone write for it." Adams continued:

> For twenty years, more or less, I have been trying to persuade people that I don't come from Boston. . . . If I stood on Fifth Avenue . . . and in a state of obvious inebriety hugged and kissed every pretty woman that passed, they would only say that I was a cold Beacon Street aristocrat, and read the New York *Nation* regularly. The *E[vening] P[ost]* will always be in the same position. I doubt whether anyone will believe it capable of committing a popular folly.[19]

For several months things ran smoothly under Schurz's direction, but privately Godkin was restive. In August he admonished the editor-in-chief: "In a talk with Villard today, he repeated a criticism which I have lately more than once heard from others—that we run some topics into the ground in the *Post*—that for instance there were too many articles on Conkling and Civil Service reform."[20] And to an unreceptive Henry Adams, Godkin complained that Schurz was sentimental. "If you dry one of his tears," Adams shot back, "I will denounce you at a stock-holders meeting. Every tear he sheds is worth at least an extra dollar on the dividends. Cultivate them! collect them!"

> You are no good yourself in the sobbing business, but you can effect a decent respect for real sympathy. I have always told you that your fatal defect was the incapacity to make a *popular* blunder . . . all your blunders are on the wrong side; they don't even make friends. What I want to see is some good, idiotic, gushing, *popular* blundering. We shall thrive on that.[21]

"The world doesn't begin to know what a man Schurz

was," claimed Henry Holt, who knew intimately and admired both Godkin and Schurz. "He was no sentimentalist, but his capacity of loving people and making them proud and happy by telling them so was a thing rare among great men—and rarer still among small ones."[22] Whatever the problems posed for Schurz and Godkin by their clashing personalities, it was obvious by the end of the first year that they would differ on policy. When Schurz went on vacation in the summer of 1882 Godkin used the occasion to alter *Evening Post* editorial policy. In one instance, he attacked Republican leader James G. Blaine, who had expressed a belated affection for civil service reform, charging that Blaine, as secretary of state, had "wallowed" in spoils like a "rhinoceros in an African pool."

The resultant uproar from the Blaine camp fell on Schurz's head. Blaine, in retaliation, reviewed Schurz's administration as secretary of the interior and alleged that he had employed the spoils system. Schurz fought back, but privately he remonstrated with Horace White about Godkin's conduct. Clover Adams—the wife of Henry Adams—was one of Godkin's readers at this time who sharply criticized his "foolish remarks." "He would carry more weight," she declared, "if he made fewer snap judgments."[23]

Schurz was also sulking over Villard's unauthorized interference in *Post* policy. As Schurz complained to White in October:

> To keep the *Ev[ening] Post* . . . not only above reproach but also above suspicion has been the object of constant care, as I also felt it to be a matter of duty and honor. You can readily imagine my sensations when, point after point, I learned that the columns of the *Ev[ening] Post* had been disposed of, by an understanding with a banking house, for the publication of a long paper in the interest of certain great railroad enterprizes, which publication could not have been brought out without exposing the character of the *Ev[ening] Post* to the gravest suspicions.[24]

By this time Godkin's notes to Schurz had taken on an undisguisedly patronizing tone. A matter of sensitivity between them was the sort of editorial writing each wanted for the *Post*. Schurz brought to the *Evening Post* something Godkin lacked, a public following and a first-hand acquaintance with public affairs. He objected to Godkin's superficial treatment of issues and his habit of substituting irony and personal invective for argument. But Schurz never complained of Godkin's writing; it was Godkin who complained of Schurz's.

Reared in the tradition of William Cobbett and of generations of Irish agitators, Godkin valued pungency over accuracy. Personalities, exaggeration, and ridicule were the legitimate tools of polemic. A stock complaint of Godkin against the scholarly contributors to the Nation was the heaviness of their writing. Schurz, a literary stylist rather than a polemicist, measured writing by more exacting standards. Godkin would have said of Schurz, as Charles Francis Adams, Jr., did of his brother Henry, that his writing reflected "the German professional belief that vivacity is trickery, and that there is some positive merit in dullness."

One facet of the disagreement between Godkin and Schurz is suggested by a note Godkin sent Schurz in the summer of 1883, advising him not to publish the widely discussed Harvard Phi Beta Kappa address of Evening Post stockholder Charles Francis Adams, Jr.:

> People will read a little about such things, but only a little in a daily paper in hot weather. And our business is to make the Post readable and attractive, and raise our circulation and increase our dividends, and not to publish long essays on the Comparative Merits of Classical and Modern Literature. . . .[25]

Technically Godkin was right, but the publicity the press gave to Adams's address proved Schurz right, and Godkin belatedly directed Garrison to publish the address in the Nation.

Despite these and other incidents relations between the two editors remained outwardly friendly until the spring of 1883. In April Schurz attended a dinner party at Godkin's home in company with Clover Adams, Henry James, and others.[26] But the next month Godkin issued his long-deferred declaration of independence. By-passing Schurz, he arranged an audience with Villard and White and demanded Schurz's title and authority—the alternative, he would retire from the Post and take the Nation with him. As he told White:

> The *Post* suffers . . . from heaviness and monotony. . . . We
> are not gaining circulation, and I can't say I think we deserve
> it. Half our editorial matter every day is dull reading on un-
> interesting subjects. I certainly should never think of reading
> it if I could help it. . . . I found Garrison yesterday in despair
> at the prospect as regards the *Nation*.[27]

After much discussion Villard and White gave in. Godkin
would get Schurz's job for two years; if by then things
were not calmed down, White would become editor-in-chief.
But Schurz knew nothing of this until June. Then, while
Schurz was preoccupied with fending off attacks on himself
by the Jay Gould newspapers, White broached the subject.
At length Schurz agreed to surrender the editorship to Godkin. White somewhat naively proposed that Schurz himself
effect the arrangements with Godkin and left with his ailing
wife for Europe.

Until now Schurz had heard nothing of the scheme from
Godkin. But on 18 June Godkin, impatient at not having
received from Schurz a formal capitulation, addressed the
editor-in-chief:

> Not hearing from you, and not knowing what [Horace White]
> actually said to you, I think it desirable that I should repeat
> the substance of what I said to him. I do so in the friendliest
> spirit toward you personally, and with the strong hope, that
> you will take it as simple *business,* as far as I am concerned.
> It was that I considered after two years' observation, that the
> *Evening Post* experiment, as at present managed, was a fail-
> ure. . . . though you and I agree on most public questions, we
> differ as to the *quality* of the writing. . . . [White and Villard]
> agree with me in general terms, and White informed me that
> you were willing to turn the control over to me whenever you
> went on your vacation. I should be glad to know now when
> that will be. . . .[28]

"As far as you are concerned," Godkin added, "I am desirous
that all this should cause you as little inconvenience of any
kind as possible. I am acting, as I say simply from business
motives which at my time of life I cannot overlook."

To this Schurz sent a courteous reply, but his words did
not mask his annoyance at his colleague's tactics:

> I did not speak to you [about your scheme to supplant me as
> editor-in-chief] because I expected, as I thought I might, that
> you would speak to me. In fact, I am inclined to think it would
> have been better had the whole plan from the beginning been

discussed between us. . . . Of course, I do not object to anything thought necessary or desirable for the furtherance of interests which are those of others as well as my own. I told White that I had intended to begin my vacation about the 1st of August, which he thought would be satisfactory. But we may talk this over.[29]

Saturday, 15 July 1883, dawned hot and humid in New York City. Godkin pulled his stout frame astride his ubiquitous saddle horse and rode to Dobbs Ferry to confer with Villard. Later in the day rain began to fall steadily, and Godkin and his horse remained weatherbound overnight at the financier's. The two men talked at length of the deteriorating *Post* editorial situation. Villard proposed that "in order to prevent future embarrassments Schurz be invited to go to Europe for a year as a correspondent of the *Post*." Godkin eagerly assented.[30]

But when Villard conveyed the proposal to Schurz, Schurz demurred. All that was needed to apply a match to the tinder was an editorial crisis. It came within days when a nationwide strike of railway telegraphers erupted. Without consulting Godkin, Schurz set about to align the *Evening Post* alongside the *Times* and the *Herald* in a policy of neutrality, the strikers enjoying some public sympathy. Thereupon Godkin brushed Schurz aside and penned a vigorous attack on the workers.[31] Without waiting for clearance from Schurz, he put his editorial into type and left for the Berkshires on a holiday. When Schurz read the editorial, he countered with one of his own, "Two Sides of the Telegraphers' Strike," and the dispute was joined. Further to exacerbate things, Godkin ordered Garrison to reprint his editorial in the *Nation* and ignore Schurz's. The *New York Herald* reacted to Godkin's editorial by saying that the *Evening Post* "thinks telegraph operators ought not to be allowed to strike at all. Laws ought to be passed, it seems, to forbid them to do so."[32]

Schurz, who was still striving to maintain an appearance of editorial unity, countered with a few lines in defense of Godkin's editorial. This only irked Godkin, who would not have stooped, he contemptuously told Garrison, to reply to criticism from the *Herald*.

Meanwhile, Schurz sent back to Godkin, with proposals for minor change, another outspoken editorial on the strike.

This was too much for Godkin, who snorted to Garrison: "The way Schurz's courage oozes out towards the end of my article, and makes him put in a shilly-shally qualifying paragraph is very comic." To assure himself of Garrison's loyalty in the tilt, Godkin added, "If anything goes wrong with you I will retire into a monastery."[33] To Schurz he wrote more explicitly:

> I do not agree with . . . you. . . . The basis of my position is that the telegraphers have a duty to the public, and . . . choosing the time when they can inflict most damage on the public to strike, aggravates their offense. . . . I think . . . it is wise policy for the *Post* . . . to be the paper which in times of excitement, when the others are running amuck, and talking wild nonsense as the *Herald* and *Times* are now, holds on to law and common sense. We shall gain not lose subscribers in this way and attacks by other newspapers are simply advertisements.[34]

Bowing to the editor-in-chief's objections, Godkin told Schurz he would cancel the editorial. But then, to Schurz's dismay, he forwarded it to Garrison to print it in the *Nation*. (As the *Post*'s weekly edition, the *Nation* was technically under Schurz's editorial supervision, but, instead, Garrison took his orders from Godkin.)[35] A week later Schurz left on his vacation and, as arranged, Godkin stepped into his shoes as editor-in-chief. But the deposing of Schurz, far from ending the dispute, only heated it up. On the eighth of August Godkin editorially flayed the telegraph strikers in the *Evening Post*, asserting that "the ten thousand to forty thousand men which some of our modern corporations now employ in telegraphic or railroad service are an army, and have to be governed on the same principles as an army."[36] This was more than the combative Schurz, nursing his wounds in the Catskills, could stand. Angrily he wrote Godkin:

> I dissent emphatically. . . . No man has to be "governed" on army principles except those who enlist in the army. . . . The relations between those who sell their labor by the day and their employers, whether the latter be great corporations or single individuals, are simple contract relations, and it seems to me monstrous to hold that the act of one or more laboring men ending that contract by stopping their work is, or should be, considered and treated in any sense as desertion from the army is considered and treated.[37]

Schurz conceded that the public had an interest in questions that the "employment of large numbers of men by corporations has brought forth," but: "Whatever legislation we may have on that subject . . . should proceed from the point of view that, while the business of transportation and telegraphing should not be at the mercy of every demagogue, the laboring man should not be at the mercy of the corporations . . . when the latter indulge in such practices as stock-watering and the like and then seek to grind out dividends by cutting down the wages of their working men. . . ." Instead of laws interfering with the right to strike, as Godkin proposed, Schurz urged laws for the arbitration of labor disputes. Then men would not have to leave their jobs in order to gain redress of their grievances. Unless the *Evening Post* changed its ways, declared Schurz, it would become known as a corporation organ, in which case he would leave the paper.[38]

Godkin's acerbic reply was written but never sent; his usual intermediary, White, still being absent in Europe, he chose to give Schurz an especially spirited answer in person. But what Godkin said in his unsent letter is instructive:

> I am very sorry you do not like the article in yesterday's *Post*. I was equally touched by those of yours on the same subject, as on many others during the past two years. But I do not see that any good would result from our discussing the matter. . . . I informed Horace White before he left that I would under no circumstances remain connected with the *Post* under your editorship . . . and I conveyed the same information to Mr. Villard, they being the persons who had invited me to join the paper. They agreed, thereupon, that I should assume the editorship and the responsibility of the paper. . . .[39]

The *Post*, Godkin's unsent letter continued, henceforward would reflect Godkin's views and he was "not afraid of being thought the organ of a corporation." Schurz, reluctantly persuaded that he must sever his connection with the paper, hurried to Dobbs Ferry to confer with Villard, spending the night of 13 August there. Little came of the meeting; Villard was preoccupied with the stock market crisis and his troubles arising from it, so that he had little time for those of his German-American compatriot. Cooperation with Godkin, Schurz dejectedly wrote his children, seemed impossible.[40] Schurz went back to the mountains and resumed his sulking.

Meanwhile the victor in the tilt was making the most of his new status. When the margins on Godkin's stock market speculations became imperiled by the financial crisis, he called on Villard for help. From Mrs. Villard, Godkin borrowed more than $16,000—repayment of which she obtained only with difficulty. Simultaneously, at his own request, the new editor-in-chief put aside his duties for a six-week Northern Pacific outing with Villard and his party in the west. "Mr. Godkin is anxious to go to the opening of the Northern Pacific with me; so I suppose you will have to stay," Villard told a disappointed Horace White. The occasion was the opening of the main line of the railway, for which Villard imported at great expense a party of distinguished guests from Europe.[41]

When Godkin returned to New York early in October the situation was unchanged. His remarks to Schurz before his departure for the west had been harsh. Apprised of Schurz's still wounded feelings, Godkin dispatched through White a note of regret, while privately to a friend he voiced a rare expression of sentiment: "I am going about with the sensation which makes me miserable of having wounded and alarmed an excellent man, for whom I have the utmost esteem."[42] But the situation was beyond repair, as was evident from Schurz's rejoinder to Godkin's note:

> White gave me your note of today and I need hardly tell you that I was sincerely glad to receive your disclaimer of unkind intentions in the conversation referred to, and that I accept it in a corresponding spirit. . . . If there are "irreconcilable differences of opinion" between us which it is "idle to discuss," or which cannot be solved or accommodated by discussion, it seems impossible that we should work together and sustain common responsibilities.[43]

Having said this and more to Godkin, Schurz prepared to leave the Evening Post. Both men were now in wretched humor. Schurz was facing an uncertain financial future and was paying for the bickerings and worries of late with insomnia and attacks of palpitations; Godkin was venting his irritation in letters. To Norton he ill-temperedly wrote in November, ". . . I suppose you have seen a good deal of Matthew Arnold. I got only one glimpse of him. The fact is that the way Englishmen of distinction have fallen into delivering themselves over on their arrival here to obscure, illiterate, and disreputable people, makes it difficult to see anything of them at all."[44]

So that Godkin could obtain the services of Joseph B. Bishop, a colorful editorial writer for the *Tribune*, he asked for authority to fire the *Post*'s managing editor Robert Burch. The task of notifying Burch, "a worthy middle-aged man, hard-working, faithful, with a wife and family," proved a challenge to Godkin's instinctive aversion to compassion.

For several weeks in the fall of 1883 Schurz's impending departure from the *Post* was a matter of notoriety in newspaper circles. But there had been no formal announcement to the press, chiefly because Godkin was opposed to airing their differences over the telegraphers' strike. White, who as Villard's agent was the real power in the *Evening Post* syndicate, had throughout the dispute taken the line of least resistance, which meant giving in to Godkin's demands.[45] But now Schurz took the offensive. In a session with White on 8 December Schurz lost his temper and denounced Godkin, leaving the usually imperturbable White shaken. Hastily White agreed to publish an account of Schurz's resignation in accordance with Schurz's wishes. The announcement, as it appeared in the eastern newspapers on the eleventh of December, stated that "in consequence of serious differences of opinion between himself and his associates concerning the treatment of important public questions in the editorial columns," Schurz was withdrawing from the paper.[46]

In his session with White Schurz had threatened to make public Godkin's conduct if the notice did not appear as agreed. Apprised of this by White, Godkin rushed back into the fray. Addressing Schurz the same day, Godkin threatened to retaliate in kind to any criticisms of him.[47] Schurz's reply was not calculated to still the troubled waters. For the first time he spoke openly of the "underhanded way" in which his removal as editor had been accomplished. To this Godkin shot back that his colleague's insinuation was "very offensive" and would "prevent any friendly intercourse between us until it is remitted."[48] Schurz retorted: "Of course I do not want to insult you, and I willingly withdraw any word which may look as if I intended to do so," but then he advanced to the charge:

> This, however, does not change the fact that the manner in
> which the things referred to were brought about, 'jarred very
> harshly upon my notions of fair and frank dealings.' . . . When
> I found that there had been conferences about our affairs be-
> hind my back and secret understandings touching myself . . .
> and the dropping of the conversation now and then when I
> entered your room unexpectedly, it was, I must confess, a very
> painful shock to me.[49]

By this time the newspapers had taken up the dispute.
The *New York Times* and the *Springfield Republican* printed
interviews with the combatants that emphasized their editorial differences.[50] "While I was gone on my summer vacation," Schurz told a reporter from the *Republican*, "articles
were published about the telegraphers' strike against which
I protested. I have taken no part in the editorial management
since then." Asked by the *Republican* reporter if he wrote the
articles to which Schurz referred, Godkin answered yes.
"They fully expressed my views, which are the same as I
have always entertained, and were opposed to the strikers."

Before the publication of the above interview, the *Republican*—apparently on the basis of a remark by Godkin to
Evening Post trustee David A. Wells—printed the false story
that Schurz was stepping down as editor because he found
"close editorial work from day to day was irksome to him."
Angry letters now flew back and forth daily between the
disputants, Schurz demanding that Godkin deny responsibility for the untrue story in the *Republican*. Godkin obliged
but the next day fired back a suspiciously different version,
along with further disparaging remarks about Schurz's writing. Schurz retaliated: "As you have confided to me the
'grievous mistake' you made [in joining the *Evening Post*
combination with me] I will in conclusion confide to you
mine. It was that, when we formed our association, my easy
confidence in human nature . . . led me to disregard the
warning of some friends who predicted substantially what
has now come to pass."[51]Godkin shot back that his adversary
was trying to make himself out a "better writer than me,"
to which Schurz accurately responded with a denial and the

plea: "You cannot possibly [be] more tired of this discussion than I am. By all means, let us have peace and take my good wishes."[52]

But there was more. During all this Schurz had been setting down for the *North American Review* his views on the telegraphers' strike.[53] The article appeared late in January 1884 and did not mention Godkin or the *Evening Post* by name. But when Godkin read it he angrily picked up his pen again to accuse Schurz of feigning his attitude toward the strikers because "as a public man" he intended "to run for office again." To this Schurz retorted that it was not the first time he had "known a man who felt himself discomfited in an argument, to resort of the expedient of attacking his opponent's motives."[54]

"Such quarrels are excessively distasteful to me . . ." Schurz declared, "But you have injured me so much and in so many ways already, that I should not be expected . . . to submit to much more." With that Schurz gained the last word. The "editorship of all the talents" had fallen, opined the *Tribune's* Isaac Bromley, because there were "too many mules in the pasture." Although there was a deeper reason for the quarrel, it was true that in the inordinately self-confident Schurz, Godkin had met a worthy adversary. "Schurz possessed an unquestionable gift for friendship," declares Arthur Hogue, "but he also seems to have had a gift for irritating people and . . . enjoyed controversy and the clash of wills — always of course in defense of his 'principles.' "[55]

With Schurz ousted Godkin now turned to Villard. At the height of the Schurz-Godkin embroglio the *Post's* proprietor had been prostrated by financial worries. Sensing in Villard's illness an opportunity to gain financial control of the *Evening Post*, Godkin set about to obtain backers. To James Bryce went a veiled explanation of why he was cancelling his trip to the British Isles in the summer of 1884: "Villard's breakup . . . coupled with Schurz's withdrawal made it necessary I should stick to my post, *in more senses than one*."[56] Irritated by Godkin's attempts to supplant him, Villard gave thought to returning him the *Nation* in order to be rid of him. But prodded by Garrison and other Godkin supporters, the proprietor at length consented to sell Godkin Mrs. Villard's controlling interest in the *Post*.

At this point Godkin's credit met with obstacles; failing to obtain in England the capital he sought, he turned instead to Wall Street. April 1886 found him writing William C. Whitney—whom privately he found "a bad fellow"—"Has it ever come in your way to speak to Mr. Payne again about the matter of the stock? The chance of getting hold of the paper is a good one which may pass away, and which is very important to me. . . ."[57] August still found Godkin, as Garrison informed his sister, "sanguine of being able to effect a purchase of the *Post* (including H. White's interest)." And to one of his financial backers, Frederick Sheldon, Godkin wrote the following month: "I am waiting Villard's arrival in a week or two to push on the affair. . . . Pierpont Morgan seems at present disposed to behave handsomely, *but this is strictly confidential.*"[58]

The full extent of Godkin's financial involvement with J. P. Morgan remains a secret, but it is known that, in addition to seeking Morgan's aid to buy the *Evening Post,* he was indebted to the financier for other loans in the amount of $23,000. Once Villard chided his editor for seeking so controversial a patron, whereupon Godkin irascibly replied that "no money would have induced me to 'serve under' Pierpont Morgan or anyone else. The proposed plan of purchase of the *Evening Post* involved no such risk." Morgan thought so well of Godkin's views that he was one of several New York financiers who in 1903 aided in endowing the Godkin Lectures at Harvard University.

Villard ultimately elected to keep the *Evening Post* and with it Godkin as editor-in-chief. Periodically during the next fifteen years their dealings were punctuated by flareups. Godkin sometimes let go his frustrations in letters to Villard, sometimes in letters to others. In an 1893 altercation he took up with Villard a long-festering issue, the periodic charge in the press that he was "editing a railroad organ under Villard's orders, for dishonest purposes." Though not denying to Villard that when he joined the *Evening Post* he knew "all about the connection of the *Post* with the Northern Pacific perfectly well," nonetheless, Godkin complained, it had been very unpleasant for him as editor "to have this sort of thing going around the country."[59] To James Bryce Godkin's bad temper spilled out: "Our old friend Villard sailed for Egypt a week ago, I may say, in disgrace. He has been kicked out of every enterprise he was connected with here, and is universally denounced as a visionary, if not worse, who has made money at the expense of other people."[60]

Meantime Schurz kept his resolve not to reenter public life; instead he sought for a time to rebuild his shattered journalistic career. In 1885 Godkin learned that his former colleague was trying to buy a controlling interest in the Boston *Post*, whereupon he wrote Bryce: "Schurz, I am sorry to say, is going to try another newspaper venture . . . in which I am quite sure he will make another failure."[61] Simultaneously Garrison was expressing to Fanny Villard wonderment that Schurz "could so misconceive his talents as to re-embark in journalism."[62] The purchase of the Boston *Post* failing, Schurz applied for the vacant editorship of the *Boston Daily Advertiser*, only to be refused after Godkin's views were presented to the stockholders. Although Schurz knew this and regarded his meddlesome former associate as the author of his continued misfortune, he wisely refrained from reopening the controversy.[63] In the years that followed Schurz occasionally corresponded with Godkin about public questions, but he never restored his former cordiality with the younger man. With the death of George William Curtis in 1892, Schurz returned to journalism as Curtis's anonymous successor as chief editorial writer of *Harper's Weekly*. He retained this post until 1898, when he withdrew in opposition to *Harper's* policy favoring America's drift toward war with Spain.

For a generation sensitivity about the Schurz-Godkin-Villard altercations persisted in the *Evening Post* family. Partly to avoid a clash with Godkin and partly in an effort to hide the squabbles, Garrison and Villard aided Godkin in publicly fostering the illusion that Godkin, not Schurz, had been made editor-in-chief of the *Post* in 1881. Mainly through Godkin's efforts more than a dozen standard reference works came to attest to 1881 as the date he assumed the editorship. Godkin went further; he dropped hints in the press that he instead of Villard had obtained financial control of the

Evening Post in 1881. In the face of this the Villards, always touchy about their role in Schurz's ouster, maintained either a discreet silence or else joined Godkin and his family in supplying inexact data about Schurz's connection with the *Evening Post*.

What did the Schurz-Godkin imbroglio signify? Did Schurz — as Godkin, Garrison, and several historians imply — by surrendering his editorial post to Godkin perform a service to journalism? Probably not. In the first place Schurz's integrity and his literary powers — greater, as time was to prove, than Godkin's — were needed in daily journalism. In an era of economic and social transformation in the United States, Schurz's pen, whatever its didactic limitations, held greater authority than Godkin's. Godkin, the embattled spokesman for laissez-faire and a fading genteel tradition, lacked the expanded outlook that the new United States demanded. The *Evening Post* addressed itself to a cultivated and influential audience; under Schurz's leadership — and without overstating that mugwump's attachment to the new liberalism — the paper might conceivably have gained tutelage over the new forces. Instead, under Godkin and his early twentieth-century successors, it shrank into the corporate organ that an 1890s versifier deplored:

> Godkin the righteous, known of old
> Priest of the nation's moral health
> Within whose *Post* we daily read
> The Gospel of the Rights of Wealth.[64]

The *New York Times* doubtless spoke with a degree of truth when it expressed the opinion that Godkin had obtained the editorship of the *Evening Post* "by a series of maneuvers of which an honest man would have no special reason to be proud."[65]

Chapter Ten
Mugwumps For Cleveland

Oh, we are the salt of the Earth
And the pick of the people too;
We're all of us men of worth
And vastly better than you!

. . .

Chorus
Sing ho! the political flirts!
The moral immaculate few!
There's Curtis and Godkin and Corporal Schurz
And the Boston 'Tizer, too.

In 1884 Godkin momentarily set aside his differences with Schurz while they joined Horace White and other independents in supporting the Democratic presidential aspirations of Grover Cleveland.

Returning in the 1880s to New York to live, Godkin set about cultivating friendly relations with influential leaders in the business world, among them Andrew Carnegie, William C. Whitney, and J. P. Morgan. Frequenting the leading clubs, he spent many hours at the fashionable Century Club. He seldom saw his old patrons Olmsted, Brace, and Norton now, and the bitterness attending the election of 1884 would put an end to his friendly relations with Whitelaw Reid and Henry Cabot Lodge.

In 1884 Godkin, now fifty-three, married thirty-eight-year-old Katharine B. Sands of the wealthy and socially prominent Sands family of New York and London. A woman of sharply opposite appearance and mien from the statuesque and sociable Fanny Godkin, Katharine Godkin nonetheless made the marriage a successful one. Winters the two spent with Lawrence in their apartment at 115 East 25th Street, and summers they spent in an antique summer hotel near New Rochelle that they leased from Henry Holt. There were no additional children; Lawrence, a recent graduate of Harvard

Law School, lived a bachelor's life at home most of his life.

That fall the Board of Overseers of Harvard, who earlier had assented to granting Godkin an honorary Master of Arts and to his appointment as a Visitor to the College, further honored him by approving his selection as "Lecturer in Free Trade for the year 1884-85." The lectures were not given.

A topic of drawing-room speculation during the Gilded Age was the authorship of two brash, anonymous novels satirizing politics and manners, *Democracy* and *The Breadwinners*. Detecting similar crudities of style in them, Charles F. Adams, Jr., proposed to Godkin in 1884 that the *Nation* publish his finding that the novels were by the same author. Unknown to Adams, Godkin was in on part of the secret of the authorship. He at once forwarded the Bostonian's letter to Charles's brother, Henry, with the query, "What shall I say to this?" Reading Charles's description of the "coarse, half educated" execution of the novels sent Henry—who with Clover and their bosom friend John Hay had concocted the literary hoax—into paroxysms of laughter. What Henry, in his glee at having hoodwinked his older brother, did not know was that Godkin relished being on both sides of an intrigue and had long been keeping secret from Henry that it was Charles who wrote the critical review in the *Nation* of Henry's *Albert Gallatin*. But Henry now had come to regard Godkin as a meddlesome and unsafe confidant, and their friendship had cooled.

Tradition has it that Charles A. Dana had Godkin in mind when he acidly affixed the name "Mugwump," from an Algonquin word meaning "chief," to the eastern intellectuals and politicians who bolted the Republican Party during the 1880s to become independents in politics.

In 1884 Godkin and White horrified some of their readers by bringing the *Evening Post* and the *Nation* out in support of the presidential aspirations of Democrat Grover Cleveland. To many of the northern public, conditioned to the post Civil War tactic of "waving the bloody sheet" in order to keep the Republican party in power, this was nothing short of treason. But Godkin and White saw a moral issue; the Republican nominee, they believed, had used an official position for private gain. "The Blaine Movement," Godkin assured

James Bryce, "is really a conspiracy of jobbers to seize on the Treasury, under the lead of a most unprincipled adventurer."[1] (Privately the New York *Tribune*'s Whitelaw Reid remonstrated with Horace White about the charges of the *Evening Post* against Blaine, pointing out that he knew all about White's whiskey speculations while serving in an official capacity during the Civil War.) Cheerfully accepting the Mugwump label, other reform-minded Republicans joined the Democratic revolt. A few hundred New York votes determined the election, which went to Cleveland by a narrow margin.[2]

Godkin emerged from the contest battle-scarred but content with its results. Among his reverses was a law suit for falsely alleging in the *Evening Post* that a Blaine backer in the clergy had been charged with moral turpitude. Cleveland generously paid half the cost of his defense. Editorially Godkin viewed the Democratic triumph as a vindication of his policy of putting the "public welfare ahead of party loyalty."[3] Other editors now set about to declare the political independence of their papers.

Cleveland's first administration met with the qualified approval of Godkin and his colleagues; editorially the *Evening Post* viewed it as one of the bright spots in an otherwise dreary decade. Godkin was heartened by Cleveland's announced support of tariff reduction, civil service reform, and economy in government.[4] Ready to overlook the sexual indiscretions of the president—which Godkin editorially found in the tradition of great Americans of the past—his bibulous habits, which to a slight extent the editor shared, and his broken election promises—which could be blamed on the party rather than the man—the *Nation* and the *Evening Post* were genuinely sorry to see the president go at the end of his term.

With no major developments in foreign policy, Godkin found less to criticize than in any previous administration. This, together with his liking for Cleveland's hard money policy, kept his relations with the president on an amicable level. The Clevelands entertained the Godkins in the White House, and the Godkins once called on the Clevelands at their retreat at the Saranac Inn in upstate New York.

Some hint of the respect in which the editor was held at the White House during Cleveland's first term is contained in the Thomas F. Bayard correspondence. Cleveland's secretary of state was repelled by the patronizing tone of the *Evening Post*, which he found was published "upon such a height of superiority and egotism that everything that comes from it towards a Democrat has an insufferable flavor of condescension." Yet Bayard often consulted with the *Post's* editors on matters relating to administration policy, which, except for the early days of the Hayes administration, was a novel experience for White and Godkin.[5]

Although Godkin occasionally exchanged letters with Cleveland and with his secretary of state, the bulk of the official correspondence was between Secretary Bayard and White, whom Bayard regarded as the official spokesman of the *Evening Post*. White, associate editor and president of the *Evening Post* Publishing Company, usually held an identity with Godkin on public questions, and some of his editorials were so pessimistic that they were mistaken for those of Godkin. The following passage from a letter that White wrote to Bayard in 1886 could have been written by Godkin:

> I thank you for sending me a copy of the President's message relative to the Chinese Treaty stipulation. I shall take it home and read it tomorrow, and shall *endeavor* to agree with you, for I always find that a comfort. It is hard to keep civilization going. Sometimes I think Bismarck's way is best.[6]

When a frustrated Bayard stepped down from his post in 1889, White consoled him: "Your management of the State Department will be vindicated by history, and will be better appreciated by your contemporaries when, if ever, Mr. Blaine essays to do something besides peddle consulships to his friends."[7]

White was obliquely pointing to one of the complaints of the *Evening Post* against Cleveland, that he had failed to live up to his campaign promise to bring about consular reform.[8] Especially irritating to White and Godkin was the unfitness of some of Cleveland's appointees. Once Godkin wrote the president in a vain attempt to block a cabinet appointment, although later he found reason to praise the official in question, Secretary of the Treasury Daniel Manning. To Secretary Bayard he protested a diplomatic assignment, and, when the able Republican Henry White was dismissed from his post as first secretary of the American legation in London, Godkin complained directly to the president about it. Afterwards Godkin's son Lawrence told White his dismissal was the one regret his father had about the new administration.[9]

One Cleveland appointment that proved embarrassing was that of Godkin's friend, Sedgwick, who in 1886 was sent to Mexico as a special agent of the Department of State to inquire into the vexatious Cutting case.[10] While in the Mexican capital Sedgwick became the center of a scandal. He was charged with having submitted himself and his country to insult at the hands of drunken Mexican male companions and having been found dead drunk in a whorehouse. Although the weight of evidence was against Sedgwick, the charges appeared to have been politically motivated, and Cleveland refused to recall him. In the *Evening Post* Godkin defended Sedgwick, whom he had personally introduced to Washington officialdom, but privately he conceded that the scandal had ruined his colleague as a diplomat.[11]

In 1888 Cleveland lost his bid for reelection. The *Nation* and the *Evening Post* heightened the bitterness of the campaign by intimating that Republican contender Benjamin Harrison was "not a safe man to be President." After the election Godkin and his Mugwump associates made it clear that they had no intention of supporting the new president.[12]

One of the problems awaiting Harrison as he took the oath of office was the Bering Sea (fur seal) question.[13] The outgoing Cleveland administration could hardly have chosen a stickier dispute to bequeath to its successor, a dispute Godkin found made-to-order for attacking the new administration. The particular object of his wrath was Harrison's Secretary of State James G. Blaine. Blaine ignited the fur seal controversy, Godkin in 1891 implied in the *Evening Post*, when he "took the law into his own hands by authorizing or permitting American cruisers to seize British ships in the open sea, and carry them into port as lawful prizes."[14]

In actuality the aggressive policy of which Godkin

complained was an inheritance from the Cleveland administration. Blaine reentered the State Department in 1889 to be
confronted by a Democratic *fait accompli,* supported by
Congress and an approving public opinion. Discretion would
have dictated a reversal of policy, but Blaine set about to
make the best—or, as Godkin would assert, the worst—of
the situation. In January 1891, at the height of the battle of
words with England, Godkin described what he characterized as the "strictly journalistic" diplomacy of the secretary
of state:

> He always begins his discussions, as we said the other day,
> horns down. He assumes from the outset that his adversary
> is a tricky, grasping, light-headed fellow, whom he is deter-
> mined to expose in his true light to a disgusted world. How
> the affair will end, whether in peace or war, he cares but
> little, if he can achieve his own rhetorical triumph.[15]

Undeniably the ailing Blaine in his diplomatic duel with Lord
Salisbury was pompous and irascible. But to allege, as Godkin did, that his handling of the legally indefensible position
handed to him by his predecessors was wholly inexpert was
hardly fair. If ever a situation called for Blaine's ability "to
raise up a cloud of words," as Godkin described it, this was it.
But when a court of arbitration in 1893 decided the controversy in favor of England, the *Nation* hailed the verdict as
proving Blaine's history "to be fiction; his geography pure
fancy, and his international law a mere whim."[16] Encouraging
Godkin in his stand was his acquaintance Sir Charles Russell,
chief counsel for Great Britain in the arbitration.[17]

In the midst of the Bering Sea controversy, the Barrundia
affair became a minor *cause célèbre* early in 1891. An American naval officer, Commander Reiter, was relieved of the
command of his ship and reprimanded by the secretary of
the navy for failing to offer asylum to the Guatemalan fug-
itive, General Barrundia. Barrundia was shot to death by
Guatemalan authorities while resisting arrest on an American merchant ship anchored near Reiter's vessel in the
harbor of San José. Godkin joined critics of the administration in censuring the Navy Department for disciplining the
officer, declaring that it is not "incumbent on American
commanders to pursue refugees with offers of asylum."[18] The

editor's legally sound but otherwise intemperate position in
the Barrundia dispute sprang largely from his hostility toward his one-time friendly acquaintance Henry Cabot Lodge,
who had condemned Commander Reiter's course. In his approval of Reiter's stand Godkin quoted what he termed the
"rational and weighty" remarks of a doughty and sometimes
irresponsible Blaine antagonist, Congressman Boutelle of
Maine: ". . . I have little sympathy with the idea that the
principal duty of the United States Government and its navy
is to send its ships around the globe to hunt up the political conspirators, revolutionists, anarchists, and nihilists of
other countries in order to aid them in their attempts to
overthrow established and orderly governments. . . ."[19]

On another occasion, during the New Orleans Mafia incident of 1891, Godkin surmounted his partisan feelings
toward Secretary of State Blaine and endorsed the administration's course. On 14 March eleven persons of Italian ex-
traction were dragged from jail by a mob of citizens and
lynched as an aftermath to the unsolved murder, supposedly
at the hands of the Mafia, of the New Orleans chief of
police.[20] To the protests of an indignant Italian government,
Blaine replied that the affair was not one of federal jurisdiction. For once Godkin agreed with the Man from Maine,
his only criticism of the secretary being that Blaine was too
conciliatory towards the Italians. "There is," the captious
editor concluded, "really hardly any material in the case
for diplomatic discussion."[21]

While Blaine was seeking to placate the outraged Italian
government, public attention shifted to Chile. There, early
in 1891, a long-standing feud between President Balmaceda
and Congress erupted into a civil war in which the United
States shortly became involved. Early in May a rebel (congressional) vessel, the Itata, put in at San Diego, California,
preparatory to taking on a shipment of arms purchased in the
United States for the rebel cause. The attorney-general of
the United States, fearful of complications with the legal
Balmaceda government, ordered the Itata detained as a
would-be offender against the neutrality laws of the United
States. But on 6 May the vessel escaped from the harbor—
kidnapping a United States deputy in the process—and

headed for Chile. A United States cruiser gave chase, and for a time a clash seemed imminent.[22]

In the *Evening Post* and the *Nation* Godkin left no doubt of his congressionalist sympathies. Citing authorities on international law, he contended that the rebels were entitled to belligerent rights; attacking the *Itata* on the open sea would be a violation of neutrality "by taking part in the hostilities on the side of President Balmaceda."[23] He brushed aside the argument of the attorney-general and the *New York Times* that United States neutrality laws obligated it — under the Geneva findings in the *Alabama* case — to pursue the *Itata,* asserting that there was neither "in the correspondence, or negotiations, or litigation arising out of the *Alabama* claims, the shadow of a suggestion, much less an assertion, that Great Britain was bound or had the right to pursue any of the escaped Confederate cruisers on the high seas."[24]

The position of Godkin and other anti-administration spokesmen was upheld by the courts, and the *Itata,* which had surrendered to the United States authorities, was returned to its owners. But in his argument in favor of the British-backed congressionalist rebel faction, Godkin was being inconsistent. During the War of the Pacific, he argued that *de facto* control, rather than approval of a regime, was the sole criterion for United States recognition.[25] Now he put forth the opposite argument, that because Balmaceda had control of the government did not justify the United States in "countenancing" this "impeachable traitor and usurper."[26] Balmaceda, Godkin to the contrary notwithstanding, was, in fact, the legitimate Chilean head of state.

In September the civil war ended in a congressional vic-tory, a revolutionary junta assuming power pending formal elections. But the end of hostilities did not bring tranquility to Chile; a relentless persecution of the defeated followers of President Balmaceda followed. The luckier among them found asylum in foreign legations and on foreign cruisers, while Balmaceda, who had been offered asylum in the Argentine legation, committed suicide. Antiforeign feeling ran high, especially against the United States for having persisted in its policy of recognizing the Balmaceda government. To rub salt in the wounds, American Minister Patrick Egan opened his legation doors to fleeing Balmacedists.

In mid-October 1891 occurred the *Baltimore* incident, in which some American sailors on shore leave were set upon in Valparaiso by a Chilean mob. Two died and many more were stabbed or beaten, while Chilean police intervened with reluctance. After vainly waiting a week for an explanation from Chile, Acting Secretary of State Wharton—Blaine was ill at his home in Maine at the time—cabled, through the American minister, a strong protest to the Chilean government.

Godkin put the blame for the *Baltimore* outrage on the Harrison administration, finding the incident "the natural outcome of our whole treatment of Chili [*sic*] since the present Administration came into power."[27] He focussed his editorial anger on Blaine:

> That such an affair should be looked upon for one moment as likely to imperil seriously the good relations of the two countries, is a striking commentary on the way in which our diplomacy . . . has been conducted since the unfortunate day, in 1881, when Mr. James G. Blaine was converted into a Minister of Foreign Affairs.[28]

Forthrightly the editor set about to defend Chile: "If our Government had had to put up with a similar series of annoyances and slights from the British Minister and Navy during the rebellion, we venture to say British sailors in uniform would have run considerable risk in appearing on our streets in 1862. . . ."[29] The number one "slight" to Chile was United States Minister Egan, an "illiterate foreign adventurer" whom Blaine had imposed on the "cultivated, proud and sensitive men who represent the Chilian Republic." "We cannot recall in diplomatic history any such slight offered by a great Power to a friendly nation," extravagantly concluded Godkin.[30] Elsewhere in the *Evening Post* he explained with more candor that the appointment of the Irish Egan was "irritating to England and to her friends in Chili."[31]

In reality the amateur diplomat Egan appears to have performed his duties with ability and tact. Despite the attacks of the Cleveland press, he remained at his post, serving to the end of the Harrison administration. Theodore Roosevelt rated him almost on a par with Henry White, whom he thought "the most useful man in the entire diplomatic service."[32]

Accuracy was patently not Godkin's forte when he was angry. Blaine, alleged he, had provoked the latest crisis; had the secretary been a "civilized man," he would "have studiously avoided the faintest appearance of a resort to force until the resources of negotiation in this matter of the attack on the American sailors in Valparaiso had been completely exhausted."[33] (In reality, during the developments of which Godkin spoke, Blaine was ill in his Maine home; it was not he, but Acting Secretary Wharton in consultation with the president, who took the steps that Godkin denounced.[34]) Chile had shown "great patience," announced the editor, in the face of bullying from the United States. He retraced for his readers his version of the events of the civil war. When Balmaceda set about to "overturn the Republic,"

> . . . we at once . . . showed our sympathy with the traitor, and treated him—a rebel in arms—as the lawful Chilian government. When the men who . . . represented all that was left of the Constitution, tried to buy a few cases of arms in the United States, we pounced on them almost with fury as public enemies, and started one of the new cruisers, with great noise, to "blow them out of the water" for committing a misdemeanor.[35]

There was conclusive evidence, Godkin indicated, that the flagship of the United States squadron had been used during the civil war to furnish President Balmaceda with "important information about movements of the Congressional army." Moreover the United States minister had served Balmaceda as "an accomplice in a conspiracy for the overthrow of the Government to which he was accredited" and had been privately engaged with the Chilean president in a financial speculation.[36] The charges relating to the United States flagship were undoubtedly true, but there is little to support Godkin's other accusations.[37]

While Godkin was indiscriminately attacking the administration for its Chilean policy, the days stretched into weeks without a word of regret or explanation from Chile about the attack on the American sailors. The Chilean reply to Wharton's remonstrance of 23 October was considered inacceptable, and it remained unanswered. With tension mounting in the United States, President Harrison in his annual message to Congress on 9 December alluded to the dispute in terms unmistakably threatening to Chile, a message Godkin denounced in the *Evening Post* as "full from first to last of the grossest insults to the Chilian government, which in private life no civilized man would think of uttering without expecting to be knocked down by the person on whom they were heaped."[38] Hot-headed Chilean Foreign Minister Matta agreed; he replied to Harrison's message with an ill-tempered note, and editorial tempers flared on both sides. Godkin, his patriotism under attack, defended himself by attacking the chauvinism of his opponents. As he wrote:

> We never have the smallest difference with a foreign Power, when our newspapers and some of our public men do not at once begin to talk of an appeal to arms, to count our ships and guns, to accuse the other side of "arrogance and insult," and "mendacity," and "hypocrisy," and "deceit," and to assure the President of the support of Congress in case he should immediately resort to hostilities.[39]

Professional patriots of the Blaine stripe, charged Godkin in the *Evening Post* on 19 November, "seem to thank God that they have a country to disgrace by lying, cheating, double-dealing, sophistry, and humbug, and proposing to thrash any one who complains."[40] He compared American conduct with European standards and found the United States wanting. In Europe the "model of diplomatic discussion" was that of "two gentlemen seated at a table trying to clear up a misunderstanding or make a contract on a matter of business," whereas the model of the United States "often seems to be that of two hostile 'toughs' who have met by chance in a bar-room, and are bent on clearing off old scores, each watching closely lest the other should 'get the drop' on him."[41]

Godkin was now sixty and in uncertain health. Although he retained his rich sense of humor, he was not meeting his advancing years gracefully; he wasted an unconscionable amount of precious time envying young people. He was obsessed with the idea that the war hawks represented youth—the "young men," as he contemptuously styled journalists of the *New York Tribune* school. In one editorial, citing as his evidence a letter written by an adolescent, he defined jingoism as a juvenile plot—the work of "patriots under eighteen." "In every country in the world, it is the minors who are readiest to rally round the flag and hurl defiance against a world in arms. . . . But in no country but our own are these youths allowed to stir up bellicose passions in the public press and propose to fight first and negotiate afterwards."[42] Especially irritating to Godkin was the talk of "national honor." He offered this analogy:

> A man elopes with your wife, which is a deadly insult . . . and you are therefore "dishonored" if you do not fight him. . . . But even if you kill him, it does not restore your wife or your domestic peace. . . . The duel proves nothing except that neither of the disputants is afraid to fight.[43]

The controversy ended in January 1892, when Chile, bowing to a virtual ultimatum from President Harrison, acceded to United States demands and offered full satisfaction for the *Baltimore* incident. The public greeted the settlement with relief, but the circumstances surrounding the Chilean surrender—Harrison had hurried a warlike message to Congress while a reply from Chile to his ultimatum was daily expected—stirred the Cleveland press to renewed attacks on the administration.[44] In an emotional editorial entitled "The Shame of It," Godkin cried that "no episode nearly so discreditable is to be found in the annals of American diplomacy." He summed up the role of his country:

> We began the process of alienating and irritating the Chilians by the appointment of Egan as our Minister—in itself contemptuous to the verge of insult. We continued it by open displays of sympathy with Balmaceda during the civil war; by our seizure and pursuit of the *Itata*, in disregard of the law as laid down by our State Department; by permitting our naval officers during four months to sneer at, abuse, defy, and threaten the Chilians, with the permission or approval of our Navy Department and the loud encouragement of our Government press. When the riot occurred, we forced on

the Chilians, with an absolute disregard of the decencies of diplomatic intercourse, a view of governmental responsibility for mob violence which we had ourselves [in the New Orleans Mafia incident] a short time previously utterly repudiated.[45]

While Godkin was explaining to his readers that the behavior of President Harrison in the Chilean dispute had made him "an object of ridicule in Congress, and in fact all over the world,"[46] in Bridgeport, Connecticut, another jingo incident was making headlines. Godkin took editorial license later in describing it:

> . . . someone started the notion in Bridgeport, Conn., that it was an "insult" for a foreign vessel to come into an American port flying any flag but the stars and stripes. Within a day or two in came a British ship flying the Union Jack. Instant preparations were made by the local patriots to board her and mob the captain. Before the eruption actually took place, however, some one suggested telegraphing to the State Department to find out whether it was an insult or not for a foreign vessel to fly her own flag in our ports.[47]

None of the events of the Harrison years had reconciled Godkin to the defeat of Grover Cleveland for reelection four years earlier. Although he disagreed on some matters with the expresident, he spoke approvingly of Cleveland's conservatism, and in 1892 he once again supported him for reelection. Committed to the support of the Democratic national ticket, the *Evening Post* during the campaign that eventuated in Cleveland's victory omitted its customary campaign exposé of Tammany Hall politicians seeking reelection. Critics of Godkin were unable to contain their amusement. "Now the *Post* has always held," noted Harry T. Peck, "that one should act in municipal matters without any thought of party, and never mix considerations of expediency with a plain civic duty." Yet during the second Cleveland campaign the paper

> had not a word to say regarding the Tammany candidates; nor did it print its customary "Voters' Directory," in which it always describes the Tammany men as "thugs," "murderers," "felons," and other equally unpleasant things. Some wicked Republican . . . offered to pay for the insertion of its "Directory" at the regular advertising rates. The offer was refused . . . and general hilarity reigned among the unregener-

ate at finding Mr. Godkin playing the "practical politician" and
turning his back on his own civic ideals.[48]

Cleveland, on his inauguration for a second term, set about
to reverse some of his predecessor's policies. Gratifying
to Godkin was the Democrat's opposition to expansionism,
especially his stand against President Harrison's scheme
for annexing the Hawaiian Islands. In 1892 a band of white
planters in Hawaii carried out a successful revolt against
the rule of Queen Liliuokalani, a revolt assisted by United
States troops brought ashore at the request of the jingoistic
American minister. A treaty of annexation was rushed to
Washington, but before it could be gotten through the Senate, Harrison had left office.

Godkin—who, contrary to Professor Robert Beisner and
other uninformed writers, stopped short of being an antiimperialist—was alert to the commercial potentialities of the
islands, but to his practical mind they could be exploited
more profitably as a protectorate than as a possession.
Accordingly he favored maintaining an American sphere of
influence in Hawaii, while avoiding the expense of governing the islands. "We could not by annexation at this moment
gain anything which we do not now possess," he editorialized, "except the privilege of paying the expenses of the
Hawaiian government."[49] Annexation, he believed, posed the
danger of speedy elevation to statehood, bringing with it a
new batch of "ignorant, superstitious, and foreign tongued"
voters.[50]

When antiimperialist Edward Atkinson sent Godkin a
letter-to-the-editor calling for an American withdrawal from
Hawaii, Godkin declined to print it, and in the Evening Post
he offered this advice to the planters of Hawaii: "You have
United States troops on your soil now, and if it would make
you feel easier, we will leave them permanently, but we do
not care to undertake the task of governing your very motley
population, on condition of allowing it to help to govern us."[51]

The death of James G. Blaine shortly before Inauguration Day gave the tactless Godkin a renewed opportunity
to attack the former secretary of state. Blaine's role in
the Hawaiian annexation scheme, he declared, was "the
last conception of a disordered and virulent ambition."[52]

Asserting that Blaine had instigated the revolt in Hawaii that resulted in the deposition of the queen, Godkin demanded to know whether there was "a single feature" in the annexation scheme that "does not find a parallel in the great historic robberies and usurpations?"[53]

Another frontier of budding American imperialism receiving Godkin's scrutiny in the *Evening Post* and the *Nation* was Samoa. There, under the terms of an 1889 treaty, the United States, Great Britain, and Germany were in joint control. In 1894 growing friction between them, helped along by a native civil war, brought demands at home that the United States get out of the archipelago. The *Literary Digest* spoke for the antiimperialists when it asserted that the public was opposed to any further outlay of money for combating native factions in Samoa.[54] Simultaneously Godkin, in an oblique reference to the Pullman strike just beginning, editorially lamented in the *Evening Post*: "Our trying to keep the Samoans in order when we cannot protect our great lines of railroads from armies of tramps, is surely a grotesque spectacle. . . ."[55] He urged the United States to get out of Samoa, but the next week, when he learned that some of the Cleveland opposition, including the jingo Senator Hunt of Alabama, had consented to withdrawal, he qualified his position to endorse American retention of the harbor of Pago Pago.[56]

Within a year of Cleveland's second inauguration, the long honeymoon between Godkin and the president began to end.[57] In 1895 Godkin dramatically broke with the president over Cleveland's intervention in the boundary controversy between England and Venezuela. The controversy, of long standing, centered around British contentions that the western boundary of British Guiana included Point Barima, which commanded the mouth of the Orinoco, as well as other territory occupied by Venezuela. The first of these contentions, the status of Point Barima, was supported by the British-sponsored Schomburgk survey of 1840. Later England made a tentative offer to surrender Point Barima to Venezuela, with the rest of the boundary to follow the Schomburgk line.[58] The Venezuelan government demurred, arguing that Point Barima was not within the authority of

England to surrender, pointing out that in 1836 British Chargé d'Affaires Sir Robert Ker Porter proposed to Venezuela that she erect at Cape Barima a beacon to guide ships coming into the area, a tacit admission—although Porter's course was probably unauthorized by his government—of Venezuelan ownership.[59]

The United States became involved in the dispute when Cleveland's cautious Secretary of State Gresham, who was a favorite of Godkin because of his refusal to interfere with the British invasion of Nicaragua in 1895, decided that the position of England toward Venezuela was "contradictory and palpably unjust." Writing to American Minister Bayard in London in March 1895, Gresham noted that England had enlarged her claims periodically to include territory that "she previously recognized as belonging to Venezuela," and he predicted that "if Great Britain undertakes to maintain her present position on that question, we will be obliged, in view of the almost uniform attitude and policy of our government, to call a halt."[60]

Two months later Gresham died, and the problem fell into the lap of his none too cautious successor, Richard Olney. In July 1895 Olney drafted his famous "twenty inch gun" note to the British Foreign Office. Approved by Cleveland, the note invoked the Monroe Doctrine and added this bombastic corollary to it: "Today the United States is practically sovereign on this continent, and its fiat is law upon the subjects to which it confines its interpositions."[61]

After four months with no reply from the British government, Congress reconvened in a bellicose mood. Senator Cullom, chairman of the Foreign Relations Committee, keynoted the popular feeling when he declared on the Senate floor in December, "The time has come for a plain, positive declaration of the Monroe Doctrine, and then, if necessary, plain, positive enforcement of it against all comers."[62] The public caught the spirit. An ex-Confederate commander tendered Cleveland his services in a war against England, declaring that the American people were a unit in favor of enforcing the Monroe Doctrine. The Indianapolis *Journal* editorialized that "when it comes to resisting British aggression, there will be no Republicans and no Democrats. We shall all be

Americans, and if Grover Cleveland is President when the crisis comes, we shall all be Cleveland men."[63] Not calculated to pour oil on the troubled waters was the receipt in December of a somewhat supercilious reply from Lord Salisbury to Olney's note.

Against this ominous background, President Cleveland dispatched a message to Congress on 17 December 1895, asking for an appropriation to send a commission to Venezuela to study the boundary question between that country and British Guiana. In effect Cleveland was proposing that the United States draw the boundary line and require England to abide by its decision.[64] War fever was running dangerously high in the United States, with the jingoistic *New York Tribune* cable correspondent rejoicing from London that "Mr. Cleveland has been an English idol but he is now dethroned." The popular generals Lew Wallace and O. O. Howard, charged Godkin, were "furious for war."[65] Support for the administration was not restricted to the sensational press, as a glance at the editorial pages of the sedate *New York Times* and the Springfield *Republican* shows.[66]

At first the *Evening Post* and the *Nation* declined to take a stand in the dispute; it was as if Godkin were waiting for opposition to the president to form. On 5 December the *Nation* noticed "nothing of an exciting character in our foreign relations."[67] The following week appeared an editorial with slight criticism of the administration. A week later Godkin mildly censured the president's message to Congress on 17 December.[68] But then, after a weekend that saw opposition to the administration erupt in eastern business circles, Godkin excitedly unleashed his papers. Cried the *Nation*:

> . . . on Friday and Saturday [Cleveland] was overwhelmed with the execrations of business men; on Sunday he received the most unanimous and crushing rebuke that the pulpit of the country ever addressed to a President. He made his appeal to the conscience of the mob; he has now heard from the conscience of the God-fearing people, and their judgment upon him leaves him morally impeached of high crimes and misdemeanors.[69]

Calling Cleveland an "anarchist," Godkin attacked the president with fury, devoting seven pages of the 26 December *Nation* to the controversy. Cleveland's message was a "dishonorable and traitorous attempt to imperil peace," a "betrayal of the nation," and a "mad appeal to the basest passions of the mob." "Was there ever such another case of a civilized man throwing away his clothes and joining the howling savages?"[70]

> Mr. Cleveland says now just what Debs said in the summer of 1894. Law or no law, Debs and his fellow-anarchists gloried in being "masters of the situation." It is a melancholy thing to find the President who put them down with a firm hand, now displaying himself as the greatest international anarchist of modern times.[71]

The attack caught Cleveland, who deeply mistrusted newspapers, flat-footed.[72] Godkin, whom with White he had trusted virtually alone among editors, who had applauded his stand for "sound" money, and who cheered loudest when he "preserved the national credit and saved the country from repudiation," now was heaping the bitterest press denunciation of all on the president. Godkin reexamined Cleveland's message to Congress that the *Nation* earlier found "unexciting" and pronounced its statements "ignorant and reckless" and "criminally rash and insensate."[73] Cleveland had flung his "terrible firebrand" into that "body of idle, ignorant, lazy, and not very scrupulous men," Congress, and that "brutish" body had responded by surrendering its war-making power to the president "without a word of deliberation or remonstrance." If Cleveland "began hostilities to-morrow, a wild yell of patriotic fervor is all that he would hear from either branch of the Congress."[74] Years later, when someone asked Cleveland if he still read the *Evening Post,* he wryly replied that he read only the joke column, "the Waifs."[75]

It is reasonable to conclude, with Harry T. Peck, that the chief concern of Godkin in the Venezuelan boundary crisis was the threat it posed to Wall Street securities. Patriotism, the editor declared, ought not to be permitted to interfere with the "money market." In an editorial, "Patriotism and Finance," he remarked that nowhere in the world do people

> show more sanity, not to say shrewdness, than Americans. Every financial transaction . . . is based on a perfect knowledge of human nature. . . . The total failure of this sense in international matters goes far to confirm the belief of a great many people that the "patriotism" which has been diffused

among the masses during the past thirty years, and even
taught to the children in the schools, is a species of madness.[76]

The Venezuelan boundary crisis subsided as voices less
strident than those of Godkin and the overheated patriots
whom he opposed made themselves heard.[77] Cleveland
achieved his purpose. Venezuela got Point Barima; the shaky
stock market recovered; and Godkin turned to other editorial
"rows," as he affectionately termed his polemical forays.

How significant was Godkin's role in the controversy? On
29 December, as the crisis passed its peak, he egotistically
informed Norton that his editorial course was "the greatest
success I have ever had and ever known in journalism."
"We were literally overwhelmed with laudatory and congratulatory letters, as well as oral applause of every description,
and our circulation rose 1,000 a day." But somewhat in an
opposite vein, he told his old friend: "I am just now the great
object of abuse, and the abuse is just what you would hear
in a bar-room row."[78]

Was Godkin thus, as some scholars assert, a "sober, detached critic"? Hardly. His was not the calm voice to soothe
passions and set in motion the wheels of conciliation. A
protégé, Joseph Bucklin Bishop, has written of him:

> Never was his enjoyment of a "row" keener than when he
> himself was the object of attack, as was very often the case.
> He would read all the hard things said of him in one paper
> after another, fairly shaking with pleasure, and then say:
> "What a delightful lot they are! We must stir them up again."[79]

Many level-headed Americans, unaffected by the hysteria
whipped up by the jingo press, were convinced of the under-
lying correctness of the American position. Godkin, by the
intemperateness of his attack on that position, opened himself to the charge of special pleading. From his admirer
William James came some pertinent advice. While compli-
menting Godkin on his courage, James cautioned him against
using expletives, and he urged the editor in the future to
be more "patiently explanatory." Singling out for criticism
Godkin's allusion to Cleveland and the public as "howling
savages," James concluded that jingoism was caused not by
savagery but by ignorance.[80]

Godkin's editorial posture in the Venezuelan boundary

crisis reflected his mounting Anglophilia. The most gratifying personal event of his later years was his rediscovery of
England. During the 1880s he wrote a few pieces for British
journals, mainly in support of home rule for Ireland, but he
had not been in England for many years. In 1888 James Bryce
invited him to contribute to the *Handbook of Home Rule*,
produced by the Liberal Party to advance Prime Minister
Gladstone's bill for Irish home rule.

The next summer Godkin revisited England for the first
time in a quarter of a century. To his intense satisfaction Bryce arranged for him to meet with Gladstone, and a
glittering gathering of peers and upper-middle-class tastemakers showered him with attentions. Later, between hearty
laughs, Godkin described to friends his visit to Gladstone.
The loquacious statesman was nearing eighty, and, according to Godkin, talked uninterruptedly for a full hour; then,
rising to allow his visitor to take his leave, he told Godkin
how much he had enjoyed "our conversation." To Katharine
in New York—who had begged off from the trip because she
was subject to sea sickness—Godkin exulted from London:
"The people here are so polite, and there are so many well
dressed, educated men, and life is so well ordered, I am
thinking I am not worth a cent as a 'good American.'"[81]
Afterwards, except for two years, Godkin spent some part of
each year abroad with Katharine, staying part of the time in
London with the Bryces or with his friend Henry James.

From 1889 onward, Godkin's Anglophilism was a favorite
topic of banter from his friends as well as censure from
his enemies. One evening at the Century Club, when Godkin missed a billiard shot, Clarence King wittily explained
to onlookers that it was a typical Godkin shot, "too much
English, and on the wrong side."[82]

Chapter Eleven
The Imperial Years

> *What can you expect of a city in which every morning the SUN makes vice attractive, and every night the POST makes virtue odious?*
>
> (Variously attributed)

Godkin had limited respect for his profession and, except for brief friendly associations with Whitelaw Reid and Richard Watson Gilder, he held himself aloof from other editors. His style and manner, thought a contemporary, were that of "a gentleman in the easy chair of his club."[1] Nevertheless hard-boiled editors read him and rephrased his arguments for use in their own papers. Governor David B. Hill of New York, who often encountered Godkin's editorial wrath, is said to have complained of the *Evening Post*: "I don't care anything about the handful of Mugwumps who read it in New York. The trouble with the damned sheet is that every editor in New York State reads it."[2] A well-substantiated legend has it that the *Evening Post* was the favorite daily of Joseph Pulitzer. Asked why he did not make the New York *World* like the *Evening Post*, he retorted: "I want to talk to a nation, not to a select committee."[3] Henry Steele Commager has aptly described that "committee." "They had gone to the best schools—one sometimes feels that a college degree was a prerequisite to admission to their club—associated with the best people, belonged to the Century or Harvard Club, read *The Nation* and *The Independent*, and knew politics, for the most part, at second hand." Commager continued:

> They recognized few evils that learning could not diagnose and honesty could not cure. They had the same abiding faith in the efficacy of moral sentiments that H. G. Wells ascribes

to the English liberals of the period in his *New Machiavelli,*
and the English example was constantly in their minds. Good
government, they believed, would follow axiomatically from
the merit system and the participation of gentlemen in politics, and when they thought of gentlemen they thought of
each other.[4]

Professor Commager might have mentioned the Saturday
Club of Boston, to which Godkin and many *Nation* readers
belonged.[5] To these men Boston was the Hub, the mecca,
and most of them shared Godkin's aversion to the rest of the
country. Like the not unperceptive Henry Adams, who in a
moment of pique found that "West of the Alleghanies, the
whole country could have been swept clean, and replaced
in better form within one or two years," Godkin, as has
been noted, found the individualism of the west unsuited
to his own independent spirit.[6] The westerner's economic
heresies, his uncouthness and his all-around flouting of the
laws of "civilized society" disquieted him. As he told a
friend: "Your account of Southern California would have
made my teeth water if it were possible for anything west
of the Alleghenies to make any impression on me, but no
scenery I had to share with the Western people would
charm me."

One of Godkin's avid readers in the 1890s was young
Upton Sinclair, whom he taught that social evils were caused
by individuals—such as the men who infested Tammany
Hall—rather than by a system. "I had not yet found out
'big business,'" Sinclair recalled, "and of course I would
not, until I had outgrown Godkin of the *'Evening Post'*
and Dana of the *'Sun'.*" Sinclair pointed out that his capitalist education blinded him to "our civilization of class
privilege":

> It . . . managed to make me regard the current movements,
> Bryanism and Populism, which sought to remedy this evil, as
> vulgar, noisy, and beneath my cultured contempt. . . . While
> emotionally in revolt against Mammon-Worship, I was intel-
> lectually a perfect little snob and tory. . . . I expected social
> evils to be remedied by cultured and well-mannered gentle-
> men who had been to college and acquired noble ideals.[7]

Godkin is claimed to have been the first editor of a major
newspaper to separate the editorial page of his paper from

the business side. The germ of truth in this is that, because he held only a 2 percent interest in the Evening Post, he did not hesitate to undertake editorial combats that cost Villard's paper advertising revenue. Yet his partisanship in behalf of the economic status quo was notorious. In an even more partisan way, private enemies tended under his pen to become confused with public enemies. Some of his most withering editorial blasts were reserved for persons whose desire for honest government was at least as great as his own. Critics of Godkin declared, with reason, that he painted the political scene and the men in it so black that he frightened idealistic young men away from politics and often hurt good causes more than he helped them.[8]

Central to the problem was that the proprietors of the Evening Post and the Nation had never been firm in their liberal moorings. Ever since Godkin and White had taken editorial control of these journals, intolerance in them had been growing. Undaunted by their failure in 1894 to obtain the dismissal of the liberal Richard Ely from the University of Wisconsin because of his opposition to classical economics, Godkin and White continued to support academic purges, such as the dismissal two years later of the pro-Silver Professor E. Benjamin Andrews of Brown University. White voiced the sentiments of both editors when to a friend he exulted over Andrews's dismissal: "In Colorado I am credibly informed that [Andrews] wore a silver pin in his shirt front and called attention to it, as an indication of his soundness, like a demagogue politician."[9]

Joseph H. Choate is said to have described the Godkin Post as "that pessimistic, malignant, and malevolent sheet, which no good citizen ever goes to bed without reading."[10] Choate, who along with James C. Carter represented Godkin in his frequent legal battles, was scarcely in a position to be objective, but the pretensions of Godkin to infallibility found even his followers enjoying his discomfiture whenever chinks in his moral armor were detected. After all Godkin was the High Priest of Criticism in the Gilded Age, and he schooled a generation to be critics. If he had been able manfully to admit his own mistakes, he would have been better liked.[11] Critics were understandably jubilant whenever he was caught red-handed in sin, as on the occasion when he lamely sought to justify his profer of a five-dollar bribe to a policeman who came to his home at an inconvenient hour to arrest him for slander.[12]

On another occasion Godkin's editorial campaign for an international copyright law backfired when he singled out the firm of John Wanamaker for attack because it was merchandising a "pirated" edition of the Encyclopedia Britannica.[13] Opponents thereupon alleged that not only were the Nation and the Evening Post accepting advertising for similar "pirated" editions, but the Post was pirating stories from English magazines and reprinting them in its Saturday supplement.[14]

Because the respect of Godkin for the press was low, he could not count on the support of other editors in his controversies. The leading weekly opponents of the Nation in the early days were the Commonwealth of Boston and, in Brooklyn, Henry C. Bowen's Independent, under the editorship of Theodore Tilton. Among the dailies the leading recipients of Godkin's scorn were the Herald, the World, the Sun, and, after 1884, the Tribune. In 1870 he confessed to "a burning longing to help to train up a generation of young men to hate Greeley and Tilton and their ways."[15] Charles A. Dana, the proprietor of the New York Sun, was one of the editors who welcomed Godkin's challenge to combat, although their set to's usually produced more heat than light. To Mrs. Frederick Bellamy, Nevins attributes the variously ascribed query: "What can you expect of a city in which every morning the Sun makes vice attractive, and every night the Post makes virtue odious?"[16]

In the testy Dana, Godkin met his match. Before the Brooklyn Bridge was opened in 1884, engineers tested its strength by sending over it huge trucks loaded with heavy weights. Dana, operating on the theory that Godkin's paper was just as heavy as it was "dull," proposed that the trial be limited to a single wagon containing a copy of the Evening Post.[17]

One thing about which Godkin and Dana were wholly compatible, however, was their lack of sympathy for the toiling masses. This was illustrated during the difficult winter that followed the Panic of 1893, when there was widespread unemployment and suffering in the United States. An urgent question was what to do about the unemployed. Godkin was willing that they be aided through organized charity as long as they were "resigned and patient," but not if they showed themselves "grasping or discontented or anarchical."[18] He scolded social gospellers among the clergy for setting aside the "theological gospel" in favor of the "gospel of social endeavor," alleging that they and economists of the new school were inciting the masses to discontent.[19]

During this period, the *New York Herald* offered readers this sketch of Godkin:

> He is of medium height, strongly built, is about fifty eight years old, wears a full gray beard and his intense personality is unmistakable even to the most observant.
>
> Mr. Godkin usually drives to the *Post* office in a closed carriage from his residence in Ninth Street, arriving about half-past nine o'clock. From that time until one o'clock no one is permitted to interrupt him. Formerly Mr. Godkin rode horseback frequently in Central Park, but he was thrown from his horse last year and since that time has seldom been seen galloping along the bridle paths.[20]

"The Century Club is Mr. Godkin's Mecca after the day's toil is over," added the *Herald*, "and those who read his attacks on Health Officer Jenkins last year during the cholera scare would be surprised to see how amiable and genial a gentleman Mr. Godkin really is at his club and among friends."

The paradox of Godkin's personableness toward his peers and his brusqueness toward others struck many. An *Evening Post* chum of Woodrow Wilson apologetically begged off from attempting to speak to the editor-in-chief in Professor Wilson's behalf, explaining to Wilson that Godkin was a "very positive Irishman."[21] Some of his staff writers the editor did not know by sight; most were afraid to approach him.

An equally disquieting paradox, not wholly accounted for by the pressures of that stern editorial taskmaster, the deadline, was Godkin's inconsistency. To illustrate the difficulties of generalizing about him, one need only turn to his writings on war. He is commonly believed to have been a crusader for international peace, a legend that sprang partly from his widely quoted remark, on his retirement in 1899, that he acquired a loathing for war in the Crimea.[22] Yet his Crimean letters do not show him opposed to war, and his subsequent writings reveal him as cool to peace movements.[23] Why, then, his vociferous reaction to jingoism? The answer is chiefly that as a Cobdenite, Godkin was against anything that might interfere with the "laws of trade." It was the United States, he explained in 1892, "which first introduced into international relations the practice of negotiating as business men, and not as soldiers."[24] To him, declared Harry T. Peck, "no war could be justifiable, because it cost money. No threat of war was ever to be made, because it depreciated the value of stocks and bonds."[25] What irritated Peck was this kind of Godkin outburst:

> Our present Congressmen are the product of thirty years of government by intrigue, concealment, and bribery. . . . To have an assembly of breech-clouted warriors, who are daily shaking their tomahawks at all strangers, presiding and legislating for a nation which has a stock exchange and banks in every town, and in which the poorest man is interested in the condition of the money market, is an absurdity. No such regime can last.[26]

Nevertheless endorsements of war appear throughout Godkin's writings. To Norton in 1865 he praised the "love of military glory."[27] "It will be a sorrowful day," he declared in 1870, "when . . . men come to consider death on the battle-field the greatest of evils, and the human heart will certainly have sadly fallen off when those who stay at home have neither graditude nor admiration for those who shoulder the musket. . . ."[28] During the *Virginius* crisis of 1873 with Spain he wrote: "Civil and religious tyranny have so debauched the Spanish people that though individually brave they have lost the capacity for combined and protracted effort even in military enterprises, which is one of the highest marks of civilization."[29] However, the war with Spain found him opposing the conscription of youths of the upper middle classes on the grounds that the "killing of public enemies," although a legitimate calling, was nevertheless the "meanest office in any state after that of the public executioner,"[30] a statement that one of the principal

architects of the Godkin legend, Oswald G. Villard, bowdlerized and attributed to Godkin as "some day the soldier [will]
find himself properly ranked after the hangman."[31]

Central to the appeal of Godkin for readers was his claim
to sober detachment in his verdicts. But his penchant for
attacking that which caused him personal discomfort did not
go unnoticed. Henry Adams for a time considered the editor
one of his best friends, but he believed that Godkin ruined
his influence by his "insistence on points of morals" when he
"avowedly pursued [his own] interests in politics."[32] An
illustration of this was Godkin's widely divergent editorial
treatment of the cholera epidemics of 1865 and 1892. During
the epidemic of 1865-66 Godkin resorted to sustained dia-
tribe in the Nation to indict the New York Board of Health
for not quarantining the port of New York.[33] But in 1892
personal circumstances impelled him to take an opposite
stand. Returning from one of his annual junkets to Europe
in a ship on which several passengers had taken ill with
cholera, he and his fellow passengers found themselves in
quarantine in New York harbor, whereupon he heaped some
of his choicest editorial invective on the New York Board
of Health. Allan Nevins describes it with admiration: "His
letters to the Evening Post were delightfully scorching, he
kept up the attack till the quarantine officers were panic-
stricken, and he demolished their last defense in an article in
the North American Review that is a masterpiece of de-
structiveness." Nonetheless Evening Post proprietor Villard
heatedly objected to Godkin's course, as did much of the
press.[34]

One of Godkin's trademarks, as well as one of his weaknesses, was his tendency to base foreign affairs arguments
on what "the textbooks say." But he was hardly so naive as
to believe that mere recitation of the texts gave force to the
law of nations. In 1869, while the Alabama controversy
was focusing attention on the need for amplification of
international usage, he penned an earnest plea for the codification of international law and the strengthening of international law.[35] The following year in a Nation critique of the
work of peace societies he urged advocates of peace to stop
talking about the horrors of death on the battlefield and to

start bringing about the supremacy of international law.[36] As if in answer to his plea, the period following the Franco-Prussian War saw renewed efforts toward the codification of international law and the arbitration of international disputes.[37] Yet Godkin greeted all these efforts with skepticism. In an 1875 editorial he assailed the activities of organizations for the advancement of international law, proposing that the "philosophers and professors" meeting at the Hague instead turn their talents to reforming people. He wrote:

> Now, in ethics it would be at once recognized as somewhat of an absurdity for a body of distinguished clergymen, leading fathers of families, and editors to get together and hold a convention for the study and reform of morals over the world. Yet there is really much greater reason why this should be done than that a number of jurists and philanthropists should undertake to amend and codify the law of nations.[38]

In brief, contended Godkin, "the notion that there is any tendency among nations to submit themselves to an international code, or that if they did they would abide by it, is absurd."[39] Several months later, in the next diplomatic "row" to engage his attention, Godkin again changed position and recited international law to his readers.[40]

In 1878 a huge international peace gathering was held in Paris. Commenting on it in the *Nation*, Godkin condemned peace societies for seeking to establish universal peace by "mechanical contrivances," i.e., by the "creation of courts of arbitration and the draughting of rules for government of disputants when they get angry. . . ."[41] Seven years later, editorializing on the dispute between England and Russia over Afghanistan, he was inattentive to proposals that the dispute be submitted to arbitration, explaining that the "existing condition of human nature" was opposed to the peaceful settlement of international difficulties.[42] Despite his fears the dispute was successfully arbitrated.

But it was not Godkin's inconsistencies that angered some of his critics. Theodore Roosevelt was in established company when, in one of his soberer moments, he asserted that the editor of the *Evening Post* was "not a patriotic man."[43] Godkin, who managed to get under the skin of the high-spirited Rough Rider as did no other editor, had been called "un-American" almost from the day the first number of the *Nation* appeared. Even the sophisticated *Springfield Republican* took offense in 1869 when the *Nation* editorially sneered at what it called the "American view" of foreign relations.[44] Never American in spirit, critics argued, ashamed of the Ireland of his birth, Godkin chose England for his final resting place. That he was more British than American was not considered a matter for debate. Luckily for him some of his critics' most potent ammunition lay out of reach—in his personal letters. Ever since the memorable voyage of 1889 when he first experienced the delights of English society,[45] he had been spending increasing portions of each year in the British Isles. It was from England in the summer of 1897 that he justified to his friend Arthur G. Sedgwick his intention of permanently quitting the United States:

> There are many things [in England] which reconcile me to America, but there is no country in the world to-day in which you can be very happy if you care about politics and the progress of mankind, while there are many in which you can be very comfortable, if you occupy yourself simply with gardening, lawn tennis and true religion. [England] is one of them.[46]

The stridently antiadministration position that Godkin took in the Venezuelan boundary crisis was only one of the signs of the disaffection that would soon lead to his expatriation to England. It was during that crisis that his old enemy, the New York *Sun*, exulted:

> People who could stand in ordinary times the dismal egotism and unrelieved snarl and sneer of Godkin's editorial manifestations refused absolutely to tolerate him when he turned his pen to defamation of the American flag and abuse of all that American patriotism holds dearest. The most hardened readers of the *Evening Post* were ashamed to be seen in public places with that sheet in their hands.[47]

Attacks like these did not bolster Godkin's affection for his adopted country. But he was perfectly capable of defending himself. "It is a fixed idea, with a certain class of publicists among us," he scolded in the *Evening Post*, "that in any controversy with a foreign power our own

Government shall be supported, whether it is right or wrong. That is to say, that any political adventurer like Blaine, who scrambles into the State Department, is at liberty to get up with foreigners disputes. . . ."[48]

In keeping with his announced detestation of chauvinism, Godkin bemoaned expressions such as "Good American" and "Americanism."[49] There was one mark of a "Good American," he cogently pointed out in 1893, that never failed; such a person "is constantly reminding you that he is a 'good American,' and inquiring whether you are. To be a 'good American' quietly and unostentatiously is something he cannot bear, and he is equally unwilling that you should."[50] On another occasion Godkin set about to analyze the word "Americanism":

> It is evidently a state of feeling, but its nature is ascertainable only by observing the things which are done or proposed by persons who declare themselves animated by it. . . . That is to say, 'Americanism,' or 'intense Americanism' has to be diagnosed, like any abnormal bodily condition, by simple observation.[51]

By this empirical method, Godkin concluded that persons "afflicted with the mental trouble known as 'Americanism' . . . bestow no attention on political problems which do not contain materials for a row with some foreign power, their patriotism being entirely bellicose."[52]

Godkin's contempt for superpatriots was compatible with his cosmopolitanism and his tendency to hold mixed feelings in diplomatic contests to which the United States was a party. Less understandable was the aloofness that he displayed toward the outside world, as, for example, his opposition to American participation in the Congo Conference and to the Pan American plan of James G. Blaine. "The United States of America was founded in order to get a portion of the civilized world out of this Donnybrook fair," he asserted in the *Evening Post*, "to provide a corner of the earth in which men could live without having constantly enemies to watch and suspect."[53] Robert E. Osgood explains it this way:

> Political and social reformers, like Carl Schurz, Moorfield Storey, and E. L. Godkin, and liberal-minded intellectuals, like David Starr Jordan, William James, Charles Eliot Norton, Mark Twain, and William Dean Howells, attributed America's moral prestige, the progress of her democratic government, and her

marvelous material development in large part to her relative
isolation from the turbulent affairs of European nations. These
men were not impressed by Mahan's prophecies. . . . To them
the White man's burden meant the ordeal of governing an
ignorant and hostile people, while embroiling the nation in
a contest for foreign markets, territorial aggrandizement, and
even larger armaments.[54]

Yet the pacifist Richard Cobden had upheld his country's
navy. Why not Godkin? The answer is that at first he did.
But by 1896 he had come to the conclusion that there "is
not in our past the smallest support for the theory that we
need a large navy. . . ." He explained:

The use of the navy is to punish people who think we are afraid
to fight. . . . In short, when we get our navy and send it round
the world in search of imputations on our honor, we shall have
launched the United States on that old sea of sin and sorrow
and ruffianism on which mankind has tossed since the dawn
of history. . . . We shall have abandoned as a failure the
greatest experiment any government ever made.[55]

In an 1892 editorial Godkin took aim at Alfred T. Mahan:

We believe the theory on which much of Captain Mahan's
advocacy of a great navy is based, that the world contains
a great many thrones, principalities, and powers only too
ready to insult, revile, trample on, and annoy the United
States if they can get a chance to do so with impunity, is
the hallucination of an able man who has devoted himself too
long and too deeply to a single topic.[56]

Mahan was "deliberately misleading the public" when he
said he was "not seeking a navy equal to the British," Godkin
persuasively argued in 1893. "Capt. Mahan and a great many
of his comrades do desire, and mean to get it if they can, the
largest and most powerful navy ever seen, and they want it
not for reviews or parades, but to fight somebody."[57]

The rest of the Godkin story—of his effort to stem the pre-
cipitate flight into war with Spain in 1898, his participation
in the unsuccessful fight to prevent the acquisition of the
Philippine Islands, his final disillusionment with the United
States and his expatriation to England—is well known.[58]
Less known is that during these events, which in two short
years catapulted the United States into the front rank of
world powers, Godkin took an editorial back seat to his
associates. By 1898 the editor had lost much of his fire and

zest for combat. Dogged increasingly by rheumatism, he was working less and writing less each year.[59] Never much of an administrator, the anecdote told of him after he joined the *Evening Post*—"I see no one before one o'clock, and at one o'clock I go home"—came increasingly to apply. Then there were the long vacation periods in Europe, during which he wrote virtually nothing. It was not so much his scorching pen as that of his younger colleague, Rollo Ogden, which moved a harassed President McKinley in 1898 to consider charging the *Evening Post* with treason.[60]

Yet the war with Spain, as his personal letters attest, aroused Godkin's deepest and, many feel, finest sentiments. In the *Evening Post* he blasted American navalism, jingoistic patriots, and the thirst for colonies, scarcely comprehending that they were unavoidable trappings of the imperialism he favored. For it was not expansion the censorious Godkin objected to so much as the men who were leading it. In an 1899 article in *Forum*, "The Conditions of Good Colonial Government," he tendered his prescription for governing the new American empire, but he had no hope that his advice would be heeded. "The one thing which will prevent expansion being a disgrace," he complained to a woman acquaintance, "is a permanent colonial civil service, but who is doing or saying a word about it?"[61]

By now the captiousness of Godkin and his *Evening Post* colleagues was legendary. One popular after-dinner story described a timid lady living in the country, who instead of getting herself a watch dog, arranged to have the *Evening Post* delivered each evening to her doorstep. "It just lay there and growled all night."[62]

In December 1899 Godkin offered a partial explanation of his decreased editorial activity to one of his women friends, Louise Dawson:

> I do not like to talk about the Boer war, it is too painful. . . .
> When I do speak of [it] my language becomes unfit for publication. . . . Talking of the Philippine war has the same effect upon me, and I have therefore ceased to write about McKinley. Every one who believes in the divine government of the world must believe that God will eventually take up the case of fellows who set unnecessary wars on foot, and I hope he won't forgive them.[63]

Editorially the embittered Godkin took time to call for a national referendum on expansionism.[64]"We have not, no thinking man has," he declared in the *Evening Post*, "the smallest doubt how this 'imperialist' movement will end. The history of America under it will, in all human probability, be that of a calamity greater by far than the fall of the Roman Empire. . . ."[65] It was during the war with Spain that his mounting fury against sensationalism in journalism boiled over and left him, in the words of Walter Millis, "reduced to helpless rage." Of the behavior of the yellow journals, notably the *New York World* and the *Journal*, before and during that conflict, the following *Nation* and *Evening Post* quotations are descriptive.[66] On 24 February 1898, nine days after the sinking of the *Maine*, the *Nation* announced:

> Nothing so disgraceful as the behavior of two of these newspapers in the past week has ever been known in the history of American journalism.[67]

A week later, as the sales of William Randolph Hearst's *Journal* reportedly topped five million copies:

> Certainly if ever the ministry feels itself called upon to withstand the active powers of darkness, the need of opposing and exposing the diabolical newspapers which are trying to lie the country into war must be obvious.[68]

Two weeks later, unimpressed by a Senate speech of Senator Proctor of Vermont giving eye-witness testimony to civilian suffering in the Spanish *reconcentrados* in Cuba:

> No one—absolutely no one—supposes a yellow journal cares five cents about the Cubans, the *Maine* victims, or anyone else. A yellow journal is probably the nearest approach to hell, existing in any Christian state.[69]

On 30 April appeared a memorable Godkin editorial in which he charged that the multitude had set up in the United States a "régime in which a blackguard boy [William Randolph Hearst] with several millions of dollars at his disposal has more influence on the use a great nation may make of its credit, of its army and navy, of its name and traditions, than all the statesmen and philosophers and professors in the country."[70]

Godkin had not exaggerated to Miss Dawson in 1899 his feelings about President McKinley.[71] Ironically his estimate of the president was quite different a year earlier when, in the tension-packed weeks before the outbreak of war with Spain, he had praised him in one column of the *Evening Post* while damning Congress in the other.[72] But by February 1899 he found that McKinley had come out of the Spanish war "drunk with glory and flattery." Then followed his memorable indictment of the president for murder.[73] Nothing less than a complete physical collapse in February 1900 robbed the sixty-nine-year-old Godkin of his burning ambition "to express by anticipation the judgment of posterity on McKinley. . . ."[74]

Godkin did not overlook the clergy in his strictures, asserting that "it is the eager support of the clergy which has launched McKinley on his career of conquest."[75] In his eyes the church bore a heavy responsibility with McKinley for the atrocities committed in the Philippines. The accounts he gave of American cruelties there rivalled yellow press descriptions of the Spanish in Cuba. Godkin searched the Judeo-Christian tradition for moral justification of the use of bayonets to "civilize" the natives of Luzon; finding none, he encouraged the Filipinos to fight on. To Bishop Huntington, he lamented: "The disposition of the church almost everywhere to take pains not to rise above the morality of the crowd has been one of the afflictions of my later years." Domestically the dispute over the Philippines was at its hottest when, in March 1899, Godkin declared in the *Evening Post* that the United States had "not a particle of claim to [Filipino] allegiance except what is based on a bogus purchase from a bankrupt vendor. . . ."[76]

Having said these and a few equally cogent things, Godkin departed for Europe and, as it transpired, to unofficial retirement in May 1899. To Marian (Mrs. James) Bryce he wrote in November 1899:

> I am on the whole not sorry for your experience [the Boer War]. You now know what we have been through, seeing a perfectly avoidable war forced on us by a band of unscrupulous politicians, the permission of whom to exist and flourish on the part of the Almighty always puzzles me; and behind them a roaring mob. . . . We are dragging wearily in the old way, killing half a dozen Filipinos every week, and continually "near the end." The folly of ignorance and rascality we are displaying in the attempt to conquer and have "subjects"

would disgrace a trades union. You do not see a quarter of
it in England.[77]

Responsible for those disgraceful events, Godkin discerned, was an "immense democracy, mostly ignorant" and
fed by a "villainous press." A recurrent theme in his editorials throughout the 1890s had been his mounting distaste
for popular government.[78] An example was Tammany Hall.
The sins of that organization arising, as Godkin believed, out
of universal manhood suffrage, irritated him—as has been
noticed—more than the sins of Tammany's respectable Republican opponents. Harold Laski perceived that, like other
one-time philosophical radicals who found democracy useful
for attaining bourgeois control, Godkin detected the warts on
it when the masses demanded a share of the power. "One
has only to compare the inability of a distinguished journalist
like E. L. Godkin to understand the relation between politics
and business with the insight which dawned on Lincoln
Steffens, as he investigated municipal corruption. . . ."[79]

The reason Tammany flourished in New York, Godkin
believed, was that most of the city's voters were "unen-
dowed with the self restraint and discrimination of men bred
to the responsibilities of citizenship." This was especially
true of recent immigrants, he argued. Whatever "a man's
abstract right to vote may be, the fact is that he cannot vote
without either benefitting or injuring his neighbor."

During Cleveland's first administration, as has been noted,
the Evening Post soft-pedalled its criticisms of Tammany
Hall in deference to national Democratic party wishes, but,
with the departure of Cleveland from office, Godkin and
White mounted an editorial offensive that included the
circulation of a pamphlet scurrilously attacking Tammany
leaders—an anti-Irish Voter's Directory containing thumb-
nail biographies of the "Pats," "Barneys," and "Mikes"
who dominated Tammany Hall. One after another those
whom the Evening Post accused of malfeasance took Godkin to court; one after another the criminal libel charges
against him were dismissed. A rumor arose—encouraged by
the Evening Post—that the editor was marked for physical
retaliation, but the closest he ever came was earlier, when
a streetcar conductor that he was upbraiding shoved him

from his car.[80]

Some of the editor's charges against the Tammany leaders were true, others false. One of the most irritating things about Godkin was his unreadiness to engage in dialogue with those with whom he disagreed. Neither the *Nation* nor the *Evening Post* under his editorship were the marketplace of ideas they might have been.

In recognition of Godkin's role in the defeat of Tammany Hall in 1894, seventy New York women bought him a silver loving cup at Tiffany's and inscribed it: "From friends in grateful recognition of fearless and unfaltering services to the City of New York." Bishop Potter presented it to the editor, with appropriate speeches by Joseph H. Choate and others, at a New Year's Eve gathering at the home of Mr. and Mrs. G. E. Kissell.[81]

By overthrowing the New York City Democratic machine, the Republicans and their mugwump allies traded the rule of Tammany Hall for that of the state Republican machine headed by Thomas C. Platt. The mugwumps ironically now found themselves making deals with the Platt forces, whom Godkin and his friends found more acceptable than Tammany Hall.[82] The result was infighting in the reform movement in New York City. In the *Evening Post* and the *Nation* Godkin attacked John Jay Chapman, a leader of the Good Government (Goo-Goo) faction who regarded the *Evening Post* as a corporation organ and the anti-Tammany Committee of Fifty as a group of self-serving plutocrats eager to make deals with the Plattites.[83]

Although Godkin's mugwump acquaintance Bishop Potter came to the defense of the Goo-Goos, Godkin did not desist in his public criticisms of "those crazy fellows," as he called Chapman and his followers. Later, in his little magazine *The Nursery*, Chapman took revenge. Comparing the two most famous New York editors, the "narrow and good" Godkin with the "cultivated and cynical" Charles A. Dana, Chapman concluded that each man hated the other because "each is the sort of hypocrite that the other most despises."

Yet to try to intimidate Godkin was, as someone said, like trying to stay the east wind. For his fearlessness in pointing out evil he gathered many admirers but few close friends.

To some powerful acquaintances—J. P. Morgan and Andrew Carnegie, for example—he granted immunity to criticism, but others never knew when it would be their turn under his editorial lash. William Dean Howells acknowledged to Charles Eliot Norton his gratitude for Godkin's kind treatment of him (Howells) in the *Nation*, but Howells was puzzled by Godkin's harshness toward others "quite as deserving."[84] William James grudgingly conceded to an acquaintance that Godkin's editorial distemper was the reason half of James's friends were opposed in 1903 to the establishment at Harvard of the Godkin Lectures.

Godkin's stand on social issues during the 1890s reflected his deepening gloom and reaction. Having many years earlier parted company with John Stuart Mill, he was now immersed in Edmund Burke; in 1899 he wrote the preface to the American edition of Burke's *Orations and Essays*.[85] Privately and in his editorials Godkin fulminated against social capitalism—which he confused with Marxism—William Jennings Bryan, whom he predictably termed an "Anarchist," and mounting worker unrest. In England he chaffed at Joseph Chamberlain's social welfare program, and at home he admonished genteel readers of the *North American Review* that to attempt to alleviate discontent among the poor "is as hopeless a task as to abolish poverty." Despairingly he told an acquaintance: "I came here fifty years ago with high and fond ideals about America, for I was brought up in the Mill-Grote school of radicals. They are now all shattered, and I have apparently to look elsewhere to keep even moderate hopes about the human race alive."[86]

By 1892 relations between Godkin and his colleagues had deteriorated. The increasing demands of the editor for extended paid vacations had become an irritant not only to owner Villard but to the whole *Evening Post* staff. The next year, when Godkin announced that he would take a four-month vacation abroad with pay, an overworked Wendell Garrison unhappily responded: "Your news of May 30 was not wholly unexpected, but there is nothing pleasant in it except on your own account. Sooner or later one's *clientèle* discovers that the principal is gone and the office boy in charge, and the business suffers."[87] On Godkin's return the

Evening Post Company decreed that, thereafter, excessive absence from the paper would be unpaid. Demurring, Godkin touted his merits to company treasurer Garrison: "The radiance of a blameless life and high intelligence is reflected in the office, no matter where [one may be] in the flesh, and has a money value."[88] Garrison, after conferring with Horace White, advised Villard to pay the temperamental editor-in-chief for the past but to "rigidly define the future."[89]

Unimpressed by the opinions of his colleagues, Godkin continued to press for longer and longer holidays. In 1897 he extended his demand to five months' vacation with pay, arguing to a reluctant Villard, "Every feature in the *Post* which distinguishes it from its contemporaries is due to me. Its high character, its independence, its veracity, its influence in this community as a moral force, are due to me. . . ."[90] A heated exchange followed, in which Villard rebuked Godkin for the "extraordinary self appreciation" that kept the editor from giving credit to his coworkers. Godkin's relations with the staff had now deteriorated to the point that he refused to meet with them at Villard's home to discuss *Post* policies.[91] Infighting in the editorial offices was becoming keen, with Bishop aspiring to supplant White, whom he and Godkin contemptuously called "Uncle."[92]

Late in 1899 the paper's embarrassed attorney, Lawrence Godkin, set about conspiring with Garrison to put the "tempery" old warrior on the shelf. Their opportunity came in September, when the editor returned from his annual junket to Europe, broken down with rheumatism and other infirmities of age. With his reluctant consent the trustees of the *Evening Post* relieved him at once of his editorial duties but permitted him to call himself editor-in-chief until 1 January 1900. Thereafter, it was agreed, he would be free to contribute to the paper signed pieces of his own choosing.

Epilogue

*I have done the state some good, and
they know it.*

Othello

Scarcely had Godkin's retirement been announced in the
press than he was back in the news for another reason. One
Christmastime evening late in December 1899, he left his
comfortable home in the Village and set out uptown. Walking to the elevated station at Eighth Street and Sixth Avenue
he moved his stout frame up the steps to the platform. While
awaiting his train his keen eyes fell on an unpleasant spectacle below: two police officers halted on their beats, heads
together in amiable conversation. Taking out his watch, Godkin timed the ten-minute exchange of pleasantries, then
descended the stairs, took the names of the officers and filed
a formal complaint against them for malingering. Three days
after Christmas he appeared on his own motion to testify
against them before the police commissioner. Retirement
obviously had not dulled Godkin's notion of civic duty.[1]

Godkin's published writings after his retirement, as well
as his personal letters, reflect his continued misgivings about
the men who were charting the new imperial course of the
United States and his sorrow over the passing of the genteel
tradition. In February 1900 he suffered a stroke in New York
while working on his memoirs, and he did not lift his pen
again for six months.[2] The next year the *Evening Post* rejected one of his signed pieces on the grounds that it was too
"extreme and pessimistic" and would make readers think its
author was "dwelling in the past."

By the middle of 1901 Godkin's health and mental facul-
ties, which had been declining for several years, would not
permit even the slight exertion of writing. Convinced, he
said, that he could not prepare for heaven in the United

States, he sailed with his wife and an attending physician to his beloved England.[3] Despite the progress reports that he regularly sent back, his American friends knew he was dying, and one by one they responded to his entreaties that they visit him in his residence in Lyndhurst in the New Forest. In August came William James, Henry James, and Henry D. Sedgwick. Death approaching, Godkin met it with fortitude. His final contribution to the *Evening Post* in August Garrison refused to reprint in the *Nation* on the grounds that it showed marks of his former chief's "mental decay."[4]

From the New Forest Godkin and faithful Katharine, who was writing all his letters for him now, moved to Torquay near the sea, where on 13 May 1902 he died.[5]

The ablest and most influential of the mugwump critics of late-nineteenth-century American civilization, Godkin left an imprint on the reporting of the period that only recent historical scholarship has partially erased. A former *Evening Post* staff member, Allan Nevins, writes of that paper and its editor: "Its dignity, integrity, scholarly accuracy, pride of intellect, and above all incisiveness, were the reflection of Godkin's own traits."[6] But elsewhere Nevins concedes Godkin's penchant for destructive criticism, noting that in each presidential campaign after 1865 the editor "printed three editorials attacking the other candidate to every one advocating his own."[7] It is interesting to compare these figures with the record of Godkin on American foreign policy. Here the ratio of censure over praise runs higher—six to one is a conservative estimate. Whether this means that Godkin believed that American domestic politics were less deserving of censure than the country's foreign relations is a matter for conjecture.

Stylistically, and in other ways, much of Godkin's writing remains as pertinent and fresh as if it were written yesterday. When he was at his best, he could not be matched for the logic, clarity, and incisive humor of his editorials. At the same time the narrow conservatism in which he wrapped himself in his later years cannot be accounted a force for good. The mugwumps were, for the most part, talented persons, but the times called for broader mental horizons. The achievements of late-nineteenth-century science and technology created a host of social problems that cried out for solution, and Godkin, to whom compassion—like sentimentality—denoted frailty, lacked the intellectual outlook the times demanded.

NOTES

Chapter 1
IRISH BEGINNINGS

1. John Fiske to Abby Fiske, 22 October 1867, quoted in John Fiske, *The Letters of John Fiske*, edited by Ethel F. Fisk (New York, 1940), p. 165.

2. "A 'Journalist' before a Police Court," New York *Sun*, 17 April 1890, p. 4. "A Career Full of Contradictions," New York *Sun*, 22 May 1902, p. 6. Frank Preston Stearns, *The Life and Public Services of George Luther Stearns* (Philadelphia and London, 1907), pp. 334-35.

3. E. L. Godkin to James Bryce, 7 June 1882, James Bryce Papers, Oxford University. Godkin, averred his former friendly acquaintance Henry Cabot Lodge in the United States Senate in 1894, "is by birth an Irishman, it is true, and by residence he is an American, but professionally he is an Englishman." *Congressional Record*, 53 Cong., 2 sess., 4528. A more appreciative observer of Godkin saw him as "an Irishman by birth, an Englishman by education, and an American by what may be called natural selection." Theodore Stanton, *A Manual of American Literature* (New York, 1909), pp. 451-52. Godkin's long-time acquaintance, the English legal scholar Albert V. Dicey, inclined toward the Lodge point of view. (Albert V. Dicey to James Bryce, 24 June 1907, Bryce Papers.) For information on Godkin's Irish backgrounds, supplied by himself, see Joseph B. Gilder, "Authors at Home; Mr. E. L. Godkin in New York," *Critic*, 30 April 1898, p. 293.

4. E. L. Godkin to F. W. Gookin, 26 October 1900, Godkin Papers (Miscellaneous Letters), Harvard University.

5. Mrs. Katharine Godkin to James Bryce, 27 October 1904, Bryce Papers. Georgina S. Godkin to Mrs. Katharine Godkin, 25 June, 3 July 1902, Godkin Papers, Harvard University.

6. "The Late Edwin Lawrence Godkin, by One Who Knew Him," *The Critic* 41, 1 (July 1902): 82. See also Brander Matthews, *These Many Years* (New York, 1917), p. 173.

7. Thomas Humphry Ward, *Men of the Reign* (London, 1885), p. 356.

8. Some of the factors behind Irish discontent are discussed in James A. Reynolds, *The Catholic Emancipation Crisis in Ireland, 1823-1829* (New Haven, 1954); Denis Gwynn, *The Struggle for Catholic Emancipation* (New York, 1928); Sir James O'Connor, *History of Ireland,*

1798-1924 (London, 1928), Volume I; Thomas N. Brown, *Irish-American Nationalism, 1870-1890* (Philadelphia, 1966), Chapter I; and Michael Tierney, "Origin and Growth of Modern Irish Nationalism," *Studies: An Irish Quarterly Review* 30 (September 1941): 321-36.

9. E. L. Godkin to John Seely Hart, 26 August 1871, John Seely Hart Papers, Cornell University.

10. *Ibid.* Thomas Doyle to E. L. Godkin, 1 August 1887, Godkin Papers.

11. Edwin Lawrence Godkin, *The Gilded Age Letters of E. L. Godkin,* edited by William M. Armstrong (Albany, 1974), p. 336.

12. Gilder, "Mr. E. L. Godkin in New York," p. 294.

13. Rollo Ogden, *The Life and Letters of Edwin Lawrence Godkin* (New York, 1907), I, 4, 6. Cited hereafter as Ogden.

14. William Dean Howells to Mrs. Katharine Godkin, 23 April 1903, Godkin Papers. Wendell P. Garrison to James Bryce, 12 November 1902, Bryce Papers. James Godkin to Whitelaw Reid, 11 January 1873, Whitelaw Reid Papers, Library of Congress. For a useful assessment of the early life of E. L. Godkin, marred only by excessive reliance on Ogden, see Louis Filler, "The Early Godkin," *The Historian* 17 (1954): 43-66.

15. Ward, *Men of the Reign,* p. 356. E. L. Godkin to John Seely Hart, 26 August 1871, Hart Papers. "Opinions of the Press," booklet of reviews of the books of James Godkin, Godkin Papers (Miscellaneous Letters). Gilder, "Mr. E. L. Godkin in New York," p. 293. James Godkin published many articles, books, and pamphlets, most of them anonymously. His principal books are *Education in Ireland* (London, 1862), *Ireland and Her Churches* (London, 1867), *The Religious History of Ireland* (London, 1873), and *The Land-War in Ireland* (London, 1870), a history of the land problem that the *Spectator* found written with "fairness and skill."

16. Ogden, I, 4.

17. Georgina S. Godkin to Mrs. Katharine Godkin, 3 July 1902, Godkin Papers. Wendell P. Garrison to Mrs. Katharine Godkin, 1, 4 June 1903, Godkin Papers. Charles Gavan Duffy, *My Life in Two Hemispheres* (New York, 1898), I, 43. Ward, *Men of the Reign,* p. 356.

18. E. L. Godkin to James Bryce, 23 November 1884, Bryce Papers. A man of imposing industry, the Reverend Abraham Hume (1814-1884) published more than one hundred books and pamphlets, mostly of an antiquarian nature. As parish vicar for over a generation in Liverpool, he played a prominent role in that city's life. In the debate over established churches, he wrote pamphlets defending the established church, while James Godkin opposed it.

19. Ogden, I, 6.

20. D. W. Simon to Rollo Ogden, 26 March 1906, Godkin Papers. H. J. Wolsterhome to Rollo Ogden, 22 March 1906, Godkin Papers.

21. Wolsterhome to Ogden, 22 March 1906, Godkin Papers.

22. Ogden, II, 31. Simon to Ogden, 26 March 1906, Godkin Papers.

23. Ogden, I, 9. E. L. Godkin to Lawrence Godkin, 22 July 1874, Godkin Papers. Thomas Doyle to Godkin, 1 August 1887, Godkin Papers.

24. Wendell P. Garrison to Mrs. Katharine Godkin, 1 June 1903, Godkin

Papers. Duffy, *My Life in Two Hemispheres*, I, 43.

25. Georgina S. Godkin to ? , n. d., typed extract, Godkin Papers. Duffy, *My Life in Two Hemispheres*, II, 33-36. For the background of events encouraging the growth of nationalism in Ireland during the 1840s, see, in addition to James Godkin's *The Land-War in Ireland* and the books of Charles Gavan Duffy cited herein, Denis Gwynn, *Young Ireland and 1848* (Cork, 1949), Michael Tierney, "Thomas Davis: 1814-1845," *Studies: An Irish Quarterly Review* (1945) and, edited by the same author, *Daniel O'Connell: Nine Centenary Essays* (Dublin, 1949). On the great famine of the 1840s and its political overtones, see R. Dudley Edwards and T. Desmond Williams, eds., *The Great Famine* (Dublin, 1956).

26. "The Rights of Ireland," by an Irish Protestant, in *Essays on the Repeal of the Union*, published for the Loyal National Repeal Association of Ireland (Dublin, 1845). The judges in the contest were Thomas Davis, Smith O'Brien, and a son of Daniel O'Connell. M. J. Barry was awarded first prize.

27. *Ibid.*, pp. 175-76.

28. Charles Gavan Duffy, *Thomas Davis: The Memoirs of An Irish Patriot, 1840-1846* (London, 1890), pp. 327-28. Georgina S. Godkin to ? , n.d., Godkin Papers.

29. Juliet Bredon, *Sir Robert Hart* (London, 1909), p. 19.

30. Godkin, *Gilded Age Letters*, p. 541.

31. For Duffy's association with Carlyle, see Charles Gavan Duffy, *Conversations with Carlyle* (London, 1892).

32. The *Nation* (Dublin), 8 April 1848, quoted in Brown, *Irish-American Nationalism*, p. 8.

33. W. C. Brownell, *The Genius of Style* (New York and London, 1924), p. 91. E. L. Godkin to Charles Eliot Norton, 3 October 1865, Godkin Papers. Henry Holt, *Sixty Years a Publisher* (London, 1923), p. 290. Despite his change of heart, Godkin, in an 1880 review of Duffy's history of Young Ireland, praised the Dublin *Nation* as a weekly of remarkable "versatility . . . fire . . . and . . . force." *Nation* (New York), 30 December 1880, p. 465.

34. E. L. Godkin, "Random Recollections," New York *Evening Post*, 30 December 1899, p. 5. The first two volumes of George Grote's *History of Greece*, with its glamorous portrayal of Athenian government "as seen through the eyes of a philosophical radical," appeared in 1846.

35. Harold Laski, *The American Democracy* (New York, 1948), p. 649. Godkin, "Random Recollections."

36. I. F. Stone, "Free Inquiry and Free Endeavor," *Nation*, 10 February 1940, p. 160. Godkin, "Random Recollections." Holt, *Sixty Years a Publisher*, p. 46. E. L. Godkin, "John Stuart Mill," *Nation* (New York), 22 May 1873, pp. 350-51.

37. Quoted in Stone, "Free Inquiry and Free Endeavor," p. 159.

38. E. L. Godkin, "The Economic Man," *North American Review* 153

(October 1891): 491-503. [Reprinted in Edwin Lawrence Godkin, *Problems of Modern Democracy* (New York, 1896), pp. 156-79.] See also [Arthur G. Sedgwick], "Mr. Godkin's Political Writings," *Atlantic Monthly* 79, 471 (January 1897): 118-20. The author of this appreciative review of Godkin's *Problems of Modern Democracy* was kept anonymous because he was a close friend of Godkin. See Arthur G. Sedgwick to E. L. Godkin, 25 December 1896, Godkin Papers.

39. Matthews, *These Many Years*, pp. 173-74. For additional commentary on the English origins of Godkin's thought, see V. L. Parrington, *Main Currents in American Thought* (New York, 1930), III, 154-68. Parrington is detailed and mostly accurate on Godkin. Superficial and inaccurate are Wendell P. Garrison [obituary], "Edwin Lawrence Godkin," *Nation*, 22 May 1902, pp. 403-4. Albert V. Dicey, "An English Scholar's Appreciation of Godkin," *Nation*, 8 July 1915, p. 52. Allan Nevins, "E. L. Godkin, Victorian Liberal," *Nation*, 22 July 1950, pp. 76-79. Godkin lucidly conveys some aspects of his thought in "Sweetness and Light," *Nation*, 12 September 1867, pp. 212-13. "Puritanism in Politics," *Nation*, 3 October 1867, pp. 275-76. "A Great Revelation," *Nation*, 5 March 1891, pp. 190-91. "The Economic Man." "John Stuart Mill."

40. Godkin, "Random Recollections."

41. E. L. Godkin to Frederick Law Olmsted, 24 February 1864, Godkin Papers.

42. Georgina S. Godkin to ? , n.d., Godkin Papers.

43. Gilder, "Mr. E. L. Godkin in New York," p. 294. E. L. Godkin to Frederick Law Olmsted, 11 April 1865, Godkin Papers. Edwin W. Morse, *The Life and Letters of Hamilton W. Mabie* (New York, 1920), p. 309. Oswald G. Villard, *Some Newspapers and Newspapermen* (New York, 1923), p. 294. Henry F. Pringle, "Godkin of the *Post*," in Edwin H. Ford and Edwin Emery, eds., *Highlights in the History of the American Press* (Minneapolis, 1954), p. 205. "I wonder if most men who are actively engaged are torn as I am by a longing for retirement," the thirty-four-year-old Godkin told Charles Eliot Norton. Godkin to Norton, 20 June 1866, Godkin Papers.

44. Georgina S. Godkin to ? , n.d., Godkin Papers. For evidence that Godkin's health problems were emotionally based, see Ogden, I, 189; John Fiske to Abby Fiske, 22 October 1867, *The Letters of John Fiske*, p. 165; Godkin, *Gilded Age Letters*, p. 541. "I have been six times examined for disease of the heart," Godkin told Frederick Law Olmsted in 1864, "and once blistered for inflammation of the pericardium. There never was anything the matter with my heart except functional derangement caused by the state of my nerves." Godkin to Olmsted, 31 May 1864, Godkin Papers.

45. Georgina S. Godkin to ? , (extract) n.d., Godkin Papers. The original of this letter, like many used by the family in the compilation of Ogden's *Life and Letters of Edwin Lawrence Godkin*, has been destroyed. After the publication of the *Life and Letters*, some of the letters were

returned to owners who requested them; of the remainder, those that were favorable to Godkin were preserved by the Godkin family and eventually sold to Harvard University. On the subject of the destruction of Godkin's letters, see Mrs. Cornelia Godkin to Thatcher Winslow, 28 March 1935, Oswald G. Villard Papers, Harvard University, and Oswald G. Villard to Mrs. Cornelia Godkin, 21 August 1936, Oswald G. Villard Papers. See also footnote 42, page 237.

46. Kate Godkin to Mrs. Katharine Godkin, 25 June 1902, Godkin Papers. Georgina S. Godkin to Mrs. Katharine Godkin, 3 July 1902, Godkin Papers.

47. Charles Loring Brace, *The Life of Charles Loring Brace, Chiefly Told in His Own Letters,* edited by his daughter (New York, 1894), p. 91.

48. *Ibid.,* p. 90. Frederick Law Olmsted, *Walks and Talks of An American Farmer in England* (New York, 1852). Frederick Law Olmsted, Jr., and Theodora Kimball, eds., *Frederick Law Olmsted; Landscape Architect, 1822-1903,* one-volume reissue (New York, 1970), p. 5. "Charles Loring Brace," *Dictionary of American Biography* (New York, 1929) II, 539-40.

49. Charles Loring Brace, *Hungary in 1851* (New York, 1852).

50. G. Barnett Smith, "James Godkin," *Dictionary of National Biography* (London, 1890) XXII, 38. Duffy, *My Life in Two Hemispheres,* I, 43; II, 35. Duffy, *Thomas Davis,* pp. 327-28.

51. Duffy, *Thomas Davis,* p. 328. Georgina S. Godkin to ? , n.d., Godkin Papers. Smith, "James Godkin." Apparently James Godkin wrote editorial leaders for the *Belfast Independent* over the pseudonym Q. E. D. Wendell P. Garrison to Mrs. Katharine Godkin, 1 June 1903, Godkin Papers.

52. Ogden, I, 13. The official date of publication was July 5.

53. E. L. Godkin to Mrs. Katharine Godkin, 19 June 1889, quoted in Ogden, II, 151. John Cassell (1817-1865), besides publishing several popular magazines, was one of the great book publishers of his day. He seems to have met James Godkin in 1848 and Edwin about two years later.

54. William E. A. Axon (letter), "E. L. Godkin and John Cassell," *Nation* (New York), 18 July 1907, p. 54.

55. *Ibid.* William M. Armstrong, *E. L. Godkin and American Foreign Policy, 1865-1900* (New York, 1957), pp. 36-37, 185-89. Chilton R. Bush, *Editorial Thinking and Writing* (New York, 1932), p. 85. Dicey, "An English Scholar's Appreciation of Godkin," p. 52. Stone, "Free Inquiry and Free Endeavor," p. 159. Allan Nevins, ed., *American Press Opinion: Washington to Coolidge* (Boston and New York, 1928), p. 300.

56. James Godkin to Whitelaw Reid, 11 January 1873, Whitelaw Reid Papers, Library of Congress.

57. William M. Neill to Rollo Ogden [?], n.d., quoted in Ogden, I, 14. The original of this letter is missing.

58. E. L. Godkin, "A Christmas in Rathnagru," *The Workingmen's Friend,* 25 December 1852, p. 197.

59. The chief writings of Georgina S. Godkin are: *Life of Victor Emmanuel II* (London, 1879), *The Soldier and the Monk, and Other Stories* (Florence, 1889), *Il Mal Occhio; or the Evil Eye* (London, 1894), *Stories from Italy* (Chicago, 1897), and *The Monastery of San Marco* (London and New York, 1901). Nearly all her writing was done in Italy, where she moved in the 1870s with her invalid sister Maria and their widowed mother. For further information about her, see Gilder, "Mr. E. L. Godkin in New York," p. 293, as well as *The Nation Index, 1865-1917*, Vol. II, "Contributors" (New York, 1953), p. 202, and letters from Maria and Georgina Godkin in the Godkin Papers. Edwin sometimes supplied money toward his sister Maria's medical expenses, but he did not welcome literary contributions from members of his family to his newspapers. His father contributed a few pieces on Irish affairs to the New York *Tribune* during the 1870s. See James Godkin to Whitelaw Reid, 11, 28 January, 11 March 1873, Whitelaw Reid Papers.

60. See announcement in *The Workingmen's Friend*, 8 November 1851, p. 95.

61. Edwin Lawrence Godkin, *The History of Hungary and The Magyars* (London and New York, 1853). György Klapka, *Memoirs of the War of Independence in Hungary* (London, 1850). E. de Lansdorff, "La Hongrie en 1848; Kossuth et Jellachich," *Revue des Deux Mondes* 24, new series (1848): 252-79. For the earlier parts of his book Godkin depended heavily on the Millman edition of Gibbon's *Decline and Fall of the Roman Empire*, Bonfini's *Rerum Hungaricarum Decades IV, La Hongrie Historique*, Knolles' *History of the Turks*, and Coxe's *History of the House of Austria*.

62. Godkin, *History of Hungary*, pp. 330-31.

63. *Ibid.*, pp. 366-67. After the Russian quelling of the 1956 Hungarian uprising, an American magazine reprinted the above quotation to assert that history was repeating itself in Hungary. "Eyewitness in Hungary," *Harper's* 214, 1282 (March 1957):77.

64. Godkin to Hart, 26 August 1871, Hart Papers.

65. "Sympathy," *Nation* (New York), 28 July 1870, p. 52. Except where otherwise stated, all titled articles from the New York *Nation* hereafter are Godkin's.

Chapter 2

WAR CORRESPONDENT WITH THE TURKS

1. R. A. J. Walling, *The Diaries of John Bright* (New York, 1930), p. 144. George M. Trevelyan, *The Life of John Bright* (Boston and New York, 1913), p. 229.

2. Godkin, "Random Recollections."

3. Ogden, I, 24. *Daily News*, 20, 28 January 1954.

4. *Daily News*, 11 January 1854.

5. All writers acknowledge the cruelty of Omer Pasha, but most conclude that under him the Turkish army was better organized than formerly. Emil Lengyel, *Turkey* (New York, 1941), pp. 163-64. H. W. V. Temperley, *England and the Near East; The Crimea* (London, 1936), pp. 215-18. William Miller, *The Ottoman Empire and its Successors, 1801-1927* (London, 1936), pp. 153, 313.

6. *Daily News*, 11 January 1854.

7. *Ibid.*, 17, 24 January, 10 April 1854. Sir Joseph A. Crowe, *Reminiscences of Thirty-five Years of My Life* (New York, 1895), pp. 117-18. Maxwell, an officer in the Bengal Artillery, later became a major-general in the British army. The London newspapers often used officers as special correspondents.

8. Crowe, *Reminiscences*, pp. 117-18. Late in life Crowe, an authority on Italian art, was knighted by Queen Victoria. For Godkin's recollections of the period, see the biographical sketch of him in John S. Hart, *A Manual of American Literature* (Philadelphia, 1873), p. 413, based on Godkin's letters to Hart of 26 and 28 August and 5 September 1871, John Seely Hart Papers.

9. *Daily News*, 28 January 1854.

10. *Ibid.*, 31 May 1854, 22 March 1855.

11. *Ibid.*, 9 February 1854.

12. *Ibid.*, 28 January 1854.

13. *Ibid.*, 9 February, 12 April 1855.

14. *Ibid.*, 18 February 1854, 8 March 1854.

15. *Ibid.*, 22 March 1854.

16. Harold Temperley calls Iskender Bey a Pole; Godkin describes him as a Tartar, formerly Count Illinsky, who once owned estates under the czar. Apparently a resolute, able soldier, Iskender failed to receive promotion from the sultan purportedly for political reasons. Temperley, *England and the Near East*, p. 217.

17. Crowe, *Reminiscences*, pp. 122-23.

18. *Ibid.*, p. 123. Godkin to Norton, 1 September 1866, Godkin Papers. Besides Govone and Maxwell the allied military observers in the Kalafat area were Captain Thompson of the 17th (British) Hussars and Major Tombs and Captain Austen of the Bengal Artillery. Some years later General Govone took his own life in the aftermath of an Italian political scandal.

19. *Daily News*, 22 March 1854.

20. Crowe, *Reminiscences*, pp. 125, 142. *Daily News*, 10 April, 13 May 1854.

21. *Daily News*, 13 May 1854. *Cf. Ibid.*, 10 August 1854.

22. *Ibid.*, 13 May 1854.

23. In April, for example, Godkin informed the *Daily News* that the Turkish commander in the Dobrudja was guilty of incompetence.

24. *Daily News*, 15 May 1854. *Ibid.*, 3 May 1854.

25. *Ibid.*, 16 May, 11 August 1854.

26. *Ibid.*, 15 May, 1 June 1854.

27. *Ibid.*, 15 May 1854.

28. *Ibid.*, 6, 9 September 1854.

29. *Ibid.*, 26 August, 16 May 1854.

30. *Ibid.*, 31 May 1854. The quantity of baggage and wives in the British entourage elicited ridicule from their French ally. For enlisted men the official allowance in wives was supposed to be six per hundred men, but additional wives were smuggled aboard the troop transports. Christopher Hibbert, *The Destruction of Lord Raglan* (Boston and Toronto, 1961), pp. 18-19.

31. Ogden, I, 26.

32. *Daily News*, 6 June 1854.

33. *Ibid.* One of the hardships the Turks had patiently borne, found Godkin, was the obligation to hand over army commissions to untrained foreigners "as if it were a genteel speculation." Arriving in Constantinople with letters of introduction to the British and French ambassadors, these adventurers "are received by the Turkish government 'with smiles that might as well be tears,' . . . and forthwith invests them with Commissions, and sends them off to the army." In such manner sergeants miraculously became captains, and captains were transformed into colonels and even pashas "with rations for half a dozen horses and pay that would astonish an archbishop." *Ibid.*

34. Ogden, I, 26-27.

35. *Daily News*, 13 June 1854. Shortly after this the czar, learning that an Austrian army was poised to enforce the wishes of England and France, ordered the lifting of the siege of Silistria and a Russian withdrawal from the Principalities. The order came just in time to save the Bulgarian fortress from being overrun by its besiegers.

36. *Daily News*, 15, 17 June 1854. Hibbert, *The Destruction of Lord Raglan*, pp. 23, 24.

37. *Daily News*, 27 June 1854.

38. *Ibid.*, 10 July 1854. Ogden, I, 101. *Cf.* Hibbert, *The Destruction of Lord Raglan*, p. 14.

39. *Daily News*, 10 July 1854.

40. *Ibid.*, 11 August 1854.

41. E. L. Godkin, "The Present Russian Campaign and that of 1853-54," *Nation* (New York), 14 June 1877, p. 347. *Daily News*, 10 August 1854.

42. Ogden, I, 27.

43. *Daily News*, 26 August 1854.

44. Ogden, I, 28.

45. *Daily News*, 22 August 1854.

46. *Ibid.*, 18, 28 August 1854.

47. Godkin, "Random Recollections." *Daily News*, 26 August 1854.

48. Rupert Furneaux, *The First War Correspondent*, p. 37. Ogden, I, 103-04.

49. *Daily News*, 21 August 1854.

50. *Ibid.*, 26 August 1854.

51. *Ibid.*
52. *Ibid.*
53. *Ibid.* See also *Ibid.*, 3 May 1855.
54. *Ibid.*, 9 November 1854. See also *Ibid.*, 27 September 1854.
55. *Ibid.*, 9 September, 13 October, 30 August 1854.
56. *Ibid.*, 9 November 1854.
57. *Ibid.*, 17 October 1854.
58. *Ibid.*, 13 October, 7 and 27 November 1854. In his hatred of the Austrians Godkin concluded that the late Russian occupiers of Bucharest, however "greasy, filthy to the last degree [and] malodorous beyond description," were preferable to the present Austrian occupiers.
59. *Ibid.*, 19 September 1854. Csitate is spelled Cetatea elsewhere herein.
60. *Ibid.*, 3 October 1854.
61. *Ibid.*, 10 October 1854.
62. *Ibid.*, 6 December 1854.
63. *Ibid.*
64. *Ibid.*, 7 February 1855.
65. *Ibid.*, 9, 10, 26 March, 12, 18 April 1855.
66. *Ibid.*, 7, 12 April 1855.
67. *Ibid.*, 18 April 1855.
68. *Ibid.*, 17 August 1855.
69. *Ibid.*, 3 May 1855. See also *Ibid.*, 17 August 1855.
70. *Ibid.*, 28 June 1855.
71. Godkin, *Gilded Age Letters*, p. 399.
72. *Daily News*, 10 March, 4, 23 July 1855.
73. *Ibid.*, 10, 19 July 1855. See also *Ibid.*, 23, 27 August 1855.
74. *Ibid.*, 23 August 1855.
75. *Ibid.*, 3 September 1855. See also *Ibid.*, 5, 18, 21 September 1855.
76. "The Present Russian Campaign and That of 1853-54," p. 347.
77. E. L. Godkin, "England and Russia," *Evening Post* (New York), 21 September 1899. See also E. L. Godkin, "The Crimean War," *Nation*, 11 December 1890, p. 466. For Godkin's later finding that the Turk is a "despicable soldier," see "The Present Campaign and that of 1853-54," p. 347.
78. See Volume I of J. B. Atkins, *The Life of W. H. Russell* (London, 1911). F. L Bullard, *Famous War Correspondents* (Boston, 1914). Sir Edward Cook, *Delane of The Times* (London, 1915). Furneaux, *The First War Correspondent*. Joseph J. Matthews, *Reporting the Wars* (Minneapolis, 1957). Hibbert, *The Destruction of Lord Raglan*, pp. 219-22 et seq. After the war, Russell published an edited and rewritten two-volume selection of his Crimean dispatches, and in 1895 he published a retrospective work on the war. [William H. Russell, *The War, 1855-56*, 2 vols. (London, 1857). William H. Russell, *The Great War with Russia* (London, 1895).] A more recent work of limited value because it employs the 1857 bowdlerized text of Russell's dispatches is Nicholas Bentley, ed., *Russell's Dispatches from the Crimea, 1854-56* (London, 1966). Accounts

of other Crimean War correspondents are found in Nicholas A. Woods, *The Past Campaigns*, 2 vols. (London, 1855) and Crowe, *Reminiscences*. 79. Ogden, I, 102.

Chapter 3
BELFAST TO AMERICA

1. Godkin to Norton, 7 April 1868, Norton Papers, Harvard University. Holt, *Sixty Years a Publisher*, p. 291. Godkin berated the British caste system in "The Tyranny of the Majority," *North American Review* 104 (January 1867): 226.

2. *Daily News*, 24 March 1856.

3. Godkin to James Bryce, 31 March 1887, Godkin Papers. Isaac J. Murphy to Godkin, 8 October 1886, Godkin Papers. Godkin to Jonas M. Libbey, 23 October 1882, Edwin L. Godkin Miscellaneous Papers, New York Public Library. In 1884 an editorial opponent sneeringly remarked on the "fatuous cunning" with which Godkin sought "to conceal his Irish birth." *New York Tribune*, 12 August 1884, p. 4.

4. S. Girdwood to Godkin, 8 September 1884, Godkin Papers. Godkin to W. McKinstry, 21 November 1900, Godkin Papers. R. J. Arnold to Lawrence Godkin, 15 June 1903, Godkin Papers.

5. William M. Neill to Rollo Ogden, n. d., quoted in Ogden, I, 14. Charles Loring Brace (1826-1890) helped found the Children's Aid Society in New York in 1853, and he was active throughout his life in social work among the poor of New York. A graduate of Yale, he had been friends with Frederick Law Olmsted since their early youth. "Charles Loring Brace," *Dictionary of American Biography*, II, 539-40. *Life of Charles Loring Brace*, pp. 199-202.

6. *Life of Charles Loring Brace*, p. 211. "Charles Loring Brace," *The National Cyclopaedia of American Biography* (New York, 1909), X, 166-67. Wendell P. Garrison to Katharine Godkin, 1 June 1903, Godkin Papers.

7. "Francis Dalzell Finlay," *Dictionary of National Biography*, VII, 29-30.

8. William Dana, Jr. to Francis D. Finlay, Jr., 16 February 1903, Godkin Papers.

9. William M. Neill to Rollo Ogden, n. d., cited in Ogden, I, 111.

10. Girdwood to Godkin, 8 September 1884, Godkin Papers. Uninfluenced by the advice, Godkin proposed to a female acquaintance that she give to some good cause the change from a purchase she had made in his behalf, "but not of education of young men for the ministry." Godkin to Theodora Sedgwick, 28 November 1886, Godkin Papers.

11. "Frank H. Hill," *Dictionary of National Biography, Supplement, January 1901-December 1911*, pp. 262-63.

12. Godkin, *Gilded Age Letters*, p. 385. Jane D. Hill to Godkin, 22 July 1883, Godkin Papers. For additional information on Godkin's friendship with Mrs. Hill, see Godkin to James Bryce, 16 February 1886, Bryce Papers, Oxford University. Henry James to Godkin, 6 February, 12 March 1886, Godkin Papers. Jane D. Hill to Godkin, 26 October 1883, Godkin Papers.

13. William Dana, Jr., to Francis D. Finlay, Jr., 16 February 1903, Godkin Papers. W. P. Garrison to Katharine Godkin, 1 June 1903, Godkin Papers. Ogden, I, 112-14; II, 193. *Life and Letters of Charles Loring Brace*, p. 211. Undated clippings in the Edwin L. Godkin Miscellaneous Papers.

14. *Daily News*, 22 November 1856, p. 5. Other details of Godkin's first day in the United States appear in his "Random Recollections," *Evening Post*, 30 December 1899, p. 5.

15. *Daily News*, 22 November 1856, p. 5.

16. Frederick Law Olmsted, *A Journey in the Seaboard Slave States* (New York and London, 1856); *A Journey Through Texas; or a Saddletrip on the Southwestern Frontier* (New York and London, 1857). In 1860 Olmsted published the third volume in his trilogy, *A Journey in the Back Country*, and the next year he revised the three volumes and brought them together into a single two-volume work, *Journeys and Explorations in the Cotton Kingdom*. These and Olmsted's other agricultural and ecological writings prompted Goldwin Smith in 1864 to call him the "Arthur Young of America." Together with his later imposing career as a landscape architect, they give him an unassailable position as a pioneer American environmentalist.

17. Godkin, "Random Recollections," p. 5.

18. In 1862 an acquaintance of Olmsted, Jane Woolsey, in her diary expressed consternation at the unsympathetic attitude of William E. Gladstone toward the Union. Since he was an Englishman whom "everybody must respect," she was perplexed at his and other Englishmen's "mysterious incapacity to understand us." Anne L. Austin, *The Woolsey Sisters of New York* (Philadelphia, 1971), p. 75. Godkin sought to explain the mystique of the American Union for English readers in his letters to the *Daily News*, 10 March and 19 March 1863.

19. *Daily News*, 26 December 1862, p. 5.

20. *Ibid.*, 26 December 1862, p. 5.

21. *Ibid.*, 16 February 1857, p. 3.

22. Frederick Law Olmsted, *Journeys and Explorations in the Cotton Kingdom* (New York and London, 1861), II, 321-22, 189-90. In this work, as he had done in his 1860 *Journey in the Back Country* (pp. 61-62, 408-09), Olmsted quoted from Godkin's southern letters to the *Daily News*.

23. William Dean Howells, "A Great New York Journalist,"*North American Review* 180 (1907): 46.

24. *Daily News*, 25 March 1857, p. 3. See also Olmsted, *Journeys and Explorations in the Cotton Kingdom*, p. 322.

25. *Daily News*, 16 February 1857, p. 3.

26. *Ibid.*, 16 February 1857, p. 3; 3 January 1857, p. 2.

27. *Ibid.*, 20 January 1857, p. 5; 25 March 1857, p. 3.

28. *Ibid.*, 12 February 1857, p. 5.

29. Godkin, "Random Recollections," p. 5.

30. "Some Recent Observations in Virginia," *Nation*, 13 September 1877, p. 164.

31. *Daily News*, 29 January 1857, p. 2.

32. *Ibid.*, 25 March 1857, p. 3.

33. *Ibid.*, 3 January 1857, p. 2.

34. *Ibid.*, 16 February 1857, p. 3.

35. *Ibid.*, 3 January 1857, p. 2.

36. *Ibid.*, 20 January 1857, p. 5.

37. *Ibid.*, 3 January 1857, p. 2.

38. *Ibid.*, 19 February 1863, p. 5. *Ibid.*, 16 February 1857, p. 3.

39. *Ibid.*, 26 December 1862, p. 5.

40. *Ibid.*, 26 December 1862, p. 5.

41. "Some Recent Observations in Virginia," p. 164.

42. The *Daily News* stopped identifying Godkin's contributions as those of "An English Traveller in the United States" in April 1857. Godkin's later statements that he carried out his southern travels in 1857 and returned to New York City in the spring of that year are in error, as is much of the published autobiographical material about him. Except for a few letters that he mailed to the *Daily News* from the south in November and December 1856, most of his southern Letters were composed in New York City after his return from New Orleans in January 1857.

43. Rufus Rockwell Wilson, *New York in Literature* (Elmira, New York, 1947), p. 20.

44. Most sources give 1858 as the date of Godkin's admission to practice, although in an 1894 interview he gave the date as 1859, and in 1899 he stated that it was 1857. "E. L. Godkin," *Town Topics*, 5 July 1894, p. 15. *Who's Who in America* (Chicago, 1899). See also "Edwin Lawrence Godkin," *Lamb's Biographical Dictionary of the United States* (Boston, 1900).

45. Godkin, "Random Recollections." Harry W. Baehr, Jr., *The New York Tribune Since the Civil War* (New York: Dodd, Mead and Company, 1936), p. viii.

46. Godkin to John Seely Hart, 26 August 1871, Hart Papers. John Bigelow, *Retrospections of An Active Life* (New York, 1909), pp. 109-11. *Evening Post*, 16 November 1901, p. 6.

47. In one *Knickerbocker* essay, Godkin endorsed universal manhood suffrage. See his "Colonial System of Great Britain," *The Knickerbocker* 53, 2 (February 1859): 119.

48. "The Death of a Great Power," *The Knickerbocker* 52, 6 (December 1858): 618, 622-23. This article Godkin in his old age believed he had written for the *Evening Post*. See *Evening Post*, 16 November 1901, p. 6.

49. *Daily News*, 13 May 1857, p. 5.

50. *Ibid.*, 19 July 1858.

51. *Ibid.*, 2 November 1858, p. 5.

52. *Ibid.*, 29 June 1858, p. 5; 22 January 1859, p. 5.

53. *Ibid.*, 15 June 1858, p. 5.

54. "Colonial System of Great Britain," p. 122. *Daily News*, 23 April 1857, p. 5. *Daily News*, 1 February 1859, p. 5.

55. "The Death of a Great Power," p. 619. "Colonial System of Great Britain," pp. 116, 119.

56. *Daily News*, 20 October 1857, p. 5.

57. *Ibid.*, 1 November 1859, p. 5; 8 November 1859, p. 5.

58. "The Late Edwin Lawrence Godkin," *The Critic* 41, 1 (July 1902): 82. Wendell P. Garrison, "Edwin Lawrence Godkin," *The Book Buyer* 13, 1 (February 1896): 6.

59. George E. Waring, Jr., *The Elements of Agriculture* (New York, 1854). Waring, who retained a lifetime friendly association with Godkin, became a leading sanitary engineer in the United States.

60. "Edwin Lawrence Godkin," in James Ford Rhodes, *Historical Essays* (New York, 1909), p. 33. Godkin, "Random Recollections," p. 5. Ogden, I, 165-66. Calvert Vaux to Frederick Law Olmsted, September 1859, Frederick Law Olmsted Papers, Library of Congress. Russell Lynes, *The Tastemakers* (New York, 1954), p. 33. For Brace's introduction to Hamilton, see Charles Loring Brace to his father, 24 October 1853, in *The Life and Letters of Charles Loring Brace*, p. 183.

61. Holt, *Sixty Years a Publisher*, p. 289. Abram A. Foote, *Foote Genealogy* (Rutland, Vt., 1907) I, 89-93, 201-04. Nathaniel Goodwin, *The Foote Family* (Hartford, 1849), p. 156. Contrary to one writer Senator Foot was not Fanny Godkin's grandfather.

62. Edith P. Cunningham, *Owls Nest* (Privately printed, 1907), p. 60. Ogden, I, 170.

63. Moncure D. Conway, *Autobiography, Memories and Experiences of Moncure Daniel Conway* (Boston and New York, 1904) I, 224-225.

64. See Charles T. Greve, *Centennial History of Cincinnati* (Chicago, 1904) I, 519, 567, 648, 669, 807, 919, 932, 1038. John P. Foote, "Memories of the Life of Samuel E. Foote" (Cincinnati, 1860). Mortimer Spiegelman, "The Failure of the Ohio Life Insurance and Trust Company," *Ohio State Archaeological and Historical Quarterly* 57, 1 (January 1948): 247-65.

65. Sara Norton and M. A. DeWolfe Howe, eds., *Letters of Charles Eliot Norton* (Boston and New York, 1913) I, 247. Godkin to Frederick Law Olmsted, 15 June 1862, Olmsted Papers. "I find I am a 'homme très policé,'" Godkin told Charles Eliot Norton, "and only enjoy scenery treated and improved by man. Nature, except Switzerland, tires me." Godkin, *Gilded Age Letters*, p. 538.

66. Calvert Vaux to Frederick Law Olmsted, 2 March 1864, Olmsted Papers.

67. Godkin, *Gilded Age Letters*, p. 416. Henry James, Sr., to Mrs. Fanny Godkin, 14 March 1875, James Papers, Harvard University. Henry James, Sr., to E. L. Godkin, 15 April 1875, James Papers. Godkin to Frederick

Law Olmsted, 24 February 1864, Godkin Papers.

68. Charles Wyllys Elliott (1817-1883) studied landscape gardening and design under Andrew Jackson Downing and was one of the commissioners for the laying out of Central Park in 1857. When Godkin first met him, he was suffering from disappointment because he had not received the contract for the park that was competitively awarded to Olmsted and Vaux. With Brace, Elliott was one of the founders of the Children's Aid Society, and he wrote several books during his lifetime, beginning with *Cottages and Cottage Life* (1848). For Godkin's contemptuous assessment of him, see Vaux to Olmsted, September 1859, Olmsted Papers and Godkin to Olmsted, 25 December 1864, Godkin Papers.

69. Wickelhausen vs. Willett, March, 1860, in Austin Abbott, *Abbott's Practice Reports* (New York, 1860) X, 164.

Chapter 4
THE CIVIL WAR YEARS

1. Ogden, I, 104. Loosely translated, Govone found Godkin "a good devil, jovial, spirited and short on words." Charles Eliot Norton agreed that the aloof Godkin had a "quiet manner," a way of saying that he seldom shared his inner thoughts with anyone. Norton to Frederick Law Olmsted, 24 January 1864, Olmsted Papers. See also W. P. Garrison to James Bryce, 12 November 1902, Bryce Papers.

2. Godkin to Olmsted, 24 February 1864, Olmsted Papers.

3. Anne L. Austin, *The Woolsey Sisters of New York* (Philadelphia, 1971), pp. 37, 54-56, 59-62, 68, 74, 91-93. Frederick Law Olmsted, comp., *Hospital Transports* (Boston, 1863). Pamphlet, *Frederick Newman Knapp; Memorial Tributes* (Boston, 1899). Charles J. Stillé, *History of the United States Sanitary Commission* (Philadelphia, 1866).

4. See Olmsted to Field, 30 January 1862, Olmsted Papers. Olmsted's letters in the Olmsted Papers and in the Godkin Papers are an excellent source for the first two years of the Civil War.

5. Godkin, writing in Justin McCarthy and Sir John R. Robinson, *The 'Daily News' Jubilee* (London, 1896), p. 73.

6. Late in the war the Union League Club of New York, founded in 1862 by Bellows and others to induce business and professional men actively to support the war effort, proposed publicly to honor the *Daily News* for its support of the North. Godkin was asked to convey the proposal to the paper, but its editor tastefully declined, replying that the only testimonial the *Daily News* wanted was the confidence of the public. The *'Daily News' Jubilee*, p. 75.

7. Donaldson Jordan and Edwin J. Pratt, *Europe and the American Civil War* (Boston and New York, 1931), pp. 85-86, 234-38. Ephraim

D. Adams, *Great Britain and the American Civil War* (New York, 1925) I, 69-70, 181-82. Charles F. Adams, Jr., *Charles Francis Adams* (Boston and New York, 1900), pp. 150, 240-43, 291-93. Sir Edward Cook, *Delane of 'The Times'* (London, 1915), p. 130. McCarthy and Robinson, *The 'Daily News' Jubilee*, pp. 45, 71-77. *The Tradition Established, 1841-1884*, Volume II of the *History of "The Times"* (London, 1938), pp. 150-51. John R. Robinson, *Fifty Years of Fleet Street* (London, 1904), p. 139. Ogden, I, 189.

8. *The Times*, London, 28 November, 3 December 1861. For other jingoistic British reactions, see *Blackwood's Magazine* 91 (January 1862) and *The Annual Register* 103, 254 (1861). Cf. *The Tradition Established*, p. 370.

9. *Daily News*, 2 December 1861, p. 5.

10. *Ibid.*, 10 December 1861, p. 5.

11. *Ibid.*, 14 December 1861, p. 5.

12. *Gilded Age Letters of E. L. Godkin*, p. 7. New York editor Thurlow Weed, a close friend of Secretary of State William H. Seward, was referring to Seward's indiscreet suggestion to President Lincoln that a foreign war might forestall Southern secession. For a subsequent indictment by Godkin of the "wild and irresponsible" Northern press during the early stages of the Civil War and of the "absurdities" of the Northern war effort, see *The 'Daily News' Jubilee*, pp. 73-74.

13. Allan Nevins, *The Evening Post; A Century of Journalism* (New York, 1922), p. 318. Godkin, who was in Paris only three months during 1862, testified that he wrote nothing there for any American journal. (See Godkin to Hart, 26, 28 August, 5 September 1871, John Seely Hart Papers). Regrettably, Nevins in a number of his works attributes to Godkin words that Godkin did not write. When the author asked him why he did this—with special reference to his practice of attributing to Godkin *Nation* articles written by others—Nevins plausibly answered that Godkin, as editor of the New York *Nation*, was "responsible" for everything in that journal. But this begs the question that Godkin himself raised about controversial articles and editorial paragraphs published in the *Nation* during his frequent absences from the paper. Conversation between Allan Nevins and the author, 17 August 1955.

14. *Daily News*, 2 May 1862, p. 5.

15. Godkin to Olmsted, 15 June 1862, Olmsted Papers.

16. *Daily News*, 6 December, 25 and 29 October, 8 and 11 November 1862, p. 5.

17. *Ibid.*, 29 October 1862, p. 5.

18. *Ibid.*, 29 October 1862, p. 5.

19. *Ibid.*, 8 and 11 November, 29 December 1862, p. 5; 2 and 5 January 1863, p. 5.

20. *Ibid.*, 31 October 1862. See also *Ibid.*, 9 January 1863, p. 5.

21. *Ibid.*, 11 November, 29 December 1862, p. 5.

22. *Ibid.*, 2 January 1863, p. 5.

23. *Ibid.*, 2 January 1863, p. 5.

24. In 1864 the *Index*, the leading Confederate propaganda organ in Europe, intimated that Godkin was in the pay of the federal government. This evoked from Godkin a passionate rebuttal that his only connection with the Lincoln administration was once having accepted the hospitality of "two members of the cabinet," a reference to his 1862 Washington visit. *Index* (London), 14 July 1864. *Daily News*, 23 August 1864, p. 5. Charles C. Cullop, *Confederate Propaganda in Europe, 1861-1865* (Coral Gables, Fla., 1969), pp. 37-55.

25. *The 'Daily News' Jubilee*, pp. 75-76.

26. As the fortunes of the North rose, Lincoln veered upwards in Godkin's estimation. *Daily News*, 21 April 1863, p. 5; 24 June 1864, p. 5; 20 March 1865, p. 5 (reprinted as "A Letter on Lincoln," Riverside, Connecticut, 1913), 1 May 1865, p. 5.

27. *Daily News*, 1 December 1862; 13 January, 30 April 1863, p. 5. Olmsted to Godkin, 4 April 1863, Godkin Papers.

28. *Daily News*, 26 December 1862, p. 5; 16 January 1863, p. 5; 26 March 1864, p. 5.

29. *Ibid.*, 2 January 1863, p. 5.

30. *Ibid.*, 9 January 1863, p. 5. See also *Ibid.*, 25 July 1865, p. 5.

31. "Humanitarianism," *Nation* (New York), 23 January 1868, pp. 68-69. *Daily News*, 26 December 1862, p. 5. Godkin to Lowell, 17 November 1868, Lowell Papers, Harvard University. Godkin to Whitelaw Reid, 14 February 1882, Whitelaw Reid Papers, Library of Congress.

32. Evelyn Page, ed., "After Gettysburg: Frederick Law Olmsted on the Escape of Lee," *Pennsylvania Magazine of History*, 75 (October 1951): 436. Olmsted to Godkin, 4 April, 15 and 19 July 1863, Godkin Papers. *Daily News*, 7, 13 August, 1863, p. 5.

33. *Daily News*, 19 March 1863, p. 5.

34. Godkin to John Seely Hart, 26 August 1871, Hart Papers.

35. Because several writers assert that Godkin at this time was a member of the staff of the New York *Times*, it is useful to quote him. In 1871 Godkin told the compiler of a reference work that "my connection with the New York *Times* has never been anything more than a contributor of two articles a week, on topics selected by myself. I never had any closer connection with the paper, seldom went to the office, and had but a slight acquaintance with the late Mr. Raymond." Godkin to John Seely Hart, 28 August 1871, Hart Papers.

36. Olmsted to Godkin, 4 April 1863, Godkin Papers. Godkin, *Gilded Age Letters*, pp. 6-7.

37. George Templeton Strong, *The Diary of George Templeton Strong*, ed. by Allan Nevins and Milton H. Thomas (New York, 1952), III, 324.

38. *Ibid.*, III, 325. Frederick Law Olmsted to John (?) Olmsted, 2 August 1863, Olmsted Papers.

39. Olmsted to John (?) Olmsted, 2 August 1863, Olmsted Papers.

40. Olmsted to Godkin, 1 August 1863, Godkin Papers.

41. Olmsted to Godkin, 15, 19 July, 25 December 1863, Godkin Papers.

42. Arthur Charles Cole, *The Irrepressible Conflict: 1850-1865* (New York, 1934), p. 376. Rollo Walter Brown, *Lonely Americans* (New York, 1929), p. 170.

43. Fisk, *Letters of John Fiske*, p. 165. Norton to Olmsted, 24 January 1864, Olmsted Papers. Kermit Vanderbilt, *Charles Eliot Norton: Apostle of Culture in a Democracy* (Cambridge, 1959), p. 96. E. L. Godkin, "Francis Parkman," *Nation* 71 (6 December 1900), p. 441. Francis Parkman to Godkin, 15 December 1885, 22, 29 November 1887, 23 February 1889, Godkin Papers. Godkin, *Gilded Age Letters*, p. 336.

44. Godkin "is here," Hale noted, "to see what encouragement he can get in undertaking a new weekly journal, political and literary—to be called perhaps 'The Week'. . . ." Quoted in Edward Everett Hale, *The Life and Letters of Edward Everett Hale*, ed. by Edward Everett Hale, Jr. (2 vols., Boston, 1917), I, 366-68.

45. Oswald G. Villard to Frank Preston Stearns, 12 October 1910, O. G. Villard Papers, Harvard University.

46. Godkin to Olmsted, 24 February 1864, Godkin Papers. From California Olmsted was mourning, "Why don't I hear something of your paper? . . . I don't think I should have been much for it, as my health turned out." Olmsted to Godkin, 25 December 1863, Godkin Papers.

47. Godkin to Olmsted, 24 February 1864.

48. Holt, *Sixty Years a Publisher*, p. 289.

49. *Daily News*, 20 June 1863, p. 4; 12 April 1865, p. 4. See also *ibid.*, 9 February 1863, p. 5.

50. Godkin to Olmsted, 24 February, 25 December 1864, Godkin Papers.

51. Godkin to Olmsted, 31 May 1864, Godkin Papers.

52. Godkin to Norton, 12 October 1864, Norton Papers. Godkin to Norton, 14 October 1864, Norton Papers.

53. Godkin to Norton, 30 November 1864, Norton Papers.

54. Norton to Olmsted (copy), 24 January 1864, Olmsted Papers.

55. Godkin to Olmsted, 25 December 1864, Godkin Papers.

56. Olmsted to Godkin, 25 December 1863, Godkin Papers.

57. Olmsted to Whom It May Concern, 19 February 1864, Olmsted Papers.

58. Godkin to Olmsted, 31 May 1864, Godkin Papers.

59. Godkin to Olmsted, 24 February 1864, Godkin Papers.

60. *Ibid.*

61. Godkin to Olmsted, 12 April 1865, Godkin Papers.

62. Calvert Vaux to Olmsted, 2 March 1864, Olmsted Papers.

63. *Ibid.*, Vaux to Olmsted, 24 March 1864, Olmsted Papers. Godkin to Olmsted, 24 February, 31 May, 25 December 1864, Godkin Papers.

64. Norton to Godkin, 17 November 1863, 5 March 1864, Godkin Papers; Norton to Godkin, 10 March 1864, Norton Papers.

65. "The Constitution and Its Defects," *North American Review* 99 (July 1864): 117-45.

66. Godkin to Norton, 10 May 1864, Norton Papers.

67. Godkin to Olmsted, 25 December 1864, Godkin Papers.

68. "Aristocratic Opinions of Democracy," *North American Review* 100 (January 1865): 194-232.

69. Oddly, students of the origins of the frontier thesis do not mention Godkin (see especially Lee Benson, "The Historical Background of Turner's Frontier Essay," *Agricultural History* 25 [April, 1951]: 96, n. 86). Turner, as Benson and other scholars suggest, may have been led to his conclusions partly from reading James Bryce's *American Commonwealth* (1888), but the evidence pointing to Godkin as a major anticipator of both Bryce and Turner is unassailable. That Turner did not mention Godkin in his 1893 paper means nothing, since Turner was no admirer of him. Twelve years after Godkin's death, in a commencement address at the University of Washington, Turner alluded to Godkin's essay, and he quoted excerpts from it to his audience. "The West and American Ideals," in Frederick Jackson Turner, *The Frontier in American History* (New York, 1920).

70. "Aristocratic Opinions of Democracy," p. 212.

71. "The Significance of the Frontier in American History," in Turner, *The Frontier in American History*.

72. Joseph B. Bishop, "Personal Recollections of E. L. Godkin," *Century* 64, New Series 42 (September 1902): 695. Godkin, *Gilded Age Letters*, p. 487n.

73. Olmsted to Godkin, 6, 9, 10, 22, 26 January, 20 February, 12 March, 4 April, 27 May, 1 June 1865, Godkin Papers. Godkin to Olmsted, 2, 12 April 1865, Godkin Papers.

74. Godkin to Mill, 1 April 1865, John Stuart Mill Papers, Johns Hopkins University Library.

75. Ogden, II, 42-44.

76. *Daily News*, 9 January 1863, p. 5.

77. Wendell P. Garrison to William Lloyd Garrison, Jr., 23 December 1863, William Lloyd Garrison, Jr. Papers, Smith College.

78. Godkin to Norton, 20 February 1865, Norton Papers.

79. James Russell Lowell, "Reconstruction," *North American Review* 100 (April 1865): 540-59. Godkin, *Gilded Age Letters*, 21-22.

80. Godkin, *Gilded Age Letters*, p. 46. Some writers have implied that Godkin was indifferent to voting rights for the blacks because, as a realist, he was more concerned for their educational well being. Yet his personal letters show no concern for black welfare, and he contributed neither time nor money to drives for the advancement of Negro education in the south.

81. Norton to Godkin, 5 April 1865, Godkin Papers.

82. Godkin to Norton, 13 April 1865, Norton Papers.

83. "The Democratic View of Democracy," *North American Review* 101 (July 1865): 103-33.

Chapter 5
FOUNDING THE NATION

1. E. L. Godkin to John Seely Hart, 31 August 1871, Hart Papers.

2. Ogden, I, 248, 250. *Letters of Charles Eliot Norton*, II, 439.

3. Prospectus of the *Nation* in Stanford University Library.

4. Godkin to Norton, 20 February 1865, Norton Papers. Godkin to Olmsted, 2 April 1865, Godkin Papers.

5. James M. McKim to Norton, 1 April 1865. Norton to Godkin, 5 April 1865, Godkin Papers.

6. Joseph H. Richards to [McKim], 15 April 1865, Norton Papers. McKim to Norton, 29 April 1865, Godkin Papers. McKim to Godkin, 3 December 1869, Olmsted Papers. "I am quite alone in the management of the [*Independent*] and wrote the leader for this week." Garrison told his brother in April 1865, "I could not think of letting Mr. Greeley speak for [the public] in such a crisis. He is clean daft on reconstruction as he was on peace." W. P. Garrison to William Lloyd Garrison, Jr., 13 April 1865, William Lloyd Garrison Papers, Harvard University.

7. McKim to Norton, 1 April [1865]. Godkin Letters.

8. McKim to Godkin, 29 April [1865]. Norton to Godkin, 5 April 1865. Godkin to Norton, 3 October 1865, 20 June 1866, Godkin Papers. Wendell P. Garrison, "Edwin Lawrence Godkin," *Book Buyer* 13 (February 1896): 5-7.

9. Joseph H. Richards to McKim, 15 April 1865 (copy), Godkin Papers.

10. John (?) to W. P. Garrison, 7 May 1865, Garrison Papers. Conway, *Autobiography*, pp. 364, 433, 438. Stearns, *Life of George Luther Stearns*, vii. Royal Cortissoz, *The Life of Whitelaw Reid*, 2 vols., (New York, 1921), I, 137.

11. "George L. Stearns," in Ralph Waldo Emerson, *Lectures and Biographical Sketches* (Boston and New York, 1904) pp. 501-07, 621-23. Norton to Godkin, 26 January 1866, Godkin Papers. The founding of the *Commonwealth* in some respects paralleled that of the *Nation*. In 1862 the Frank Bird Club of Boston undertook discussions aimed at founding a new abolitionist weekly. In July Stearns told Moncure Conway, the abolitionist scion of a prominent Maryland slaveholding family, that he was ready to "furnish the means for the present publication of a weekly newspaper which will fearlessly tell the truth about this war." He asked Conway, who in 1860 had edited the *Dial*, to be editor. The *Commonwealth* was launched in Boston in September 1862, with Conway as editor-in-chief, James Stone as publisher, and Frank B. Sanborn as associate editor. Besides Stearns the paper's backers included Elizar Wright and Albert G. Browne. Conway declared that the *Commonwealth* was not a rival to Garrison's *Liberator,* and apparently he and Sanborn performed the difficult feat of keeping on good terms with both the Garrison and the Phillips factions of the disrupted American Anti-Slavery

Society. In the controversy over the control of the *Nation*, the *Commonwealth* supported the Stearns faction and attacked Godkin. See Conway, *Autobiography*, p. 369.

12. Edward Cary, *George William Curtis* (Boston, 1894), p. 190. McKim to Norton, 29 April [1865], Godkin Papers. Stearns, *Life of George Luther Stearns*, p. 333.

13. Stearns, *Life of George Luther Stearns*, p. 334. Cortissoz, *Whitelaw Reid*, I, 137-38.

14. Olmsted to Godkin, 12 March, 27 May 1865. Godkin to Olmsted, 2, 12 April 1865. Norton to Godkin, 5 April 1865, Godkin Papers.

15. Godkin to Norton, 6 May 1865, Norton Papers. Godkin to Norton, 25 July 1877. Norton to Godkin, 7 May 1865, Godkin Papers. Stearns, *Life of George Luther Stearns*, p. 334. *Letters of Norton*, II, 439. Godkin, *Gilded Age Letters*, p. 463.

16. Godkin to Olmsted, 5 May 1865. Olmsted to Godkin, 10 June 1865, Godkin Papers.

17. McKim to Norton, 29 April [1865]. Norton to Godkin, 9 May 1865. Richards to McKim, 15 April 1865 (copy), Godkin Papers. Ogden, *Godkin*, I, 239. Godkin to Norton, 6 May 1865, Norton Papers.

18. Stearns, *Life of George Luther Stearns*, pp. 334-35. Printed circulars, Stearns to *Nation* stockholders, 14 August, 4 September 1865, Godkin Papers.

19. Godkin to Norton, 11 May 1865, Norton Papers. Stearns, *Life of George Luther Stearns*, p. 333. C. E. Detmold to George Bancroft, 9 May 1865, George Bancroft Papers, Massachusetts Historical Society. Godkin to James Parton, 6 June [1865], James Parton Papers, Harvard University. Hans Trefousse to the author, 22 January 1958. Godkin's long enmity toward Bancroft, James Parton, Butler, Phillips, and Sumner may have related in part to their refusal of financial help to the *Nation*. Norton to Godkin, 15 February 1866, Godkin Papers.

20. Benjamin F. Butler to Edward G. Pierce (rough draft), 12 July 1865, Benjamin F. Butler Papers, Manuscript Division, Library of Congress.

21. Edward P. Mitchell, *Memories of An Editor: Fifty Years of American Journalism* (New York, 1924), p. 302.

22. Stearns to Sumner, 30 April 1865, Charles Sumner Papers, Harvard University. Stearns, *Life of George Luther Stearns*, p. 344. Stearns' letter reads in part: "Charles Norton and myself are here, making arrangements to establish a weekly newspaper to advocate advanced opinions. Its location will be New York and we expect to secure some of the best editorial talent of the country."

23. John Murray Forbes, *Letters and Recollections of John Murray Forbes*, 2 vols., edited by Sarah Forbes Hughes (Boston, 1899), II, 143-44.

24. Norton to Godkin, 13 July 1865. Godkin to Norton, 22 July [1865], Godkin Papers. Godkin to Olmsted, 23 July [1865]. McKim to Olmsted, 27 July 1865. Olmsted to his wife, 23 August [1865]. Olmsted to McKim, 7 September 1865, Olmsted Papers.

25. Godkin to Norton, 6 May 1865, Norton Papers.

26. W. P. Garrison to William Lloyd Garrison, Jr., 15 June 1865, Garrison Papers. Ogden, I, 239. Godkin to Olmsted, 23 July [1865], Olmsted Papers. Godkin to Norton, 23, 30 June [1865]. Godkin to C. C. Hazewell, 21 June [1865], Autograph Collection, Harvard University. Godkin to Norton, 6 June, 29 September 1865. Norton to Godkin, 9 June 1865, Godkin Papers.

27. Godkin to Hazewell, 21 June [1865].

28. Godkin to Norton, 26 September, 4 November 1865. Norton to Godkin, 26 January 1866, Godkin Papers. Godkin, *Gilded Age Letters*, p. 71.

29. Godkin to John S. Hart, 28 August [1871], Hart Papers. Henry J. Raymond to Godkin, 12 June 1865. Godkin to Norton, 25 July [1865], Godkin Papers.

30. Charles Nordhoff to Norton, 4 May [1865]. Norton to Godkin, 7 May 1865, Godkin Papers. Godkin to Norton, 6 May 1865, Norton Papers.

31. McKim to Norton, 11 May [1865]. Godkin to Norton, 6, 11 May 1865, Norton Papers. McKim to Pierce, 10 July 1865, Butler Papers.

32. Godkin to Olmsted, 5 May 1865. Godkin to Daniel Coit Gilman, 6 June [1865], Godkin Papers. Godkin to Gilman, 1, 28 June [1865], Daniel Coit Gilman Papers, Johns Hopkins University.

33. Norton to Godkin, 7, 8, 9, 13 May, 9, 12, 15 June 1865, Godkin Papers. Godkin to Norton, 6, 11 May 1865, Norton Papers. Godkin to Norton, 12, 26 May, 23, 30 June 1865. Edward Atkinson to Norton, 10 June 1865. Edward Austin to Norton, 26 May 1865. Charles Beck to Norton, 7 June 1865. Samuel G. Ward to Norton, 6, 13, 21 June 1865. Dennett to Norton, 20 June 1865. J. M. Forbes to Norton, 8 June 1865. James M. McKim to Norton, 11 May [1865]. Nordhoff to Norton, 4 May [1865]. E. L. Philbrick to Norton, 15 May 1865, Godkin Papers.

34. Godkin to Norton, 5 May 1865. Norton to Godkin, 9 May 1865, Godkin Papers. See also Godkin to Henry Wadsworth Longfellow, 6 November 1865, Longfellow Trust, Harvard University, and Godkin to Norton, 6 June 1865, Godkin Papers.

35. Godkin to Norton, 6 June 1865, Godkin Papers.

36. Godkin to Norton, 11 May 1865, Norton Papers. S. G. Ward to Norton, 20, 21 August 1865. E. W. Gurney to Garrison, 6 June 1865. Godkin to Norton, 26 May, 25, 27 July [1865], Godkin Papers. Ogden, *Godkin*, I, 240. Godkin to Atkinson, 17 July 1865. Stearns to Norton, 26 July 1865, and Stearns to Norton, 14 August 1865 are in Stearns' circular to the *Nation* stockholders, August 1865. Stearns to Norton, 3 September 1865, and Godkin to Norton, 23 August 1865, are both printed in Stearns' circular to the *Nation* stockholders, September 1865, Godkin Papers.

37. Called upon by the stockholders to explain the "Philadelphia pledge," Godkin pleaded expediency, whereupon Stearns, Hallowell, and Atkinson demanded his dismissal. Norton and McKim backed Godkin, and the resulting uproar was nearly fatal to the *Nation*. Godkin to Norton, 22, 27, 29 July, 19, 24, 26 August, 19 September, 20 October, 20, 22, 29 November 1865. Atkinson to Norton, 19 July, 12, 16 August 1865.

222 NOTES TO PAGES 84-88

S. G. Ward to Norton, 21 August 1865. Atkinson to Godkin, 18 July 1865, Godkin Papers.

38. Henry James, *Notes of a Son and Brother* (New York, 1914), p. 425. Henry James, "The Founding of the 'Nation,'" *Nation*, 8 July 1915, p. 45.

39. Dennett to Norton, 20 June 1865, Godkin Papers. See also Godkin to Norton, 6, 30 June [1865]. Norton to Godkin, 9, 12 June 1865, *ibid.*

40. Albert Bushnell Hart, ed., *American History as told by Contemporaries* (New York, 1929), IV, 448-52. Godkin "spent nine months journeying through the South," Hart mistakenly asserted in introducing his fragmentary reprint of "The South As It Is" under Godkin's name, "and during this time he wrote a letter for each issue of the Nation. . . ." *Ibid.*, 448. Lowell to Godkin, 25 September 1866, Godkin Papers.

41. Godkin to Norton, 6, 11 May 1865, Norton Papers. Samuel S. White to McKim, 31 August 1870 (copy), Olmsted Papers. Ogden, *Godkin*, I, 239. Godkin to Atkinson, 29 June 1871, Edward Atkinson Papers, Massachusetts Historical Society. Forbes to Norton, 12 March, 8 June 1865, 12 February, 19 April 1866. Atkinson to Norton, 10, 12 June 1865, 25 April 1866. Stearns to Norton, 31 July 1865. Hallowell to Norton, 27 July 1865. Norton to Godkin, 8, 13, 18 May, 15 June 1865, 21 June 1866. McKim to Norton, 11 May [1865]. Godkin to Norton, 26 May, 10 December [1865], 20 February, 11 March, 20 June [1866]. George C. Ward to Norton, 6, 21 June 1865. Philbrick to Norton, 15 May 1865, Godkin Papers.

42. Forbes to Norton, 12 March 1865, Godkin Papers. See Norton to Godkin, 8 May 1865, and Godkin to Norton, 12 May [1865], *ibid.* Godkin to Norton, 11 May 1865, Norton Papers.

43. Austin to Norton, 26 May 1865. Godkin to Norton, 12 May [1865], Godkin Papers.

44. Godkin to Norton, 12, 26, 28 May [1865], *ibid.*

45. Ward to Norton, 6 June 1865, *ibid.* Godkin to Gilman, 1 June [1865], Gilman Papers. McKim to Mrs. Maria W. Chapman, 6 June 1865, Chapman Papers, Boston Public Library.

46. Beck to Norton, 7 June 1865. Norton to Godkin, 13 May 1865. Forbes to Norton, 8 June 1865. Godkin to Norton, 6 June 1865, Godkin Papers.

47. Norton to Godkin, 9 June 1865, *ibid.*

48. Atkinson to Norton, 10, 12 June 1865, *ibid.*

49. Norton to Godkin, 9, 12, 15 June, 16 August 1865, Godkin Papers. Printed circular, Stearns to *Nation* stockholders, September 1865. Printed circular, Norton to *Nation* stockholders, August 1865, *ibid.*

50. Ward to Norton, 21 June 1865. Forbes to Norton, 8 June 1865, *ibid.*

51. Godkin to Norton, 23, 30 June, 27 July, 16 August [1865]. Atkinson to Norton, 12 August 1865, *ibid.*

52. Ogden, I, 239.

Chapter 6
THE WEEKLY "DAY OF JUDGMENT"

1. *New York Times*, 7 July 1865. Raymond sent an apology to Godkin for the editorial.

2. Godkin, *Gilded Age Letters*, p. 40. Contrary to Wall and Sterne, Wendell Phillips was not a stockholder in the *Nation*. Joseph Frazier Wall, review, *History; Reviews of New Books*, 3 (January 1975). Richard Clark Sterne, "The *Nation* and its Century," *The Nation*, 100th Anniversary Issue, 20 September 1965, p. 47.

3. *Nation*, 6 July 1865, p. 1.

4. Wendell P. Garrison to William Lloyd Garrison, 28 March 1875, Garrison Papers, Harvard University. Pierce to Butler, 11 July 1875, Butler Papers.

5. Quoted in Stearns, *Life of George Luther Stearns*, p. 337.

6. Addison Hogue to Lawrence Godkin, 20 April 1903, Godkin Papers.

7. Godkin, *Gilded Age Letters*, p. 47.

8. Stearns, *Life of George Luther Stearns*, p. 334. Godkin to *Nation* stockholders, 23 August 1865 (printed circular), Godkin Papers. Godkin to Charles Eliot Norton, 19 September 1865, Godkin Papers.

9. McKim to Pierce, 10 July 1865, Butler Papers.

10. Stearns, *Life of George Luther Stearns*, pp. 357, 370. Godkin, *Gilded Age Letters*, pp. 30, 40, 44-85 *passim*. Godkin's side of the controversy with Stearns is argued in Wendell P. Garrison to William Lloyd Garrison, 28 March 1875, Garrison Papers, Harvard. Wendell P. Garrison to Godkin, 28 December 1899, Godkin Papers. Godkin to Norton, 25 July 1877, Godkin Papers.

11. Godkin, *Gilded Age Letters*, p. 68.

12. *Ibid.*, pp. 60-61, 64-65, 66, 68, 71, 72, 74.

13. *Ibid.*, pp. 83-86. James Bryce, *Studies in Contemporary Biography* (London, 1903), p. 371.

14. William Roscoe Thayer, "Edwin Lawrence Godkin," in M. A. DeWolfe Howe, ed., *Later Years of the Saturday Club* (New York, 1927), p. 95.

15. Henry F. Pringle, *Theodore Roosevelt, A Biography* (New York, 1931), p. 32. Charles W. Eliot to E. L. Godkin, 18 July 1870, Godkin Papers. Godkin, *Gilded Age Letters*, pp. 148-57 *passim*, 307, 488, 311n. After consulting friends, Godkin turned down the professorship, one acquaintance urging him to remain on the *Nation* because "you are giving weekly lessons in history to hundreds of college graduates."

16. Undated verse bearing Godkin's signature, Godkin Papers.

17. James Bryce, "Two Editors: Recollections of E. L. Godkin and W. P. Garrison," *Nation*, 8 July 1915, p. 41. Matthew Arnold, *Civilization in the United States* (Boston, 1888), pp. 89, 178. James Bryce, *Studies in Contemporary Biography*, pp. 372-73.

18. Thomas Bailey Aldrich to E. C. Stedman, 30 October 1873, Special

Collections, Columbia University. On the subject of Dennett's captiousness, see also citations in Chap. 6, note 54 and Henry James the elder to Henry James, Jr., 19 March 1870, James Papers.

19. Godkin to Norton, 30 December 1865, Godkin Papers.

20. Prospectus of the *Nation*, Stanford University Library. See also *Nation*, 13 July 1865, p. 63, and 17 August 1865, p. 199.

21. Joseph B. Bishop, *Notes and Anecdotes of Many Years* (New York, 1925), p. 106.

22. "The Proper Work of the City Club," *Nation*, 21 April 1892, p. 296. See also "Personalities," *Nation*, 29 December 1892, p. 488.

23. Arthur G. Sedgwick, "The 'Nation's' Critics," *Nation*, 8 July 1915, p. 56. Godkin, *Gilded Age Letters*, pp. 88, 114n, 431.

24. Worthington C. Ford to Wendell P. Garrison, 18 April 1906. Frederick Bancroft to Wendell P. Garrison, 3 July 1906, Wendell P. Garrison Papers, Harvard University.

25. Woodrow Wilson, *Papers*, edited by Arthur S. Link and others (Princeton, 1966-) 11, 280. William Allen White, *Autobiography* (New York, 1946), pp. 144-45.

26. Worthington C. Ford to Henry Adams, 5 January 1897, Adams Papers, Massachusetts Historical Society. E. L. Godkin to Moses Coit Tyler, 25 May 1867, Moses Coit Tyler Papers, Cornell University. *Nation*, 27 November 1873, p. 354. Charles H. Farnham, *A Life of Francis Parkman* (Boston, 1901), pp. 271-72, 348. *Letters and Memorials of Wendell Phillips Garrison*, comp. by J. H. McDaniels (Cambridge, Mass., 1908), pp. 104, 159-60. Learned, *The Literature of American History: A Bibliographical Guide*, p. 308, items 2735, 2736. M. A. DeWolfe Howe, *James Ford Rhodes, American Historian* (New York, 1929), pp. 23, 45, 154, 160, 165, 168-72. Rhodes, "Edwin Lawrence Godkin," *Historical Essays*, pp. 279-88 (reprinted from *Atlantic Monthly*, September 1908). Harvey Cushing, "James Ford Rhodes," in Howe, *Later Years of the Saturday Club*, p. 349. Ellis P. Oberholtzer, *A History of the United States since the Civil War* (New York, 1917-1937). *Evening Post*, 16 November 1901, Second Historical Supplement, p. 8. Leading historians like A. B. Hart and H. E. von Holst agreed with the *Nation* on essentials but nursed private grievances against Godkin. See Albert Bushnell Hart to Wendell P. Garrison, 8 July 1906, Garrison Papers, Harvard University. H. E. von Holst to E. L. Godkin, 13 April 1878, Hermann von Holst Papers, University of Chicago.

27. Theodore Roosevelt, *Letters*, edited by Elting E. Morison, John M. Blum and others (Cambridge, Massachusetts, 1951-1954), VI, 1399.

28. James Bryce to Godkin, 24 January 1889, Godkin Papers. The reply to this letter is in Godkin to Bryce, 24 March 1889, Bryce Papers. A friend of Godkin put Bryce's reasons more bluntly. Bryce, he alleged, had refused to give Godkin his due for "fear that people would say the author was 'reproducing the *Nation*.'" Frederick Sheldon to E. L. Godkin, 6 January 1889, Godkin Papers. Godkin appears in the preface to later editions of the *American Commonwealth*. Subsequent testimonials to him

by Bryce appear in his "Two Editors: Recollections of E. L. Godkin and W. P. Garrison," *Nation*, 8 July 1915, p. 41, and his above-cited chapter on Godkin in his *Studies in Contemporary Biography*.

29. Oberholtzer, *History of the United States*, III, 477, 478; IV, 141; V, 301, and footnotes throughout all five volumes.

30. Howe, *James Ford Rhodes*, pp. 23, 45, 154, 160, 165, 168-72. See also Howe, *Later Years of the Saturday Club*, p. 349.

31. Rhodes, *Historical Essays*, pp. 279-80.

32. Howe, *Rhodes*, p. 168. Except for the digest *Public Opinion*, the *Nation* is the only authority that Rhodes cites in his Volumes VI and VII. Oddly enough not all specialists in late nineteenth-century American history are aware of the influence of the *Nation* on historians. The commentator at the session, "Reconstruction," of the 1960 annual meeting of the Mississippi Valley Historical Association, a well-known historian, wondered aloud to his audience where Rhodes got his later view of Reconstruction.

33. "The Real Weakness of American Universities," *Nation*, 3 May 1883, p. 377. See also "Professorial Salaries in America," *Nation*, 31 May 1883, p. 461. Unless otherwise indicated, all *Nation* articles and editorials cited herein were written by Godkin.

34. Charles A. and Mary R. Beard, *The Rise of American Civilization* (New York, 1928), pp. 11, 465.

35. Godkin to Norton, 23 August 1866, Godkin Papers. Godkin, *Gilded Age Letters*, pp. 56, 87-88, 91-93, 133-34, 144-45, 164, 294-95, 304, 392, 448, 499.

36. Henry F. Pringle, "Godkin of the *Post*," *Scribners Magazine* 96, 6 (December 1934): 327. J. Lincoln Steffens, *The Autobiography of Lincoln Steffens* (New York, 1931), pp. 172, 179, 180. Bishop, *Notes and Anecdotes*, pp. 87, 97-98. Nevins, *The Evening Post*, pp. 527-28. Villard, *Some Newspapers and Newspapermen*, pp. 293-96. Godkin, *Gilded Age Letters*, pp. 11, 88, 91, 114n, 133-34, 160, 162-63, 185, 199-200, 428-29, 447, 531. Godkin's relations with his employer Henry Villard, after 1881 the proprietor of the *Nation* and the *Evening Post*, at times bordered on a vendetta.

37. Godkin to Olmsted, 24 February 1864, Godkin Papers.

38. Barrett Wendell and Chester Noyes Greenough, *A History of Literature in America* (New York, 1907), pp. 439-40.

39. Ferris Greenslet, *The Lowells and Their Seven Worlds* (Boston, 1946), p. 322. William James to Henry James, 22 January 1876, James Papers, Harvard University.

40. A thinly supported brief for Godkin's devotion to democracy is Harold W. Stoke, "Edwin Lawrence Godkin, Defender of Democracy," *The South Atlantic Quarterly* 30 (1931): 339. Another writer reaches the yet more startling conclusion that, besides being a champion of democracy, Godkin was "popular." Barbara D. Cochran, "The Evolution of Journalism," in George F. Mott, ed., *Survey of Journalism* (New York, 1937), p. 23.

41. *Nation*, 26 October 1865, p. 527. *Ibid.*, 30 November 1865, p. 674.

Ibid., 15 July 1869, p. 45.

42. For Godkin's defense of pessimism, see his "Optimists and Pessimists," *Nation*, 24 July 1890, p. 64.

43. *Nation*, 13 May 1869, p. 369.

44. Russell Kirk, *The Conservative Mind*, (Chicago, 1953), p. 309.

45. Statement by Joseph B. Bishop to Richard W. G. Welling, Diary of Richard W. G. Welling, entry of 5 July 1907, Welling Papers, New York Public Library. The writer is indebted to Robert Muccigrosso for this information.

46. Godkin to Norton, 4 November 1866, Godkin Papers.

47. Vincent DeSantis, *Republicans Face the Southern Question* (Baltimore, 1959), pp. 50-51. An able summation of Godkin's vacillating editorial policy toward the blacks is found in Allan P. Grimes, *The Political Liberalism of the New York Nation* (Chapel Hill, 1953), pp. 5-12. His views on woman suffrage are outlined in the *Daily News* (London), 17 August 1867, p. 5 and in "Female Suffrage," *Nation*, 8 March 1883, pp. 204-05.

48. Bryce, *Studies in Contemporary Biography*, p. 372. Godkin, *Gilded Age Letters*, p. 241. The *Nation's* policy of anonymity of contributors was responsible for frequent misunderstandings. For an amusing one—it shows, incidentally, how tactless and meddlesome Godkin could be—see Evelyn Page, "The Man around the Corner," *New England Quarterly* 23 (1950): 401, and *Henry Adams and his Friends; A Collection of his Unpublished Letters*, compiled by Harold Dean Cater (Boston, 1947), pp. 96, 102-03, 105. See also *Nation*, 1 February 1866, p. 129.

49. Lowell to Godkin, 25 September 1866, Godkin Papers.

50. Godkin to Moses Coit Tyler, 25 May 1867, Tyler Papers.

51. Vanderbilt, *Charles Eliot Norton*, p. 99.

52. Virginia Harlow, *Thomas Sergeant Perry; A Biography* (Durham, North Carolina, 1950), pp. 52-55.

53. W. C. Brownell, "The *Nation* from the Inside," *Nation*, 8 July 1915, p. 42. George W. Curtis, "The Easy Chair," *Harper's* (September 1884).

54. Sedgwick, "The 'Nation's' Critics," p. 54. Ogden, I, 308. M. A. DeWolfe Howe, ed., *Memories of a Hostess* (Boston, 1922), pp. 126-27. Eleanor M. Tilton, *Amiable Autocrat; A Biography of Dr. Oliver Wendell Holmes* (New York, 1947), pp. 290-91. *The Nation: Index of Contributors*, compiled by Daniel C. Haskell (New York, 1953). Hereafter cited as *Nation Index: Contributors*.

55. *Nation Index: Contributors*. *Fifty Years of American Idealism: The New York Nation, 1865-1915*, edited by Gustave Pollak (New York, 1915), p. 17. Mrs. Henry James to Alice James, 25 August [1872?], Henry James, Sr., to Henry James, Jr., 27 April 1869, James Papers.

56. Rufus Wilson Rockwell, *New York in Literature* (Elmira, New York, 1947), pp. 45, 107-08.

57. Godkin to Norton, 26 January 1866, Godkin Papers.

58. Wendell P. Garrison, *Letters and Memorials of Wendell Phillips*

Garrison, compiled by J. H. McDaniels. Fabian Franklin, *People and Problems* (New York, 1908), p. 183. Rollo Ogden, "Wendell Phillips Garrison," *Nation*, 7 March 1907, pp. 217-19. Lounsbury Papers, Yale University Library. Lea Papers, University of Pennsylvania. The last two are a mine of information on Garrison's method of dealing with contributors to the *Nation*.

59. Godkin to Garrison, 24 July 1883, Godkin Papers. Wendell P. Garrison to Godkin, 28 December 1899, Godkin Papers. *The Outlook*, 21 July 1915, p. 642. The negative feelings of the Garrisons toward Godkin and the *Nation* are illustrated in William Lloyd Garrison to Wendell P. Garrison, 25 January 1875, and William Lloyd Garrison to Fanny Garrison Villard, 4 December 1876, Garrison Papers, Boston Public Library. William Lloyd Garrison to Wendell P. Garrison, 15 February 1878, and the same to Ellen Garrison, 7 and 10 February 1875, and Fanny Garrison Villard, 7 February 1878, Garrison Papers, Smith College.

60. Garrison to his mother, 21 April 1871, Garrison Papers, Harvard. For a list of Garrison's contributions to the *Nation*, see *Nation Index: Contributors* and William M. Armstrong, "Additions to the *Nation Index*," *Bulletin of the New York Public Library* 73, 4 (April 1969): 268.

61. James M. McPherson to the writer, 2 July 1967.

62. Cornelia Pulsifer Kelley, *The Early Development of Henry James* (Urbana, Illinois, 1965), pp. 23-26.

63. Holt, *Sixty Years a Publisher*, p. 52. Henry Holt, "A Young Man's Oracle," *Nation*, 8 July 1915, p. 47. Richard Hofstadter, *Social Darwinism in American Thought* (New York, 1959), pp. 23-24.

64. Sidney Lanier, *The Centennial Edition of the Works of Sidney Lanier*, edited by Charles R. Anderson and A. H. Starke (Baltimore, 1945) X, 7. Cf. *Ibid.*, II, xxvii; IX, 211-12.

65. Thomas Bailey Aldrich to James R. Osgood, 21 December 1874, Rogers Room, Harvard University.

66. Godkin, *Gilded Age Letters*, pp. 257-61 *passim*.

67. William Dean Howells to Thomas Bailey Aldrich, 27 October 1866. Thomas Bailey Aldrich Papers, Harvard University.

68. Harlow, *Thomas Sergeant Perry*, pp. 55, 126. Garrison, *Letters and Memorials*, p. 104, and *Nation Index: Contributors*.

69. Ernest Samuels, *The Young Henry Adams* (Cambridge, Massachusetts, 1948), pp. 172, 188-90. *Nation Index: Contributors*. For the secret contributions of Schurz to the *Nation*, see Armstrong, "Additions to the *Nation* Index."

70. *Nation*, 24 June 1869, p. 490. See also *Ibid.*, "Opinion-Moulding," 12 August 1869, pp. 126-27. "The Boston Press," 17 March 1892, pp. 206-07. "Journalistic Dementia," 14 March 1895, pp. 195-96. Bryce, *Studies in Contemporary Biography*, p. 379.

71. Charles F. Wingate, ed., *Views and Interviews on Journalism* (New York, 1875), p. 211.

72. Ogden, II, 51.

73. Godkin, *Gilded Age Letters*, p. 73.

74. Quoted in *Nation*, 7 January 1869, p. 6.

75. "The Impeachment," *Nation*, 18 October 1866, p. 310. "The Result of the Trial," *Nation*, 21 May 1868, p. 404. "The Executive Legislating," *Nation*, 5 April 1866, p. 423. Cf. *Nation*, 1 March, 9 August, 20 September 1866, pp. 262, 110, 233.

76. "The End at Last," *Nation*, 19 May 1870, p. 314. "Police Duty," *Nation*, 27 April 1871, pp. 284-85. "The Law and the Facts in Louisiana," *Nation*, 14 January 1875, p. 20. Scholars sometimes overplay Godkin's role in the Radical cause, as in the inflated depiction of him as a Radical spokesman by David Montgomery, *Beyond Equality; Labor and the Radical Republicans, 1862-1872* (New York, Alfred A. Knopf, 1967), pp. 80, 85, 203-40, 247, *et seq.*

77. "'Radicals' and 'Conservatives,'" *Nation*, 13 July 1871, p. 21.

78. "Socialism in South Carolina," *Nation*, 16 April 1874, pp. 247-48.

79. Merle Curti, *The Growth of American Thought* (New York, 1943), p. 487. Roger W. Shugg, "The Liberal Ideology and Reconstruction," paper read at a joint session of the American Historical Association and the Southern Historical Association at Chicago, *c.* 29 December 1953. "The Negro's Claim to Office," *Nation*, 1 August 1867, p. 90. "The Republican Party and the Negro," *Forum* 7 (March 1889): 246-57. Addison Hogue to Lawrence Godkin, 20 April 1903, Godkin Papers. Godkin, *Gilded Age Letters*, p. 249.

80. "Some Recent Observations in Virginia," *Nation*, 13 September 1877, p. 163.

81. Gabriel Kolko, *Railroads and Regulation 1877-1916* (Princeton, 1965), p. 12, quoting from Godkin's "The Late Riots," *Nation*, 2 August 1877, p. 68. Allan P. Grimes, *American Political Thought* (New York, 1960), pp. 487, 489.

Chapter 7
"ANNEXATION FEVER" AND IMMIGRATION FOLLY

1. *Nation*, 1865, 13 July, p. 34, 20 July, p. 79, 27 July, p. 100, 3 August, pp. 143-44, 10 August, p. 177, 17 August, p. 193, 24 August, p. 225, 31 August, p. 271, 14 September, pp. 323-24, 21 September, p. 356; *ibid.*, 2 August 1866, p. 81.

2. Armstrong, *Godkin and American Foreign Policy*, p. 70.

3. *Nation*, 1867, 4 April, p. 266, 11 April, p. 286, 18 April, p. 305, 21 November, p. 496 and 19 December, p. 493; *ibid.*, 1868, 2 January, pp. 4-5, 13 February, p. 122, and 21 May, p. 403; *ibid.*, 10 December, 1874, p. 374.

4. *Nation*, 29 November 1866, p. 432.

5. J. M. Callahan, *American Foreign Policy in Canadian Relations, 1849-1874* (New York, 1937), pp. 12, 193.

6. "The Annexation Fever," *Nation*, 15 April 1869, pp. 289-90. For contradictory claims by Godkin of British and Canadian opinion toward annexation, see Armstrong, *Godkin and American Foreign Policy*, pp. 106, 221n.

7. Quoted in L. B. Shippee, *Canadian-American Relations, 1849-74* (New Haven, 1939), p. 211. Cf. *Blackwood's Magazine* 106 (1869): 196. *North American Review* 108 (1869): 637-39. For a detailed study of American agitation for the annexation of Canada, see Donald F. Warner, *The Idea of Continental Union* (Lexington, Kentucky, 1962).

8. "The Annexation Fever," p. 289.

9. *Nation*, 4 October 1866, pp. 270, 271; *ibid.*, 2 June 1870, p. 374. U. S. Department of State, *Papers Relating to Foreign Relations of the United States* (Washington, D. C., 1865) II, 96-97. *A Compilation of the Messages and Papers of the Presidents, 1789-1897*, prepared by James D. Richardson (New York, 1911) V, 3595, 3540, 3655, 3718. U. S. Congress, *The Congressional Globe*, 39 Cong., 1 Sess. (Washington, D. C., 1866-1867), pp. 493, 3085, 4049, 4193, 4274. U. S. Congress, House, *House Report* No. 100, 39 Cong., 1 Sess. (Washington, D. C., 1866).

10. "Fenianism as a Swindle," *Nation*, 2 June 1870, p. 347. For British attitudes as reflected in the correspondence of two British representatives in the United States, see Shippee, *Canadian-American Relations, 1849-1874*, pp. 216, 218. For secondary accounts of American Fenianism from the Anglo-Saxon vantage point, see *ibid.*, pp. 213-39 and C. P. Stacey, "Fenianism and the Rise of National Feeling in Canada at the time of Confederation," *Canadian Historical Review* 12 (1931): 238-61.

11. "The Fenian Sop," *Nation*, 4 October 1866, p. 271.

12. "Eighteen Hundred and Sixty-Six," *Nation*, 27 December 1866, p. 519. "The Latest Phase of Fenianism," *Nation*, 2 January 1868, p. 5. "The Rising in Ireland," *Nation*, 14 March 1867, p. 213.

13. "The Latest Phase of Fenianism," p. 5.

14. "Protectorates," *Nation*, 21 January 1869, pp. 44-45. For the details of the Hawaiian reciprocity treaty, see Sylvester K. Stevens, *American Expansion in Hawaii, 1842-1898* (Harrisburg, Pennsylvania, 1945), pp. 97-105, and John Patterson, "The United States and Hawaiian Reciprocity, 1867-1870," *Pacific Historical Review* 7 (1938): 14-26. On the use of bribery in the purchase of Alaska, see F. A. Golder, "The Purchase of Alaska," *American Historical Review* 25 (1920): 419. W. A. Dunning, "Paying for Alaska," *Political Science Quarterly* 27 (1912): 386. R. H. Luthin, "The Sale of Alaska," *Slavonic Review* 16 (1937): 171.

15. "Protectorates," p. 45.

16. "The Annexation Fever," p. 289.

17. "Protectorates," p. 45.

18. "Sympathy," *Nation*, 28 July 1870, p. 52.

19. *Ibid.*, p. 52.

20. "The Latest Phase of Fenianism," p. 6. "Sympathy," p. 52. Cf. *Nation*, 23 January 1868, p. 63.

21. "Sympathy," p. 52.

22. *Nation*, 21 July 1870, p. 36.

23. "Culture and War," *Nation*, 8 September 1870, pp. 151-52. Friedrich Kapp to E. L. Godkin, 7 October and [21?] November 1870, Godkin Papers.

24. "Neutrals and Contraband," *Nation*, 15 September 1870, p. 166.

25. J. F. Rippy, *The Caribbean Danger Zone* (New York, 1950), pp. 117-20.

26. Allan Nevins, *Hamilton Fish* (New York, 1936), pp. 260-61, 318.

27. Richardson, *Messages and Papers*, VI, 4053-55.

28. "The Santo Domingo Row," *Nation*, 29 December 1870, p. 432.

29. *Ibid.*

30. *Ibid.*

31. See C. C. Tansill, *The United States and Santo Domingo, 1798-1873* (Baltimore, 1938), pp. 366, *et. seq. Atlantic Monthly* 76 (1895): 167-68. U. S. Congress, Senate, *Senate Exec. Doc.* No. 34, 41st Cong., 3 Sess. (Washington, D.C., 1871), pp. 2-5.

32. J. V. Fuller, "Hamilton Fish," in Bemis, *American Secretaries of State and Their Diplomacy*, VII, 162.

33. "The Washington Imbroglio," *Nation*, 16 March 1871, p. 172.

34. *Ibid.*, p. 172. (Italics are the writer's.)

35. Nevins, *Fish*, p. 463.

36. "The Santo Domingo Row," p. 432. (Italics are the writer's.)

37. "The American Diplomatic Service," *Nation*, 27 February 1868, pp. 248-49.

38. *Ibid.*

39. *Saturday Review* (London), 22 August 1868, pp. 248-49.

40. "The Coming of the Barbarian," *ibid.*, 15 July 1869, p. 45. On this point, see Mary Coolidge, *Chinese Immigration* (New York, 1909), p. 21.

41. "The Coming of the Barbarian," p. 45.

42. *Ibid.*

43. "The Chinese Invasion," *Nation*, 14 July 1870, p. 20.

44. "The Coming of the Barbarian," p. 45.

45. "The Chinese Invasion," p. 20.

46. Frothingham to Godkin, 17 July 1870, Godkin Papers.

47. "Tertullian at the Amphitheatre," *Nation*, 22 September 1870, p. 187.

48. *Ibid.*

49. Quoted in C. C. Tansill, *The Foreign Policy of Thomas F. Bayard* (New York, 1940), p. 131. Cited hereafter as Tansill, *Bayard.*

50. On the subject of discriminatory legislation toward the Chinese in California, see Lucille Evans, *History of California Labor Legislation* (Berkeley, 1910), pp. 105-25.

51. F. W. Taussig, *Principles of Economics* (New York, 1911), Vol. II, p. 140.

52. *Nation*, 9 December 1880, p. 402. For other comment by the *Nation* on the Morey letter case, see these issues of 1880: 28 October, p. 297, 4 November, p. 316, 18 November, p. 349.

53. Cited in *Nation*, 21 February 1884, p. 154.

54. Henry Adams, *The Education of Henry Adams* (New York, 1918),

pp. 280, 336.

55. Russell Kirk makes a persuasive case for putting Godkin in the American conservative tradition in his *The Conservative Mind*, pp. 294, 304-10. Louis Filler presents the case for Godkin's "liberalism of dogma" in his "East and Middle West: Concepts of Liberalism in America during the Late Nineteenth Century," *American Journal of Economics and Sociology* (January, 1951), 179ff.

56. "The Decision on the Geary Act," *Evening Post*, 16 May 1893. On Godkin's inconsistencies, see Armstrong, *Godkin and American Foreign Policy*, pp. 29, 30, 45, 210n, 240n. Historians unacquainted with Godkin occasionally dispute his inconsistency, as, for example, the uninformed review by Joseph Dorfman of Allen P. Grimes, *Political Liberalism of the New York Nation, 1865-1932* (Chapel Hill, 1953) in the *American Historical Review* 59 (1954): 455.

57. "The Proper Sieve for Immigrants," p. 312.

58. Quoted in Howard K. Beale, *Theodore Roosevelt and the Rise of America to World Power* (Baltimore, 1956), p. 29. For Godkin's views on Anglo-Saxon superiority, see Godkin, *Gilded Age Letters*, pp. 13, 101, 144. Godkin, *History of Hungary*, pp. 368-69. "An English Dream of 'Americanization'," *Nation*, 5 April 1883, p. 290. "The Proper Sieve for Immigrants," *Nation*, 16 April 1891, p. 312. Bryce, *Studies in Contemporary Biography*, p. 376. *Nation*, 4 March 1869, p. 166. Denis T. Lynch, *"Boss" Tweed* (New York, 1927), pp. 371-74.

59. Godkin, *Gilded Age Letters*, p. 27. *Nation*, 13 July 1876, pp. 20-21. Parrington, *Main Currents in American Thought*, III, 160. Again Godkin was not consistent. Once he argued that there was no nobler word in the literature of politics than liberty. "Better that ten men should loaf," he similarly declared in an 1892 article in which he defended the idle rich in their right to be idle, "than one should lose his liberty." It is on isolated evidence such as this that O. G. Villard erroneously concluded that Godkin "never compromised on any issue of human liberty," refashioned by Edward C. Kirkland into the equally preposterous "Godkin never wavered on freedom." E. L. Godkin, "The Prospects of the Political Art," *North American Review* 110, 398 (1870). E. L. Godkin, "Idleness and Immortality," *Forum* 13, 341 (1892). O. G. Villard, *Fighting Years; Memoirs of a Liberal Editor* (New York, 1939), p. 119. Kirkland, *Business in the Gilded Age*, p. 24. "The Substitute for Hanging," *Nation*, March 20, 1873, pp. 193-94.

60. *Nation*, 14 June 1877, p. 346. "Crazes," *Nation*, 26 November 1891, p. 406. "Protection and Socialism," *Nation*, 15 March 1894, pp. 189-90. "The Organized Tramp, *ibid.*, 26 April 1894, p. 396. "The Farmer as a Business Man," *ibid.*, 27 October 1896, pp. 322-23. "Mob Violence," *ibid.*, 27 October 1896, p. 322. For the author's argument that the laissez-faire liberalism ascribed to Godkin was "hardly more than a conditioned economic reflex," with his writings lacking "real philosophical underpinnings," see William M. Armstrong, "Godkin and Chinese Labor; a Paradox in 19th Century Liberalism," *The American Journal of Economics*

and Sociology 21, 1 (1962): 91-102.

61. Godkin's antilabor views are outlined in William M. Armstrong, "The Godkin-Schurz Feud," *New-York Historical Society Quarterly* 48, 1 (1964): 18-25; and in Nevins, *The Evening Post,* pp. 455-56.

62. "The Government of Our Great Cities," *Nation,* 18 October 1866, p. 312.

63. "Foreign Immigration," *Evening Post,* 20 March 1896. For various of the views of Godkin on immigration, see his editorial in the *Nation,* "The Government of Our Great Cities," 18 October 1866, p. 312, and his editorials in the *Evening Post:* "The Proper Sieve for Immigrants," 11 April 1891, "The Harm of Immigration," 14 January 1893, "Mr. Morton's Coachman," 23 October 1894, and the chapter "Criminal Politics," in Godkin, *Problems of Modern Democracy,* p. 131 (reprinted from *North American Review* [June 1890]).

64. "The Harm of Immigration," *Nation,* 19 January 1893, p. 43.

65. "The Government of Our Great Cities," p. 312. Godkin's notion of civil service reform is outlined in his "Henry G. Pearson, A Memorial Address." Privately printed for the Civil Service Commission of New York, 1894.

66. Ogden, I, 302. In supporting the proposed new constitution, Godkin pointed out to the Rev. Henry W. Bellows that "democracy to be successful must rest on intelligence . . . an ignorant citizen is but one degree removed from a traitor or alien enemy." Godkin to Bellows, 4 February 1867, H. W. Bellows Papers, Massachusetts Historical Society.

67. "'The People' And The Municipal Government," *Nation,* 19 December 1872, p. 400.

68. Whitelaw Reid to Godkin, 12 and 16 March 1877, Whitelaw Reid Papers, Library of Congress. C. L. Barrows, *William M. Evarts* (Chapel Hill, 1941), pp. 194-96. New York State Assembly Document No. 68, 1877, "New York Commission to Devise a Plan for the Government of the Cities in the State of New York." Report . . . May 6, 1877. New York (State) Governor, *Messages from the Governors of the State of New York,* edited by Charles Z. Lincoln (Albany, 1909), VI, 825-44. John Bigelow, *The Life of Samuel J. Tilden,* 2 vols. (New York, 1895), I, 265. The commission, besides Godkin and chairman Evarts, included Simon Sterne, Oswald Ottendorfer, Samuel Hand, Henry F. Dimick, William Allen Butler, James C. Carter, Joshua M. Van Cott, and John A. Lott.

69. "Tweed," *Nation,* 18 October 1877, pp. 237-38.

70. Laski, *The American Democracy,* p. 232.

71. *Ibid.* The interesting 1907 exchange between Howells and Charles Eliot Norton over Godkin's stature, resulting in Howells rewriting a review somewhat critical of the editor, appears in the Howells-Norton correspondence in the Norton papers and in the Howells papers at Harvard University. The manuscript of Howells' review, showing his changes, is at Rutgers University.

72. Grimes, *The Political Liberalism of The Nation,* p. 120.

73. Nevins, *American Press Opinion,* p. 299.

Chapter 8
THE LIBERAL REPUBLICAN MOVEMENT OF 1872

1. "An Erie Raid," *North American Review* 112 (April 1871): 242. This article is mistakenly attributed to Charles Francis Adams, Sr., in Ralph Henry Gabriel, *The Course of American Democratic Thought* (New York, 1940), pp. 143-44.

2. *Nation*, 6 April 1871.

3. "Commercial Immorality and Political Corruption," *North American Review* 107 (July 1868): 252-53.

4. Gabriel, *The Course of American Democratic Thought*, p. 149.

5. *Nation*, 18 June 1868, pp. 505, 507, 510, 29 October 1868, p. 345.

6. *Nation*, 18 March 1869, p. 201.

7. *Nation*, 18 January 1866, p. 65, 8 March 1866, p. 302, 22 March 1866, p. 355, 10 January 1867, p. 32.

8. Daniel Aaron, *Men of Good Hope* (New York, 1951), p. 138.

9. Godkin, *Gilded Age Letters*, p. 166n. Frederick E. Haynes, *Third Party Movements Since the Civil War* (Iowa City, 1916), p. 12. E. Mc-Clung Fleming, *R. R. Bowker, Militant Liberal* (Norman, Oklahoma, 1952), p. 90n.

10. Godkin to Woolsey, 6 December 1869, Woolsey Papers, Yale University. Godkin to Gilman, 6 December 1869, Gilman Papers, Johns Hopkins University.

11. Joseph Logsdon, *Horace White, Nineteenth Century Liberal* (Westport, Connecticut, 1971), p. 182.

12. Godkin to George P. Marsh, 6 October 1870, Marsh Papers, University of Vermont. Godkin, *Gilded Age Letters*, p. 158n.

13. Godkin to his wife, 1 December 1870, Godkin Papers.

14. Horace White, *The Life of Lyman Trumbull* (Boston and New York, 1913), p. 353.

15. Godkin to his wife, 1 December 1870. See also Haynes, *Third Party Movements*, p. 12.

16. Adams, *Henry Adams and his Friends*, p. 48.

17. *Ibid.*

18. Godkin to his wife, 1 December 1870.

19. Joseph Wall, *Henry Watterson, Reconstructed Rebel* (New York, 1956), p. 108. Fred Bunyan Joyner, *David Ames Wells, Champion of Free Trade* (Cedar Rapids, Iowa, 1939), pp. 115-16. Malcolm Moos, *The Republicans; A History of the Party* (New York, 1956), p. 137. Harry W. Baehr, Jr., *The New York Tribune Since the Civil War* (New York, 1936), p. 102. Charles Ramsdell Lindley, *Since the Civil War* (New York, 1926), p. 42.

20. Leon Burr Richardson, *William E. Chandler, Republican* (New York, 1940), p. 131. Nevins, *The Evening Post*, pp. 294-99. Earle Dudley Ross, *The Liberal Republican Movement* (New York, 1919), *passim*.

21. Logsdon, *Horace White*, pp. 185-86, 192.

22. Schurz to Godkin, 31 March 1871, Godkin Papers.

23. Godkin to Schurz, 5 April 1871, Schurz Papers, Library of Congress.

24. *Ibid.*

25. *New York Times*, 27 March 1872.

26. *New York Tribune*, 26 March 1872.

27. Adams, *Henry Adams and his Friends*, p. 49.

28. Moos, *The Republicans*, p. 137. White, *Lyman Trumbull*, pp. 356-84.

29. White to Trumbull, 4 May 1872, Trumbull Papers, Library of Congress.

30. *Nation*, 9 May 1872, p. 303.

31. Joyner, *Wells*, p. 131.

32. White, *Lyman Trumbull*, p. 381.

33. Eric F. Goldman, *Rendezvous with Destiny* (New York, 1952), p. 22.

34. Godkin to Schurz, *Private*, 19 May 1872, Schurz Papers.

35. Schurz to Godkin, *Private and Confidential*, 20 May 1872, Godkin Papers.

36. Edward Cary, *George William Curtis*, p. 230.

37. Godkin to Atkinson, 29 May 1872, Atkinson Papers. Godkin to Schurz, 29 May 1872, Schurz Papers. Godkin to Trumbull, 29 May 1872, Trumbull Papers.

38. "Grant, Greeley, and Adams," *Nation*, 13 June 1878, pp. 384-85. See also *Nation*, 30 May 1872, pp. 345, 349-50.

39. Carl Schurz, *Speeches, Correspondence and Political Papers of Carl Schurz*, edited by Frederic Bancroft (New York and London, 1913) 11, 383.

40. Schurz to Godkin, 23 June 1872, Schurz Papers.

41. Godkin to Schurz, 28 June 1872, Schurz Papers.

42. Nevins, *Evening Post*, p. 399. Wall, *Henry Watterson*, p. 108. White, *Lyman Trumbull*, p. 393.

43. White, *Lyman Trumbull*, p. 404. The foregoing is the source from which Allan Nevins got his claim that Godkin's pen did "more than that of any other writer" to defeat Greeley. Nevins, *Evening Post*, p. 398.

44. *The Penn Monthly* 3 (September 1872): 519-20.

45. Godkin to Atkinson, 31 October 1872, Atkinson Papers. Professor Perkins is in error in asserting that Godkin supported Greeley in the campaign. Dexter Perkins and Glyndon G. Van Deusen, *The United States of America: A History* (New York, 1962) II, 43.

46. Godkin to White, 11 November 1872. *Nation*, 21 November 1872, p. 328. For a diagnosis by Samuel Bowles of the causes of the Cincinnati debacle, see Bowles to David A. Wells, 13 February 1873, Wells Papers, Library of Congress.

47. Schurz to Godkin, 23 November 1872, Schurz Papers.

48. C. F. Adams, Jr., to Wells, 13 November 1873, Wells Papers, New York Public Library.

49. C. F. Adams, Jr., to Schurz, 22 December 1873, Schurz Papers. Baehr, The New York Tribune, p. 150. Schurz to C. F. Adams, Jr., 25 December 1873, Schurz Papers. Arthur F. Beringause, Brooks Adams; A Biography (New York, 1955), p. 58.

50. C. F. Adams, Jr., to Wells, 1 December 1873, Wells Papers.

51. Godkin to Schurz, 5 December 1873, Schurz Papers.

52. Wells to Godkin, 20 December 1873, Schurz Papers.

53. Evarts to Wells, 25 December 1873, Wells Papers, Library of Congress.

54. William James to Henry James, Jr., 24 November 1873, James Papers.

55. Memorandum, Godkin to Sedgwick, 7 October 1872, Godkin Papers (Nation Business Records), Harvard University.

56. See John G. Sproat, "The Best Men"; Liberal Reformers in the Gilded Age (New York, 1968), passim.

57. For Godkin's anti-Semitism, see Godkin, Gilded Age Letters, pp. 126, 145, 231, 351, 541-45. See also I. F. Stone, "Free Inquiry and Free Endeavor," Nation, 10 February 1940, p. 159, and Marian (Mrs. Henry) Adams to Godkin, 25 December 1879, Godkin Papers.

58. Godkin to Bryce, 23 November 1884, Bryce Papers, Oxford University.

59. Godkin to Lowell, 30 July 1874, Lowell Papers, Harvard University. "Chromo-Civilization," Nation, 24 September 1874, pp. 201-02.

60. W. C. Brownell, "The 'Nation' from the Inside," Nation, 8 July 1915, p. 42.

61. Godkin to Whitelaw Reid, 10 March [1873], Reid Papers, Library of Congress. Godkin to Charles W. Eliot, 20 May 1884, Eliot Papers, Harvard University. Godkin to Andrew D. White, 15 June 1872, White Papers, Cornell University. Godkin, Gilded Age Letters, 197n, 311n, 189n. Godkin to James Monroe Taylor, 14 January 1890, Taylor Papers, Vassar College.

62. Godkin to Bellows, 2 April [1873], Bellows Papers, Massachusetts Historical Society. In a verse entitled "Embalmed," poetess friend Sarah Woolsey ("Susan Coolidge") lamented Fanny's passing. Susan Coolidge, Verses (Boston, 1880).

63. Godkin, Gilded Age Letters, pp. 216-17, 218n.

64. Ibid., pp. 218-19n, 252n.

65. Unpublished memoir of Anne Ashburner in the Stockbridge, Massachusetts, library, bearing a foreword by William Dean Howells.

66. Godkin, Gilded Age Letters, p. 244n.

Chapter 9
TOO MANY MULES IN THE PASTURE

1. Mrs. Cornelia Godkin to O. G. Villard, 14 October 1931, Villard Papers, Harvard University.
2. Allan Nevins, *The Evening Post* (New York, 1922), p. 456. Frederic Bancroft and W. A. Dunning, *The Reminiscences of Carl Schurz* (New York, 1907-1908), Chapter III, p. 402. C. M. Fuess, *Carl Schurz, Reformer* (New York, 1922), p. 279. Italics are the writer's.
3. For some of these Schurz articles, see Armstrong, "Additions to the *Nation Index*," p. 271.
4. Godkin, *Gilded Age Letters*, pp. 198, 263, 264, 270-71.
5. Huntington to Bigelow, 15 June 1881, Bigelow Papers, New York Public Library.
6. Godkin to Olmsted, 21 April 1881, Olmsted Papers.
7. White to Schurz, 18 March 1881, Schurz Papers. Godkin to Olmsted, 21 April 1881, Olmsted Papers. Lodge to Godkin, 4 May, 14 June 1881, Godkin Papers. Adams to Godkin, 25 May 1881, Schurz Papers. Godwin to Godkin, 28 May 1881, Godkin Papers. Godkin to Higginson, 9 June, 15 June 1881, Godkin Papers. George C. Eggleston, *Recollections of a Varied Life* (New York, 1910), pp. 230-31.
8. *Albany Evening Journal*, 27 May 1881. Cf. Philadelphia *Times*, 26 May 1881. *Chicago Tribune*, 26 May 1881. *Boston Herald*, 27 May 1881. *Harper's Weekly*, 11 June 1881, p. 375. Schurz Papers.
9. Hay to Reid, 26 May 1881, in John Hay, *Letters and Diaries of John Hay* (Washington, 1908) II, 65.
10. Schurz to Adolph Meyer, 26 August 1881, Private Papers of Carl Schurz, Bloomington, Indiana. Godkin to Olmsted, 21 April 1881, Olmsted Papers. The writer is indebted to Arthur Hogue for the contents of the Meyer letter and of several other letters pertinent to this study.
11. Garrison described his position on the *Nation* vis-à-vis Godkin after 1881 as "limited-monarchy" or "junior partner," Ogden, II, 180. Garrison, *Letters and Memorials of Wendell Phillips Garrison*, p. 53.
12. Frederick Sheldon to Godkin, 24 May 1881, Godkin Papers. See also John L. Cadwalader to Godkin, May 1881, Godkin Papers. Italics are the author's.
13. Godkin to Lodge, 9 June 1881, Lodge Papers, Massachusetts Historical Society.
14. Henry Adams to Godkin, 19 September 1881, Godkin Papers.
15. *Boston Daily Advertiser*, 23 December 1873. Godkin, *Gilded Age Letters*, p. 192.
16. Schurz to Adolph Meyer, 22 June 1881, Private Papers of Carl Schurz.
17. The erroneous story that Villard surrendered control over *Evening Post* editorial policy first appeared in the financier's *Memoirs* and then

was given currency in Nevins' *The Evening Post*, Bancroft and Dunning's *The Reminiscences of Carl Schurz*, and various of the writings of Oswald G. Villard. The Henry Villard papers at the Harvard School of Business are rife with directives from the financier about *Post* policy.

18. Armstrong, *Godkin and American Foreign Policy*, p. 27.

19. Adams to Godkin, 6 August 1881, Godkin Papers.

20. Godkin to Schurz, 12 August 1881, Schurz Papers.

21. Adams to Godkin, 23 September 1881, Godkin Papers.

22. Holt, *Sixty Years as a Publisher*, p. 140.

23. Schurz, *Reminiscences of Carl Schurz*, pp. 404-5. Marian Adams, *The Letters of Mrs. Henry Adams, 1865-1883*, edited by Ward Thoron (Boston, 1936), p. 315.

24. Schurz to White, 14 October 1882, Schurz Papers.

25. Godkin to Schurz, July 1883, Schurz Papers. For a noted educator's view of the significance of the address, see Nicholas Murray Butler to C. F. Adams, Jr., 25 September 1895, Adams Papers, Massachusetts Historical Society.

26. Adams, *Letters of Mrs. Henry Adams*, pp. 438-41.

27. Godkin to White, 21 May [1883], Illinois State Historical Society.

28. Godkin to Schurz, 18 June 1883, Schurz Papers.

29. Schurz to Godkin, 18 June 1883, Godkin Papers. There is a similar draft of this letter in the Private Papers of Carl Schurz.

30. Henry Villard to Horace White, 17 July 1883, Villard Papers.

31. "The Threatened Strike of the Telegraphers," *Evening Post*, 17 July 1883.

32. "Wages and Water," *New York Herald*, 21 July 1883. See also "The Strike and the Public Rights," *ibid.*, 24 July 1883.

33. Godkin to Garrison, 24 July 1883, Godkin Papers. A bowdlerized version of a part of this letter appears in Ogden, II, 127.

34. Godkin to Schurz, 24 July 1883, Schurz Papers.

35. "The Public and the Strikers," *Nation*, 26 July 1883, p. 70.

36. "The Telegraph Strike," *Evening Post*, 8 August 1883.

37. Schurz to Godkin, 9 August 1883, Godkin Papers.

38. *Ibid.*

39. Godkin to Schurz, unsent, 11 August 1883, Godkin Papers.

40. Schurz to his children, 14 August 1883, Private Papers of Carl Schurz. Telegram, Villard to White, 14 August 1883, Villard Papers.

41. Details of the excursion are found in *Harper's Weekly*, 22 September 1883, and in the Villard Papers.

42. Ogden, II, 126. Ogden did not identify the object of Godkin's solicitude, but internal evidence suggests that it was Schurz. The letter from which Ogden took the quotation has disappeared, along with others he employed in his thinly researched appreciation of Godkin. On the subject of missing Godkin correspondence, see William M. Armstrong, "Manuscripts Relating to E. L. Godkin," *Manuscripts* 13, 1 (1961): 32, and footnote 45, pp. 204-5.

43. Schurz to Godkin, 3 October 1883, Godkin Papers.

44. Godkin, *Gilded Age Letters*, p. 304.

45. White's private letters reveal a lack of respect for Godkin.

46. *New York Times*, 11 December 1883. *Springfield Republican*, 11 December 1883.

47. Godkin to Schurz, 8 December 1883, draft of letter in Godkin Papers.

48. Schurz to Godkin, 10 December 1883, Godkin Papers. Godkin to Schurz, 10 December 1883, draft of letter in Godkin Papers.

49. Schurz to Godkin, 11 December 1883, Godkin Papers.

50. *New York Times*, 12 December 1883. *Springfield Republican*, 11, 12 December 1883.

51. Schurz to Godkin, 14 December 1883, Godkin Papers.

52. Schurz to Godkin, 15 December 1883, Godkin Papers.

53. "Corporations, their Employees, and the Public," *North American Review* 327 (February 1884): 101-19.

54. Schurz to Godkin, 20 January 1884, Godkin Papers.

55. Hogue to the writer, 11 September 1958. See also Lucy M. Salmon, *The Newspaper and the Historian* (New York, 1923), p. 265.

56. Godkin to Bryce, 1 June 1884, Bryce Papers. Italics are the writer's.

57. Godkin to Whitney, 18 April 1886, William C. Whitney Papers, Library of Congress. See also Godkin to Whitney, 18 October 1886, and Mrs. Godkin to Whitney, 7 February 1887, Whitney Papers.

58. Garrison to Fanny Villard, 1 August 1886, Villard Papers. Godkin to Sheldon, 19 September 1886, Godkin Papers. Godkin to Villard, 21 June 1893, Villard Papers. Commenting severely on Godkin's dealings with J. Pierpont Morgan and William C. Whitney was contemporary reformer W. H. Rainsford: "One unknown facet of Godkin's career was his willingness to traffic in his own interests with men who were known as despoilers of the public treasury." W. H. Rainsford, *The Story of a Varied Life* (New York, 1922), p. 315.

59. Godkin to Villard, 7 June 1893, Villard Papers.

60. Godkin to Bryce, 19 November 1893, Bryce Papers.

61. Godkin to Bryce, 2 November 1885, Bryce Papers.

62. Godkin to Bryce, 2 November 1885, Bryce Papers. Garrison to Fanny Villard, 1 November 1885, Villard Papers. See also Garrison to the same, 13 September 1884 and 15 November 1885, Villard Papers.

63. See especially E. W. Gurney to Godkin, 13 November 1885, Godkin Papers.

64. A verse by McCready Sykes, quoted in *American Historical Review* 13 (1907): 170.

65. Quoted in *The Sun* (New York), 17 April 1890.

Chapter 10
MUGWUMPS FOR CLEVELAND

1. Godkin, *Gilded Age Letters*, p. 315. In the *Evening Post* see these Godkin editorials: "The Blaine Boom," 7 April 1884. "Vindication," 19 April 1884. "The True Cause of the Trouble," 17 July 1884. "An Unfortunate Comparison," 18 August 1884. "Keep My Name Quiet," 10 September 1884. "The Standard of Official Morality," 12 September 1884.

2. For Godkin's role in the campaign, see *Evening Post*, "What We Think of It Now," 5 August 1884. "More of It," 15 August 1884. "The Conscience Vote," 25 September 1884. "Cleveland's Independence," 30 September 1884.

3. Godkin to Cleveland, 30 March 1890. Cleveland Papers, Library of Congress. "A Great Example," *Evening Post*, 9 November 1892.

4. See *Evening Post*, "The Mournful Past," 5 January 1885. "Memoranda," 13 March 1885. "How the Standard Has Been Raised," 30 March 1885. "The President as a Sheikh," 31 March 1885. "The President's Critics," 13 April 1885. "The Importance of the Finish," 19 April 1887. "The One Thing Needful," 25 April 1887. See also Godkin to Cleveland, 10 November 1885, and Godkin to Stetson, 16 December 1884, Cleveland Papers.

5. C. C. Tansill, *The Foreign Policy of Thomas F. Bayard* (New York, 1940), pp. xviii, xix, xx, xxi, 142, 272, 273, 274, 652. Godkin to Cleveland, 24 March 1891. Godkin to Cleveland, 11 April 1885, Cleveland Papers.

6. Tansill, *Bayard*, p. 142.

7. *Ibid.*, p. 652.

8. "The Tariff and the Consuls," *Evening Post*, 4 November 1893. "Good Work for 'Good Americans'," *Evening Post*, 3 April 1894.

9. Godkin to Cleveland, 26 February 1885, Cleveland Papers. Allan Nevins, *Grover Cleveland: A Study in Courage* (New York, 1933), p. 231. Tansill, *Bayard*, p. xxi. Godkin to Lamont, 12, 18 March 1885, Cleveland Papers. Godkin to Cleveland, 5 April 1893, Cleveland Papers. Allan Nevins, *Henry White* (New York, 1930), pp. 74, 100. One of the most controversial of Cleveland's actions was the Van Alen appointment, involving the alleged sale of a diplomatic post. For details of the case, including Godkin's protest to the president about it, see Nevins, *Cleveland*, p. 518. Godkin, "The Van Alen Case," *Evening Post*, 28 September 1893. Godkin to Cleveland, 5 April 1893. Godkin to Honey, 29 April 1893, Cleveland Papers.

10. For the details of this complicated case, see Tansill, *Bayard*, pp. 579-611.

11. *Ibid.*, pp. 591-95. Henry M. Wriston, *Executive Agents in American Foreign Relations* (Baltimore, 1929), pp. 815-17. Godkin to James A. Garfield, 9 January 1877. Garfield Papers, Library of Congress. Godkin, *Gilded Age Letters*, p. 147. For additional information about Sedgwick,

see William M. Armstrong, "Libby Prison: The Civil War Diary of Arthur Sedgwick," *Virginia Magazine of History and Biography* 81, 4 (1963): 449-60.

12. *Nation,* 12 July 1888, pp. 24-25; 19 July 1888, p. 45; 2 August 1888, p. 85; 16 August 1888, p. 124; 8 November 1888, p. 368; 28 November 1888, p. 406. For charges by Godkin that Harrison was subsidizing the press by giving political appointments to editors and owners of newspapers, see *ibid.,* 18 April 1889, p. 315; 2 May 1889, p. 355; 30 May 1889, pp. 435-36.

13. There are several good secondary accounts of this dispute. Especially useful are Tansill, *Bayard,* Chapters 14 and 15. J. B. Henderson, *American Diplomatic Questions* (New York, 1901), Chapter I, and, for the later phase, T. A. Bailey, "The North Pacific Sealing Convention of 1911," *Pacific Historical Review* 4 (1935): 2.

14. "Mr. Phelps on Mr. Blaine," *Evening Post,* 23 March 1891. See also "Some Hawaiian Oddities," *ibid.,* 22 January 1894.

15. "Humorous Diplomacy," *Evening Post,* 14 January 1891. See also "Mr. Blaine's *Tu-quoques,*" *ibid.,* 8 May 1891.

16. *Nation,* 17 August 1893, p. 113.

17. For the friendship between Godkin and Russell, see Godkin to Russell, 15 April 1889, 5 May 1894, and Russell to Godkin, 24 November 1883, 14 August 1885, 12 January 1886, 28 April 1889, Godkin Papers. See also Godkin, *Gilded Age Letters,* pp. 385, 390n, 393, 394, 395.

18. "The Barrundia Debate," *Evening Post,* 12 February 1891.

19. *Ibid.* See also *Evening Post,* "More About the Barrundia Case," 12 January 1891. "The Reiter Fog," 23 January 1891. "What the Barrundia Case Calls For," 21 February 1891. "Secretary Tracy's Duty," 23 April 1891. The State Department correspondence is in U. S. Congress, Senate, *Sen. Exec. Doc.* No. 51, 51 Cong., 2 Sess., and that from the Navy Department is in U. S. Congress, House, *House Exec. Doc.* No. 51, 51 Cong., 2 Sess. For additional material, see Tyler, *The Foreign Policy of James G. Blaine,* p. 105n.

20. J. E. Coxe, "The New Orleans *Mafia* Incident," *Louisiana Historical Quarterly* 20 (1937): 1084.

21. "The Italian Trouble," *Evening Post,* 1 April 1891.

22. Osgood Hardy, "The *Itata* Incident," *Hispanic American Historical Review* 5 (1922): 195-226. For correspondence over the incident, see U. S. Congress, House, *House Exec. Doc.* No. 91, 52 Cong., 1 Sess.

23. "The *Itata* Case," *Evening Post,* 14 May 1891. Although Godkin denied it, he appears to have been in agreement with Blaine on the *Itata* question. See Blaine to Lazcano, 13 March 1891, U. S. Congress, House, *House Exec. Doc.,* No. 91, 52 Cong., 1 Sess. Tyler, *The Foreign Policy of James G. Blaine,* pp. 139-40.

24. "The Alabama Precedent," *Evening Post,* 15 May 1891.

25. "More of Mr. Blaine's International Law," *Nation,* 24 March 1882.

26. "The Chilian Situation," *Nation,* 12 June 1891. "The Chilian Con-

flict," *Evening Post*, 3 March 1891. "Balmaceda's Defense," *ibid.*, 27 May 1891.

27. "Our Treatment of Chili," *Evening Post*, 26 October 1891.

28. "The Chilian News," *ibid.*, 29 October 1891.

29. "Our Treatment of Chili."

30. "The Chilian News." "Our Treatment of Chili."

31. "The Democratic House and War with Chili," *Evening Post*, 7 January 1892. See also William E. Curtis, *Between the Andes and the Ocean* (New York, 1907), p. 409.

32. Nevins, *Henry White*, p. v. *Cf.* Osgood Hardy, "Was Patrick Egan a 'Blundering Minister'?" *Hispanic American Historical Review* 8 (1928): 65-81.

33. "Our Treatment of Chili."

34. T. C. Crawford, *James G. Blaine* (Philadelphia, 1893), p. 617.

35. "Our Treatment of Chili."

36. "The Chilian News."

37. See A. B. Hart, "The Chilean Controversy," in *Practical Essays in American Government* (New York, 1905), p. 111, and John Basset Moore, "The Chilean Affair," *Political Science Quarterly* 8 (September 1893): 467 *ff.*

38. "The Secret of Warriorism," *Evening Post*, 17 March 1892.

39. *Ibid.*

40. "The Proper Use of a Country," *Evening Post*, 19 November 1891.

41. "The Secret of Warriorism."

42. *Ibid.*

43. "Concerning War as a Remedy," *Evening Post*, 25 January 1892.

44. See W. R. Sherman, *The Diplomatic and Commercial Relations of the United States and Chile, 1820-1914* (Boston, 1926), pp. 187-88.

45. "The Shame of It," *Evening Post*, 29 January 1892.

46. *Ibid.*

47. "Patriotism and Finance," *Evening Post*, 23 December 1895. For a slightly different British version of the affair, see *The Times* (London), 2 February 1892.

48. Harry T. Peck, "Mr. Godkin and His Book," *Bookman* 2 (1896): 486.

49. "Hawaii," *Evening Post*, 3 February 1893.

50. *Ibid.*

51. Godkin to Atkinson, 1 March 1893, Atkinson Papers.

52. "The Hawaiian Message," *Evening Post*, 19 December 1893.

53. "General Harrison on Hawaii," *Evening Post*, 15 November 1893. "'Americanism,'" *Evening Post*, 21 February 1893. For the reaction of Godkin to the events leading up to the formal annexation of Hawaii five years later, see his *Evening Post* editorials, "Jamming Through," 3 December 1897; "The Momentous Decision," 9 December 1897; "Straight Lines," 10 January 1898; "More Bureau," 20 January 1898.

54. *Literary Digest*, 26 May 1894, p. 95.

55. "The Samoan Troubles," *Evening Post*, 10 May 1894.

56. "'Scuttling' Out of Samoa," *Evening Post*, 17 May 1894. See also

"Our Samoan Trouble," *Evening Post*, 21 June 1894.

57. See *Evening Post*, "The Van Alen Case," 28 September 1893. "The Tariff and the Consuls," 4 November 1893. "The Nomination of Mr. Peckham," 23 January 1894. "Good Work for 'Good Americans'," 3 April 1894. "The Consular Reform," 24 September 1895.

58. See P. R. Fossum, "The Anglo-Venezuelan Boundary Controversy," *Hispanic American Historical Review* 8 (1928): 299-329.

59. Unpublished manuscript by the writer based on an examination of British Foreign Office records and Venezuelan documents. See also Great Britain, Foreign Office, British Blue Books, *Correspondence Respecting the Question of the Boundary of British Guiana* (London, 1896), I, 17, 26, 241-46. William M. Armstrong, "The Many-Sided World of Sir Robert Ker Porter," The *Historian* 25, 1 (November 1962): 49-50.

60. Tansill, *Bayard*, p. 695.

61. *Foreign Relations* (1895), I, 558.

62. See *Congressional Record*, 10 December 1895, pp. 108-12.

63. Quoted in *Nation*, 19 December 1895, p. 441.

64. The message is printed in U. S. Department of State, *Foreign Relations* (1895), I, 545.

65. *Nation*, 19 December 1895, p. 441.

66. See Richard Hooker, *The Story of an Independent Newspaper* (New York, 1924), pp. 165, 166.

67. *Nation*, 5 December 1895, p. 399.

68. *Ibid.*, 12 December 1895, p. 420. "Union for Cleveland," *ibid.*, 19 December 1895, pp. 441-42. The latter editorial appeared in the *Evening Post* on 11 December.

69. *Nation*, 26 December 1895, p. 456.

70. *Ibid.*, pp. 455-56.

71. *Ibid.*, p. 455.

72. James E. Pollard, *The Presidents and the Press* (New York, 1947), p. 514, *et seq.*

73. *Nation*, 26 December 1895, p. 455.

74. "Patriotism and Finance," *Evening Post*, 23 December 1895.

75. Nevins, *The Evening Post*, p. 450.

76. "Patriotism and Finance."

77. See especially the articles by Andrew Carnegie and James Bryce in the *North American Review* 162 (1896): 114, 153.

78. Godkin, *Gilded Age Letters*, pp. 475-76.

79. Bishop, *Notes and Anecdotes of Many Years*, p. 93.

80. James to Godkin, 24 December [1895], Godkin Papers.

81. Godkin, *Gilded Age Letters*, p. 384.

82. Rainsford, *Story of a Varied Life*, p. 315.

Chapter 11
THE IMPERIAL YEARS

1. Peck, "Mr. Godkin and his Book," p. 483.

2. Villard, *Some Newspapers and Newspapermen*, pp. 292-93. See also *Nation*, 21 December 1865, p. 769.

3. James Creelman, "Joseph Pulitzer—Master Journalist," *Pearson's Magazine* 21 (1909): 246.

4. Henry Steele Commager, *The American Mind* (New Haven, 1950), p. 318.

5. W. R. Thayer, "Edwin L. Godkin" in M. A. DeWolfe Howe, *Later Years of the Saturday Club* (New York, 1927), pp. 187-96. George F. Hoar, *Autobiography* (New York, 1906), pp. 422-25.

6. Adams, *The Education of Henry Adams*, p. 328. Godkin, *Gilded Age Letters*, p. 357. See also *Ibid.*, pp. 88, 195, 238, 383, 478, 480, 505. C. S. Gleed, "Mr. Godkin on the West: A Protest." "A Protest," *Forum* 21 (1896): 144. W. A. Russ, Jr., "Godkin Looks at Western Agrarianism," *Journal of Agricultural History* 19 (1945): 233.

7. Upton Sinclair, *American Outpost* (New York, 1932), p. 63. See also by the same author, *The Brass Check* (Pasadena, 1920), pp. 15, 22. For a critical estimate of Godkin by Lincoln Steffens, see Steffens, *Autobiography of Lincoln Steffens*, pp. 172, 179, 180.

8. Rhodes, *Historical Essays*, p. 277. See also Godkin, "English and American Ministers," *Nation*, 9 March 1882, pp. 200-01.

9. Logsdon, *Horace White*, p. 354.

10. *Bookman* 2 (1895): 93. See also Nevins, *American Press Opinion*, p. 301.

11. Rhodes, *Historical Essays*, p. 282. *Nation*, 4 June 1868, p. 451. *Ibid.*, 10 October 1867, p. 299. Garrison to Lounsbury, 28 May 1883, Lounsbury Papers, Yale University.

12. Fraser Bond, *Mr. Miller of the Times* (New York, 1931), p. 61. New York *Sun*, 10 April 1892. *New York Herald*, 29 December 1899. New York *World*, 8 April 1892. Peck, "Mr. Godkin and his Book," p. 486, Ogden, II, 169-70.

13. "A Unique Performance," *Nation*, 5 June 1890, p. 444. "A Blow at the Pirates," *ibid.*, 3 July 1890, pp. 6-7. On the mammoth libel suit that followed, see Nevins, *The Evening Post*, pp. 560-62. G. H. Putnam, *Memories of a Publisher* (New York, 1916), pp. 128-34. *Nation*, 23 February 1893, p. 135. Ogden to Crary, 21 June 1890; Publisher, *Evening Post*, to Robert C. Ogden, 11 March 1899; Godkin to Robert C. Ogden n. d. (1899); Robert C. Ogden to Call, 11 April 1899; Gray to Wanamaker, 14 April 1899; Wanamaker to Robert C. Ogden, 15 April 1899; Robert C. Ogden to Parkhurst, 17 April 1899; ? to Robert C. Ogden, 18 April 1899; all in Robert C. Ogden Business Letters, Library of Congress.

14. Peck, "Mr. Godkin and his Book," p. 485. For Godkin's editorial

views on international copyright, see his editorials in the *Nation*, "Who Owns an Author's Ideas?" 27 June 1867, pp. 520-22. "International Copyright," 9 November 1871, pp. 301-02. "The Working of the Copyright Bill," 19 March 1891, pp. 233-34.

15. Godkin, *Gilded Age Letters*, p. 149.

16. Nevins, *The Evening Post*, p. 546. The authorship of this bon mot has been variously attributed. See *Bookman* 2 (1895): 93.

17. Henry F. Pringle, "Godkin of 'The Post'," *Scribner's Magazine* 96 (1934): 332. For Dana's distaste for Godkin, see New York *Sun*, 9 September 1885, 15, 18 July 1886, 17, 18 February, 5 August, 6, 7, 14, 19 September 1888, 17 April, 30 June 1890, 20, 21, 22, 24 March, 10 April 1892. For Godkin's equally unvarnished opinion of Dana, see Godkin to Norton, 16 October 1869. Godkin, *Gilded Age Letters*, pp. 140, 306, 463n.

18. "What to do With the Unemployed," *Nation*, 28 December 1893, pp. 481-82.

19. "The Economic Man," *North American Review* 153 (1891): 502.

20. *New York Herald*, 14 May 1893, p. 35.

21. Wilson, *Papers*, II, 282.

22. Bishop, *Notes and Anecdotes*, p. 107. See also "Morality in Diplomacy," *Evening Post*, 28 March 1891.

23. A selection of Godkin's Crimean letters appears in Ogden, I, 22-108. A complete list of Godkin's Crimean letters appears in William M. Armstrong, "The Writings of E. L. Godkin," *Bulletin of the New York Public Library* 72 (May 1969): 306. It is instructive to compare the Godkin letters on Admiral Farragut in 1864 in Ogden, I, 216, with the sentiments expressed by him in his editorial, "Fictitious War," *Evening Post*, 27 March 1894.

24. "Navalism," *Evening Post*, 19 January 1892. "Americanism," *ibid.*, 21 February 1893.

25. *Bookman* 22 (1905): 244.

26. "Change Without Variety," *Evening Post*, 6 March 1896.

27. Godkin to Norton, 24 October 1870, Godkin Papers.

28. "Peace," *Nation*, 29 December 1870, p. 434.

29. "The 'Virginius'. The Reasons for Keeping Cool About It," *Nation*, 20 November 1873, p. 334. See also A. V. Dicey, "An English Scholar's Appreciation of Godkin," *Nation*, 8 July 1915, p. 52.

30. "The Conscription," *Evening Post*, 21 December 1898.

31. Villard, *Some Newspapers and Newspapermen*, p. 291.

32. Adams, *The Education of Henry Adams*, pp. 280, 336.

33. *Nation* (1865): 26 October, p. 514; 9 November, p. 577; 23 November, p. 641. (1866): 24 April, pp. 513, 520; 8 May, pp. 577, 594; 15 May, p. 625; 29 May, p. 690; 5 June, p. 705; 19 June, p. 770.

34. Nevins, *The Evening Post*, p. 335. (letters) "On Board the Normannia," *Evening Post*, 10, 12 September 1892. "A Month of Quarantine," *North American Review* 155 (1892): 737-43. *New York Herald*, 16 September 1892. *Brooklyn Daily Eagle*, 18 September 1892.

35. "What is the Use of International Law?" *Nation*, 13 March 1869, p. 368.

36. "Peace," pp. 433-34.

37. A. C. Beales, *The History of Peace* (New York, 1931), pp. 137-38.

38. "The Meetings at the Hague," *Nation*, 14 October 1875, pp. 241-42. Associations for the advancement of international law were not only useless, explained Godkin, but dangerous, especially when infiltrated by representatives of a foreign power with ulterior motives. He pointed in this connection to the endorsement given by the Institute of International Law to a Russian proposal to ban the use of irregular troops in wartime—a thinly disguised move, he sensibly believed, to "place Providence definitively on the side of the heaviest battalions. . . ."

39. *Ibid.*, p. 242.

40. "The Extradition Treaty," *Nation*, 25 May 1876, p. 331.

41. "The Work for Peace Societies," *Nation*, 7 November 1878, p. 281.

42. "Arbitration," *Evening Post*, 4 May 1885.

43. Theodore Roosevelt, *Theodore Roosevelt: An Autobiography* (New York, 1913), p. 202. A "malignant and dishonest liar" and "traitor to the country" were among the hardier Roosevelt characterizations of Godkin, with whom he began feuding in 1884. Roosevelt, *Letters* I, 74, 1368. See also New York *Sun*, 22 April 1895.

44. Cited in *Nation*, 29 April 1869, p. 327. The assertion of Oswald G. Villard that Godkin "was as devoted an American as ever lived," an evident paraphrase of Wendell P. Garrison's obituary description of Godkin as "an American to the core," is challenged by Godkin's personal letters. Edward W. Randall seeks to illustrate how Godkin used the *Nation* as a sounding board for his Anglophilia in "Edwin Lawrence Godkin, Anglo-American" (MA thesis in Honnold Library, Claremont, California, 1947). Yet in fairness it should be said that Godkin often censured England, especially in his early years. See Villard, *Fighting Years*, p. 119. *Nation*, 22 May 1902, p. 404. Godkin to Emily Tuckerman, 1 September 1898, MSS letter in New York Public Library. Godkin, *Gilded Age Letters*, pp. 389, 495, 507, 509. William Dean Howells, "A Great New York Journalist," *North American Review* 185 (1907): 45. "The Tyranny of the Majority," *North American Review* 104 (1867): 226. *Times* (London), 3 December 1861. The *Annual Register* 102 (1861): 254. *Blackwood's Magazine* 91 (1862): 125-127. Ogden, I, 192, 197; II, 140.

45. Ogden, II, 138-68.

46. Godkin, *Gilded Age Letters*, p. 495.

47. Quoted in Norman Angell, *America and the New World-State* (New York, 1915), pp. 194-95.

48. "Some Hawaiian Oddities," *Evening Post*, 22 January 1894.

49. See, in addition to the *Evening Post* references hereinafter cited, "Good Americans in Trouble," 1 April 1899, and "Concerning 'Going to Europe'," 21 April 1894.

50. "Good Americans," *Evening Post*, 13 November 1893.

51. "Americanism," *Evening Post*, 21 February 1893.

52. "Hawaii," *Evening Post*, 3 February 1893.

53. "'National Honor'," *Evening Post*, 14 January 1896. *Cf.* "Navalism."

54. Robert E. Osgood, *Ideals and Self Interest in America's Foreign Relations* (Chicago, 1953), p. 54.

55. "'National Honor'."

56. "The War Danger in 1892," *Evening Post*, 11 May 1893.

57. "Naval Politics," *Evening Post*, 7 March 1893. See also (letter in *Evening Post*) "'The Sea Power'," 15 September 1898. (letter in *Evening Post*) "War as a Means of Peace," 24 October 1900.

58. See especially Nevins, *The Evening Post*, pp. 496-568. Walter Millis, *The Martial Spirit* (Cambridge, 1931), pp. 29-30, 38-39, 110, 117, 198-199, 444, 506. Marcus W. Wilkerson, *Public Opinion and the Spanish-American War* (Baton Rouge, 1932), pp. 111, 123-27.

59. The *Nation Index* fosters the impression that Godkin wrote more editorials at this time, but this is because more complete records of authorship exist for this period. Of almost 500 *Evening Post* editorials reprinted in the *Nation* between 1898 and 1900 Godkin wrote less than 100, or fewer than one in five. Horace White wrote an equal number, and Joseph B. Bishop and Arthur Sedgwick together accounted for slightly more than 20 percent. Rollo Ogden dominated the editorial page, writing nearly one-third of the editorials. The importance of these figures becomes apparent when it is realized that a larger proportion of Godkin's editorials, compared to those of his associates, were reprinted in the *Nation*.

60. Morse, *Life and Letters of Hamilton W. Mabie*, p. 309. See also Villard, *Some Newspapers and Newspapermen*, p. 53.

61. "The Conditions of Good Colonial Government," *Forum* 27 (1899): 190-203. Burton J. Hendrick, *The Training of an American* (New York, 1928), p. 215.

62. Nevins, *American Press Opinion*, p. 301.

63. Godkin, *Gilded Age Letters*, p. 529.

64. "Come and Let Us Reason Together," *Evening Post*, 2 November 1898.

65. "Democratic Fatalism," *Evening Post*, 26 November 1898.

66. Godkin, *Gilded Age Letters*, pp. 516-17.

67. *Nation*, 24 February 1898, p. 139.

68. *Nation*, 3 March 1898, p. 157.

69. *Evening Post*, 17 March 1898.

70. "The New Political Force," *Evening Post*, 30 April 1898.

71. See Godkin's *Evening Post* editorials, "Expansionist Dreams," 23 January 1899; "Some Wholesome Restraints," 3 February 1899; "The President's Popularity," 3 April 1899; "*Imperium et Libertas*," 15 May 1899. See also *New York Herald*, 4 October 1900. Godkin, *Gilded Age Letters*, pp. 481, 483, 484n, 490, 494, 500, 510, 513-529 *passim*, 537, 539, 542-43, 547.

72. See "'Suspension of Judgment'," 9 March 1898. "The War in Its Right Place," 29 March 1898. "Deliberation," 2 April 1898.

73. (letter) "Modern Christianity," *Evening Post*, 27 February 1901.

74. Ogden, II, 224. Godkin to Villard, 2 October 1899, Villard Papers,

Harvard.

75. "The Clergy and War," *Evening Post*, 26 September 1900. See also J. W. Pratt, *Expansionists of 1898* (Baltimore, 1936), Chapter VIII.

76. "A Great Moral Catastrophe," *Evening Post*, 27 February 1899. Godkin, *Gilded Age Letters*, p. 525. "'Chaos'," *Evening Post*, 8 March 1899.

77. Godkin, *Gilded Age Letters*, pp. 525-36.

78. *Ibid.*, pp. 462, 475. Godkin, "The Growth and Expression of Public Opinion," *Atlantic Monthly* 81 (1898): 9. Godkin to Scott, June 1898, Villard Papers.

79. Laski, *The American Democracy*, p. 232.

80. Godkin, *Gilded Age Letters*, pp. 412-13.

81. *Ibid.*, p. 462n.

82. *Ibid.*, p. 465n.

83. *Ibid.*, pp. 469-70.

84. Howells to Norton, 15 April 1907, Norton Papers. See also Howells to Norton, 12 April 1907, Norton Papers. Norton to Howells, 14, 16 April 1907, Howells Papers, Harvard University.

85. Edmund Burke, *Orations and Essays* (New York, 1900), introduction by Edwin L. Godkin.

86. Godkin, *Gilded Age Letters*, p. 524.

87. Garrison to Godkin, 1 April 1892, Godkin Papers.

88. Godkin to Villard [23 May 1893], 7 June 1893, 21 June [1893], Villard Papers. Godkin to Garrison, 5 October 1893, Godkin Papers, *Nation* Business Records, Harvard University.

89. Godkin, *Gilded Age Letters*, p. 448n.

90. Godkin to Villard, 13 February 1897, Villard Papers.

91. Godkin, *Gilded Age Letters*, pp. 486-87n, 501n.

92. *Ibid.*, p. 524n.

NOTES TO EPILOGUE

1. *New York Herald*, 29 December 1899.

2. Godkin, *Gilded Age Letters*, pp. 535-37.

3. *Ibid.*, pp. 495, 543-45.

4. *Ibid.*, pp. 545n, 546n.

5. *Ibid.*, pp. 547, 548.

6. *History of the State of New York*, edited by A. C. Flick (New York, 1937), IX, p. 295.

7. Nevins, *The Evening Post*, p. 535.

BIBLIOGRAPHY

MANUSCRIPT COLLECTIONS

Adams Family. Massachusetts Historical Society
Aldrich, Thomas Bailey. Houghton Library, Harvard University
Atkinson, Edward. Massachusetts Historical Society
Autograph File. Houghton Library, Harvard University
Ashburner, Grace. Stockbridge, Massachusetts, Library
Bellows, Henry W. Massachusetts Historical Society
Bigelow, John. Manuscript Division, New York Public Library
Bryce, James. Bodleian Library, Oxford University
Butler, Benjamin F. Manuscript Division, Library of Congress
Carnegie, Andrew. Manuscript Division, Library of Congress
Carnegie Autograph Collection. Manuscript Division, New York Public
    Library
Century Collection. Manuscript Division, New York Public Library
Chapman, John Jay. Houghton Library, Harvard University
Child, Francis J. Houghton Library, Harvard University
Cleveland, Grover. Manuscript Division, Library of Congress
Dana, R. H. Massachusetts Historical Society
Eliot, Charles W. Harvard Archives, Harvard University
Fairchild, Charles S. New-York Historical Society
Farrer, Sir Thomas. London School of Economics Library
Foulke, William D. Manuscript Division, Library of Congress
Garfield, James A. Manuscript Division, Library of Congress
Garrison, Wendell P. Houghton Library, Harvard University
Garrison Family Papers. Smith College Library
Gilder, Richard Watson. Manuscript Division, New York Public Library
Gilman, Daniel Coit. The Johns Hopkins University Library
Godkin, E. L. Houghton Library, Harvard University
Godkin Miscellaneous Papers. Manuscript Division, New York Public
    Library
Simon Gratz Autograph Collection. Historical Society of Pennsylvania
Hart, John Seely. Cornell University Press
Harvard Archives, Harvard University
Hayes, Rutherford B. Hayes Library, Fremont, Ohio
Higginson, Thomas Wentworth. Houghton Library, Harvard University
Hoar, George F. Massachusetts Historical Society
Holyoake, George. Holyoake House, Manchester, England

James Family. Houghton Library, Harvard University
Lea, Henry C. Lea Library, University of Pennsylvania
Lodge, Henry Cabot. Massachusetts Historical Society
Longfellow, Henry Wadsworth. Longfellow Trust, Harvard University
Lounsbury, Thomas Raynesford. Beinecke Library, Yale University
Lowell, James Russell. Houghton Library, Harvard University
MacVeagh, I. Wayne. Historical Society of Pennsylvania
Marble, Manton. Manuscript Division. Library of Congress
Marsh, George P. University of Vermont Library
Matthews, Brander. Butler Library, Columbia University
Mill, John Stuart. The Johns Hopkins University Library
Mitchell, Edward P. New-York Historical Society
Nation Business Records. Godkin Papers, Houghton Library, Harvard
    University
Newcomb, Simon. Manuscript Division, Library of Congress
Norton, Charles Eliot. Houghton Library, Harvard University
Ogden, Robert C. Manuscript Division, Library of Congress
Olmsted, Frederick Law. Manuscript Division, Library of Congress
Ordway, Edward W. Manuscript Division, New York Public Library
Parton, James. Houghton Library, Harvard University
Reid, Whitelaw. Manuscript Division, Library of Congress
Schurz, Carl. Manuscript Division, Library of Congress
Private Papers of Carl Schurz. Indiana University, Bloomington, Indiana
Scudder, Horace. Houghton Library, Harvard University
Stedman, Edmund Clarence. Butler Library, Columbia University
Taylor, Bayard. Cornell University Library
Thompson, Joseph P. Beinecke Library, Yale University
Trenholm, William L. Manuscript Division, Library of Congress
Tuckerman, Emily. Manuscript Division, New York Public Library
Vilas, William E. State Historical Society of Wisconsin
Ward, S. G. Houghton Library, Harvard University
Warner, Charles Dudley. Trinity College Library
Weed, Thurlow. University of Rochester Library
Wells, David A. Manuscript Division, New York Public Library
White, Andrew D. Cornell University Library
White, Horace. Illinois State Historical Society
Whitney, William C. Manuscript Division, Library of Congress
Whitney, William D. Beinecke Library, Yale University
Woodberry, George Edward. Houghton Library, Harvard University
Woolsey, Theodore D. Beinecke Library, Yale University

DOCUMENTS

U. S. Bureau of Immigration and Naturalization, *Annual Reports.*
U. S. Congress, *Congressional Globe,* 39th Cong., 1 Sess. (Washington, D. C., 1866-1867).
U. S. Congress, *Congressional Record,* 53rd Cong., 2 Sess., 4528; December 10, 1895.
U. S. Congress, House, *House Executive Documents,* No. 51, 51st Cong., 2 Sess.; No. 91, 52nd Cong., 1 Sess.
U. S. Congress, House, *House Reports,* No. 100, 39th Cong., 1 Sess. (Washington, D. C., 1866).
U. S. Congress, *Senate Executive Documents,* No. 34, 41st Cong., 3 Sess. (Washington, D. C., 1871); No. 51, 51st Cong., 2 Sess.
U. S. *Statutes at Large,* Act of Congress, March 3, 1873; Vol. 22 May 6, 1882.

NEWSPAPERS

Albany Evening Journal, 1881.
Boston Daily Advertiser, 1873.
The Boston Herald, 1881.
Brooklyn Daily Eagle, 1892.
The Chicago Tribune, 1881.
Daily News (London), 1854-1870.
The Evening Post (New York), 1881-1902.
New York Herald, 1872-1900.
New York Times, 1865-1902.
New York Tribune, 1870-1902.
Springfield Republican, 1883.
The Sun (New York), 1885-1902.
The Times (Philadelphia), 1881.
The Times (London), 1861-1892.
The Washington Post, 1882.
The World (New York), 1892.

BOOKS

Aaron, Daniel. *Men of Good Hope.* New York: Oxford University Press, 1951.
Abbott, Austin. *Abbott's Practice Reports,* X. New York: New York Law

Book Company, 1860.

Adams, Charles F., Jr. *Charles Francis Adams*. Boston and New York: Houghton Mifflin Company, 1900.

Adams, Ephraim D. *Great Britain and the American Civil War*. 2 vols. New York: Longmans, Green and Company, 1925.

Adams, Henry. *The Education of Henry Adams*. New York: Houghton Mifflin Company, 1918.

_____. *Henry Adams and his Friends*, comp. by Harold D. Cater. Boston: Houghton Mifflin Company, 1947.

Adams, Marian. *The Letters of Mrs. Henry Adams, 1865-1883*, ed. by Ward Thoron. Boston: Little, Brown, and Company, 1936.

Angell, Norman. *America and the New World-State*. New York: G. P. Putnam's Sons, 1915.

Armstrong, William M. *E. L. Godkin and American Foreign Policy, 1865-1900*. New York: Bookman Associates, 1957.

_____, ed. *Gilded Age Letters of E. L. Godkin*. Albany: State U. of New York Press, 1974.

Arnold, Matthew. *Civilization in the United States*. Boston: Cupples and Hurd, 1888.

Atkins, J. B. *The Life of William Howard Russell*. London: J. Murray, 1911.

Austin, Anne L. *The Woolsey Sisters of New York*. Philadelphia: American Philosophical Society, 1971.

Baehr, Harry W. *The New York Tribune Since the Civil War*. New York: Dodd, Mead and Company, 1936.

Bancroft, Frederic and Dunning, W. A. *The Reminiscences of Carl Schurz*. 3 vols. New York: The McClure Company, 1907-1908.

Barrows, Chester L. *William M. Evarts*. Chapel Hill: U. of North Carolina Press, 1941.

Beale, Howard K. *Theodore Roosevelt and the Rise of America to World Power*. Baltimore: Johns Hopkins Press, 1956.

Beales, A. C. *The History of Peace*. New York: G. Bell and Sons Ltd., 1931.

Beard, Charles A. and Mary A. *The Rise of American Civilization*. 2 vols. New York: The Macmillan Company, 1928.

Bemis, S. F., ed. *The American Secretaries of State and Their Diplomacy*. 10 vols. New York: A. A. Knopf, 1927-29.

Beringause, Arthur F. *Brooks Adams; A Biography*. New York: Alfred A. Knopf, 1955.

Bigelow, John. *Retrospections of an Active Life*. 3 vols. New York: The Baker & Taylor Company, 1909-1913.

_____. *The Life of Samuel J. Tilden*. 2 vols. New York: Harper & Brothers, 1895.

Bishop, Joseph B. *Notes and Anecdotes of Many Years*. New York: Charles Scribner's Sons, 1925.

Bond, F. Fraser. *Mr. Miller of "The Times."* New York, London: Charles Scribner's Sons, 1931.

Brace, Charles Loring. *Hungary in 1851*. New York: Charles Scribner, 1852.

_____. *The Life of Charles Loring Brace, Chiefly Told in His Own Letters*, ed. by his daughter. New York: Charles Scribner's Sons, 1894.

Bredon, Juliet. *Sir Robert Hart*. London: Hutchinson and Company, 1909.

British Blue Books. *Correspondence Respecting the Question of the Boundary of British Guiana*. London: Harrison and Sons, 1896.

Brown, Rollo Walter. *Lonely Americans*. New York: Coward-McCann, Inc., 1929.

Brown, Thomas N. *Irish-American Nationalism, 1870-1890*. Philadelphia: Lippincott, 1966.

Brownell, W. C. *The Genius of Style*. New York and London: Charles Scribner's Sons, 1924.

Bryce, James. *Studies in Contemporary Biography*. London: Macmillan and Co., Ltd., 1903.

Bullard, F. L. *Famous War Correspondents*. London: Sir I. Pitman and Sons, 1914.

Burke, Edmund. *Orations and Essays*. New York: D. Appleton and Company, 1900.

Bush, Chilton R. *Editorial Thinking and Writing*. New York: D. Appleton and Co., 1932.

Callahan, J. M. *American Policy in Mexican Relations*. New York: The Macmillan Company, 1932.

Cary, Edward. *George William Curtis*. Boston: Houghton, Mifflin Company, 1894.

Cole, Arthur Charles. *The Irrepressible Conflict: 1850-1865*. New York: The Macmillan Company, 1934.

Commager, Henry Steele. *The American Mind*. New Haven: Yale University Press, 1950.

Conway, Moncure D. *Autobiography, Memories and Experiences of Moncure Daniel Conway*. 2 vols. Boston and New York: Houghton Mifflin Company, 1904.

Cook, Sir Edward. *Delane of 'The Times.'* London: Constable and Company, 1915.

Coolidge, Mary. *Chinese Immigration*. New York: Henry Holt and Company, 1909.

Coolidge, Susan (Sarah C. Woolsey). *Verses*. Boston: Roberts Brothers, 1880.

Cortissoz, Royal. *The Life of Whitelaw Reid*. 2 vols. I. New York: Charles Scribner's Sons, 1921.

Crawford, T. C. *James G. Blaine*. Philadelphia: Edgewood Publishing Company, 1893.

Crowe, Sir Joseph A. *Reminiscences of Thirty-Five Years of My Life*. London: J. Murray, 1895.

Cullop, Charles C. *Confederate Propaganda in Europe, 1861-1865*. Coral Gables: University of Miami Press, 1969.

Cunningham, Edith P. *Owls Nest*. Privately printed at the Riverside

Press, 1907.

Curti, Merle. *The Growth of American Thought.* New York: Harper & Brothers, 1943.

Curtis, William E. *Between the Andes and the Ocean.* New York: Duffield and Company, 1907.

DeSantis, Vincent. *Republicans Face the Southern Question.* Baltimore: The Johns Hopkins Press, 1959.

Duffy, Sir Charles Gavan. *Conversations with Carlyle.* New York: Charles Scribner's Sons, 1892.

_____. *My Life in Two Hemispheres.* 2 vols. New York: The Macmillan Company, 1898.

Duffy, Sir Charles and Davis, Thomas. *The Memoirs of An Irish Patriot, 1840-1846.* London: Kegan, Paul, Trench, Trübner and Company, Ltd., 1890.

Edwards, R. Dudley and Williams, T. Desmond, eds. *The Great Famine.* Dublin: Browne and Nolan, 1956.

Eggleston, George C. *Recollections of a Varied Life.* New York: Henry Holt and Company, 1910.

Elliott, Charles Wyllys. *Cottages and Cottage Life.* New York: A. S. Barnes & Company, 1848.

Emerson, Ralph Waldo. "George L. Stearns." *Lectures and Biographical Sketches.* Boston and New York: Houghton Mifflin and Company, 1904.

Farnham, Charles H. *A Life of Francis Parkman.* Boston: Little, Brown, and Company, 1901.

Fenwick, Charles G. *International Law.* 3rd Edition. New York: Appleton-Century-Crofts, 1948.

Fields, Mrs. James T. *Memories of a Hostess,* ed. by M. A. DeWolfe Howe. Boston: Atlantic Monthly Press, 1922.

Fiske, John. *The Letters of John Fiske,* ed. by Ethel F. Fisk. New York: The Macmillan Company, 1940.

Fleming, E. McClung. *R. R. Bowker, Militant Liberal.* Norman, Okla: U. of Oklahoma Press, 1952.

Foote, Abram A. *Foote Genealogy.* Rutland, Vermont: Marble City Press, 1907.

Forbes, John Murray. *Letters and Recollections of John Murray Forbes.* 2 vols., ed. by Sarah Forbes Hughes. Boston: Houghton Mifflin Co., 1899.

Franklin, Fabian. *People and Problems.* New York: Henry Holt and Company, 1908.

Fuess, C. M. *Carl Schurz, Reformer.* New York: Dodd, Mead and Co., 1932.

Furneaux, Rupert. *The First War Correspondent, William Howard Russell of THE TIMES.* London: Cassell and Company Ltd., 1945.

Gabriel, Ralph Henry. *The Course of American Democratic Thought.* New York: The Ronald Press Company, 1940.

Garrison, Wendell P. *Letters and Memorials of Wendell Phillips Garrison,* Comp. by J. H. McDaniels. Cambridge, Massachusetts: The Riverside Press, 1908.

Godkin, Edwin Lawrence. *The History of Hungary and The Magyars.*

New York: Alexander Montgomery, 1853.

_____. *Unforeseen Tendencies of Democracy*. Boston and New York: Houghton Mifflin and Company, 1898.

Goldman, Eric F. *Rendezvous with Destiny*. New York: Knopf, 1952.

Goodwin, Nathaniel. *The Foote Family*. Hartford: Press of Case, Tiffany and Company, 1849.

Greenslet, Ferris. *The Lowells and Their Seven Worlds*. Boston: Houghton Mifflin Company, 1946.

Greve, Charles T. *Centennial History of Cincinnati*. 2 vols. Chicago: Biographical Publishing Co., 1904.

Grimes, Allan P. *The Political Liberalism of the New York 'Nation.'* Chapel Hill: U. of North Carolina Press, 1953.

Gwynn, Denis. *The Struggle for Catholic Emancipation*. New York: Longmans, Green and Co., 1928.

_____. *Young Ireland and 1848*. Cork: Cork University Press, 1949.

Hale, Edward Everett. *The Life and Letters of Edward Everett Hale*. 2 vols., ed. by Edward Everett Hale, Jr. Boston: Little, Brown and Company, 1917.

Harlow, Virginia. *Thomas Sergeant Perry; A Biography*. Durham, North Carolina: Duke U. Press, 1950.

Hart, Albert Bushnell, ed. *American History told by Contemporaries*. 5 vols. New York: The Macmillan Company, 1929.

Hart, John S. *A Manual of American Literature*. Philadelphia: Eldridge S. Brother, 1875.

Hay, John. *Letters and Diaries of John Hay*. 3 vols. Washington, privately printed, 1908.

Hayes, Rutherford B. *Diary and Letters of Rutherford Birchard Hayes*. 5 vols., ed. by C. R. Williams. Columbus: Ohio State Archaeological and Historical Society, 1924.

Haynes, Frederick E. *Third Party Movements Since the Civil War*. Iowa City: The State Historical Society of Iowa, 1916.

Henderson, John B. *American Diplomatic Questions*. New York: The Macmillan Company, 1901.

Hendrick, Burton J. *The Training of an American*. New York: Houghton Mifflin Company, 1928.

Hibbert, Christopher. *The Destruction of Lord Raglan*. Boston: Little, Brown, 1951.

Hoar, George F. *Autobiography of Seventy Years*. New York: Charles Scribner's Sons, 1903.

Hofstadter, Richard. *Social Darwinism in American Thought*. New York: George Braziller, Inc., 1959.

Holt, Henry. *Sixty Years as a Publisher*. London: George Alden & Unwin, Ltd., 1923.

Hooker, Richard. *The Story of an Independent Newspaper*. New York: The Macmillan Company, 1924.

Howe, M. A. DeWolfe. *James Ford Rhodes, American Historian*. New York: D. Appleton & Co., 1929.

Hughes, Sarah Forbes. *Letters and Recollections of John Murray Forbes.* 2 vols. Boston: Houghton Mifflin Company, 1899.

James, Henry. *Notes of a Son and Brother.* New York: Charles Scribner's Sons, 1914.

Jordan, Donaldson and Pratt, Edwin J. *Europe and the American Civil War.* Boston and New York: Houghton Mifflin Company, 1931.

Joyner, Fred Bunyan. *David Ames Wells, Champion of Free Trade.* Cedar Rapids, Iowa: The Torch Press, 1939.

Kelley, Cornelia Pulsifer. *The Early Development of Henry James.* Urbana, Illinois: U. of Illinois Press, 1965.

Kirk, Russell. *The Conservative Mind.* Chicago: Henry Regnery Company, 1953.

Frederick Newman Knapp: Memorial Tributes. Boston: n.p., 1889.

Kolko, Gabriel. *Railroads and Regulation, 1877-1916.* Princeton: Princeton U. Press, 1965.

Korngold, Ralph. *Two Friends of Man.* Boston: Little, Brown and Company, 1950.

Lanier, Sidney. *The Centennial Edition of the Works of Sidney Lanier,* ed. by Charles R. Anderson and A. H. Starke. Baltimore: The Johns Hopkins Press, 1945.

Laski, Harold. *The American Democracy.* New York: The Viking Press, 1948.

Lengyel, Emil. *Turkey.* New York: Random House, 1941.

Lincoln, Charles Z., ed. *Messages from the Governors of the State of New York.* Albany: J. B. Lyon Company, 1909.

Lingley, Charles Ramsdell. *Since the Civil War.* New York: The Century Company, 1926.

Logsdon, Joseph. *Horace White, Nineteenth Century Liberal.* Westport, Connecticut: Greenwood Publishing Company, 1971.

Lynch, Denis T. *"Boss" Tweed.* New York: Boni and Liveright, 1927.

Lynes, Russell. *The Tastemakers.* New York: Harper, 1954.

Mathews, Joseph J. *Reporting the Wars.* Minneapolis: University of Minnesota Press, 1957.

Matthews, Brander. *These Many Years.* New York: Charles Scribner's Sons, 1917.

McCarthy, Justin and Robinson, Sir John R. *The 'Daily News' Jubilee.* London: Sampson, Lows, Marston and Co., 1896.

McPherson, James M. *The Struggle for Equality.* Princeton, New Jersey: Princeton U. Press, 1964.

Miller, William. *The Ottoman Empire and its Successors, 1801-1927.* London: Cambridge University Press, 1936.

Millis, Walter. *The Martial Spirit.* Boston: Houghton Mifflin Company, 1931.

Mitchell, Edward P. *Memories of An Editor: Fifty Years of American Journalism.* New York: Charles Scribner's Sons, 1924.

Moos, Malcolm. *The Republicans; A History of the Party.* New York: Random House, 1956.

Quarterly 20 (1937).

Creelman, James. "Joseph Pulitzer—Master Journalist," *Pearson's Magazine* 21 (1909).

Curtis, George W. "The Easy Chair," *Harper's* (September 1884).

de Lansdorff, E. "La Hongrie en 1848; Kossuth et Jellachich," *Revue des Deux Mondes* 24, n.s. (1848).

Dorfman, Joseph. Review, Allen P. Grimes, *Political Liberalism of the New York NATION, 1865-1932,* in *American Historical Review* 59, 455 (1954).

"Eyewitness in Hungary," *Harper's* 214, 1282 (March 1957).

Filler, Louis. "The Early Godkin," *The Historian* 17 (1954).

_____. "East and Middle West: Concepts of Liberalism in America during the Late Nineteenth Century," *American Journal of Economics and Sociology* (January 1951).

Fossum, P. R. "The Anglo-Venezuelan Boundary Controversy," *Hispanic American Historical Review* 8 (1928).

Garrison, Wendell P. "Edwin Lawrence Godkin," *The Book Buyer* 13, 1 (February 1896).

Gilder, Joseph B. "Authors at Home; Mr. E. L. Godkin in New York," *Critic,* 30 April 1898.

"Edwin Lawrence Godkin." *Lamb's Biographical Dictionary of the United States.* Boston: James H. Lamb and Co., 1900.

"E. L. Godkin," *Town Topics,* 5 July 1894.

"The Late Edwin Lawrence Godkin, by One Who Knew Him," *The Critic* 41, 1 (July, 1902).

Godkin, E. L. "Aristocratic Opinions of Democracy," *North American Review* 100 (January 1865).

_____. "A Christmas in Rathnagru," *The Workingmen's Friend,* 25 December 1852.

_____. "Colonial System of Great Britain," *The Knickerbocker* 53, 2 (February 1859).

_____. "Commercial Immorality and Political Corruption," *North American Review* 107 (July 1868).

_____. "The Conditions of Good Colonial Government," *Forum* 27 (April 1899).

_____. "The Constitution and its Defects," *North American Review* 99 (July 1864).

_____. "The Death of a Great Power," *The Knickerbocker* 52, 6 (December 1858).

_____. "The Democratic View of Democracy," *North American Review* 101 (July 1865).

_____. "The Economic Man," *North American Review* 153 (October 1891).

_____. "The Growth and Expression of Public Opinion," *Atlantic Monthly* 81 (January 1898).

_____. "Idleness and Immortality," *Forum* 13, (May 1892).

_____. Nation editorials, 1865-1900.

_____. "The Prospects of the Political Act," *North American Review* 110 (April 1870).

_____. "The Republican Party and the Negro," *Forum* 7 (May 1889).

_____. "The Tyranny of the Majority," *North American Review* 104 (January 1867).

Godkin, James. "The Rights of Ireland." *Essays on the Repeal of the Union.* Published for the Loyal National Repeal Association of Ireland. Dublin: 1845.

Hardy, Osgood. "The *Itata* Incident," *Hispanic American Historical Review* 5 (1922).

_____. "Was Patrick Egan a 'Blundering Minister'?" *Hispanic American Historical Review* 8 (1928).

Harper's Weekly, 11 June 1881; 22 September 1884.

Hart, Albert Bushnell. "The Chilean Controversy." *Practical Essays on American Government.* New York: Longmans, Green and Co., 1905.

"Frank H. Hill." *Dictionary of National Biography, Supplement, January 1901-December 1911.* London: Smith, Elder & Company, 1912.

Howells, William Dean. "A Great New York Journalist," *North American Review* 185 (1907).

James, Henry. "The Founding of the 'Nation'," *Nation,* 8 July 1915.

Literary Digest, 26 May 1894.

Lowell, James Russell. "Reconstruction," *North American Review* 100 (April 1865).

"A Month of Quarantine," *North American Review* 155 (1892).

Moore, John Basset. "The Chilean Affair," *Political Science Quarterly* 8 (September 1893).

Nation (Dublin), 8 April 1848.

Nation (New York), 1865-1950.

The Outlook, 21 July 1915.

Page, Evelyn. Ed., "After Gettysburg: Frederick Law Olmsted on the Escape of Lee," *Pennsylvania Magazine of History* 75 (October 1951).

_____. "The Man Around the Corner," *New England Quarterly* 23 (September 1950).

Patterson, John. "The United States and Hawaiian Reciprocity, 1867-1870," *Pacific Historical Review* 7 (1938).

Peck, Harry T. "Mr. Godkin and His Book." *Bookman* 2 (February 1896).

The Penn Monthly, September 1872.

Pringle, Henry F. "Godkin of the *Post,*" *Scribners Magazine* 96 (December 1924).

"A Protest", *Forum* 21 (1896).

Punch, 28 April 1876.

Rhodes, James Ford. "Edwin Lawrence Godkin," in *Historical Essays.* New York: The Macmillan Company, 1908.

Russ, W. A., Jr. "Godkin Looks at Western Agrarianism," *Journal of Agricultural History* 19 (1945).

Saturday Review (London), 22 August 1868.

Schurz, Carl. "Corporations, their Employees, and the Public," *North*

American Review 327 (February 1884).

Smith, G. Barnett. "James Godkin." *Dictionary of National Biography.* XXII, 38. London: Smith, Elder & Company, 1890.

Spiegelman, Mortimer. "The Failure of the Ohio Life Insurance and Trust Company," *Ohio State Archaeological and Historical Quarterly 57,* 1 (January 1948).

Stacey, C. P. "Fenianism and the Rise of National Feeling in Canada at the time of Confederation," *Canadian Historical Review* 12 (1931).

Stoke, Harold W. "Edwin Lawrence Godkin, Defender of Democracy," *The South Atlantic Quarterly* 30 (1931).

Stone, I. F. "Free Inquiry and Free Endeavor," *Nation,* 10 February 1940.

Sykes, McCready. (A verse), *American Historical Review* 13 (1907).

Thayer, William Roscoe. "Edwin Lawrence Godkin," in *Later Years of the Saturday Club,* edited by M. A. DeWolfe Howe. New York: Houghton Mifflin Company, 1927.

"The 'Treaty Muddle,'" *Atlantic Monthly* 29 (1872).

Tierney, Michael. "Origin and Growth of Modern Irish Nationalism," *Studies: An Irish Quarterly Review* 30 (September 1941).

INDEX

DEMCO 38

DATE DUE

AUG 1 1 1991
DEC 10 95

DEMCO 38-297

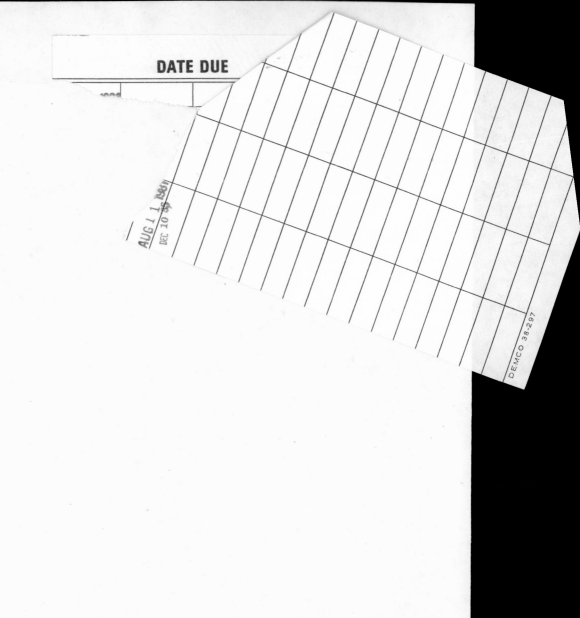